User-friendly Legal Science

Petri Mäntysaari

User-friendly Legal Science

A New Scientific Discipline

Springer

Petri Mäntysaari
Department of Accounting and Commercial Law
Hanken School of Economics
Vaasa, Finland

ISBN 978-3-319-53491-6 ISBN 978-3-319-53492-3 (eBook)
DOI 10.1007/978-3-319-53492-3

Library of Congress Control Number: 2017936953

Printed on acid-free paper

This Springer imprint is published by Springer Nature
The registered company is Springer International Publishing AG
The registered company address is: Gewerbestrasse 11, 6330 Cham, Switzerland

Preface

Legal science can and should comply with the customary requirements as to scientificity. The fact that the doctrinal study of law is not a science has increased the popularity of the interdisciplinary approach and law-and-something disciplines. They rely on the theory arsenal of non-legal disciplines. One may ask whether there is an alternative that could make legal science stronger in the competition for scientific hegemony.

The purpose of this book is to define a new legal discipline as an alternative to law-and-something disciplines and the traditional interdisciplinary approach. Its point of view is how users can use legal tools and practices to reach their objectives in different contexts. We call this new discipline User-Friendly Legal Science.

User-Friendly Legal Science is a qualitative science. It is anchored in theories on scientificity, scientific theory building and scientific methods customarily used in social sciences. Its goal is interpretive understanding. It can use abduction and grounded theory. It can also be regarded as a design science that produces constructions. These concepts are common knowledge in qualitative research. The use of such tested standard parts makes it easier to develop User-Friendly Legal Science and increase its overall usability. However, User-Friendly Legal Science itself is designed as a legal discipline.

The framework of User-Friendly Legal Science can help to upgrade many existing legal areas into scientific disciplines in legal research and education.

Since this approach is new, a detailed account of the theory and methods of User-Friendly Legal Science might seem premature. But perhaps a book at this stage of the development of the discipline shows that there is an alternative.

Vaasa, Finland

Petri Mäntysaari

Preface

Contents

Chapter 1
Introduction

> If it becomes desirable to formulate any cognition as science, it will be necessary first to determine accurately those peculiar features which no other science has in common with it, constituting its characteristics; otherwise the boundaries of all sciences become confused, and none of them can be treated thoroughly according to its nature. (*Immanuel Kant*)[1]

> It is obvious that no matter how complete the theory may be, a middle term is required between theory and practice, providing a link and a transition from one to the other . . . There are, for example, doctors or lawyers who did well during their schooling but who do not know how to act when asked to give advice. (*Immanuel Kant*)[2]

> Now the true and lawful goal of the sciences is none other than this: that human life be endowed with new discoveries and powers. (*Sir Francis Bacon*)[3]

Legal science is dominated by four broad approaches. The first was the doctrinal study of law. It has its roots in antiquity and uses legal rhetoric as its main method. The doctrinal study of law lacks scientificity and is secondary to the whims of politics, as was famously pointed out by Julius von Kirchmann in 1848.[4] The second approach was to combine the internal point of view[5] of legal dogmatics with an interdisciplinary approach. It was introduced around 1814 when Friedrich Carl von Savigny interpreted legal norms on the basis of a historical framework.[6] The third approach combines the interdisciplinary approach with an external point of view. This approach emerged after the founding of sociology by Max Weber and

---

[1]Kant I (1783), § 1.

[2]Kant I (1793), p. 61.

[3]Bacon F (1620), book I, aphorism 81: "Meta autem scientiarum vera et legitima non alia est, quam ut dotetur vita humana noviis inventis et copiis."

[4]von Kirchmann J (1848), p. 23: "As science takes the arbitrary as its object, it becomes arbitrary itself; three corrective words from the legislator, and entire libraries turn into maculature."

[5]Hart HLA (1961/ 2012), pp. 88–90.

[6]von Savigny FC (1814).

P. Mäntysaari, *User-friendly Legal Science*, DOI 10.1007/978-3-319-53492-3_1

others. Sociology provided a way to study law as the field of a non-legal discipline. In 1913, Eugen Ehrlich was the first to define the principles of the sociology of law.[7] This led to the development of a broad range of law-and-something disciplines in the twentieth century. The fourth approach is comparative. Comparative law started to flourish in continental Europe in the 1920s. While both the sociology of law and comparative law chose an external point of view, they had different knowledge interests and primary sources, and comparative law was not an interdisciplinary approach as such.

In the twenty-first century, much of normal legal science still has not exceeded the threshold of scientificity. First, the doctrinal study of law is unable to comply with the basic principles of scientific research. Since laws are a way to address conflicting interests and the outcome of political processes,[8] doctrinal research is just as political as it was when criticised by von Kirchmann, and the use of legal rhetoric, its core method, depends on subjective values and preferences.[9] Legal dogmatics lacks both statements that can be true or false[10] and scientific theory building. Second, if combined with the internal point of view, the interdisciplinary approach adds a new pool of arguments that might be perceived as legitimate without curing the fundamental problems of legal dogmatics as such. The new arguments could be historical, like the arguments used by Friedrich Carl von Savigny[11]; originate in economics, as they often do in modern legal science[12]; or have their roots in other scientific disciplines. Third, the law-and-something approach with its external point of view does not turn legal science into an independent science. In this case, law is regarded as a mere field of other scientific disciplines just as it was for Eugen Ehrlich and Max Weber. Fourth, while comparative law has scientific ambitions, its scope is limited to the comparison of sets of legal norms.

Due to the lack of scientificity, normal legal science is unable to prevail in the competition for scientific hegemony. 'It takes a theory to beat a theory',[13] but normal legal science has failed to produce theories about society outside the legal system.[14] Normal legal science has little to contribute to the scientific discourse of other disciplines. Legal science should have the means to compete with other

---

[7]Ehrlich E (1913), pp. 382–383.

[8]Heck P (1914); Stigler GJ (1971).

[9]For legal rhetoric, see White JB (2002), p. 1399; Perelman C (1977); Gast W (2015). For the effect of psychological types, see Novak M (2014).

[10]von Kirchmann J (1848); von Jhering R (1858); Larenz K (1966), p. 11; Ulen TS (2002).

[11]History was defined as the frame of reference even in von Jhering R (1858), pp. 75–76: "Denn die Geschichte selber ist, wie Hegel gesagt hat, das Weltgericht; die Sünden der Väter strafen sich an den Kindern, und wer in der Geschichte suchen will, was gut und böse, der wird es erkennen können an dem Segen, der auch hier auf der guten, und dem Fluch, der auf der bösen Tat ruht." Hegel GWF (1820/1821), § 343: "Die Geschichte des Geistes ist seine Tat, denn er ist nur, was er tut . . ."

[12]See already Holmes OW (1897).

[13]Kuhn TS (1970).

[14]For the problematic relationship between legal theory and practice, see, for example, Posner RA (2002), p. 1316; Jestaedt M (2006).

scientific disciplines on an equal footing and challenge them. There is too much one-way traffic[15] and too little two-way traffic.

If legal science does not produce useful scientific theories about societal reality, legal scholars and lawmakers feel forced to turn to other social sciences, such as sociology or economics, for guidance. This is certainly one of the factors that explain the increasing popularity of the interdisciplinary approach.[16] Unfortunately, the widespread use of the theories of other disciplines can result in a downward spiral that makes it even more difficult to upgrade legal science into an independent science. In the US, legal science is in the process of being marginalised as the scientific discipline of law professors.[17]

The lack of scientificity is not the only problem. Normal legal science is less useful than legal science could be even for two other reasons.

First, the doctrinal study of law, the core of normal legal science, does not seem to be able to do its job properly. Legal theory has failed to provide a sufficient basis for the rational interpretation and systematisation of legal norms, and the absence of useful theory building makes it more difficult to cope with the current problems of fragmentation of law,[18] legal pluralism and over-regulation. These problems seem to be connected. If legal norms are the only tool you know, you will end up with more regulation than society can bear.[19] Over-regulation is likely to increase the fragmentation of law and legal pluralism.

Second, normal legal science fails to serve the knowledge interests of the vast majority of people. While it is characteristic of normal legal science to focus on legal norms, most people are not interested in legal norms as such. Normal people have their own objectives and use legal things to reach them.

The root and cause of these ills seems to be the fact that normal legal science is too much limited to the study of legal norms. This is a problem for legal scholars as well, as was made clear by Julius von Kirchmann. The shorter the life span of legal norms, the weaker incentives there are to allocate time and effort to high-quality research about such an 'arbitrary object', and the stronger incentives there are to do short-term and well-paid advisory work. At the same time, there are stronger incentives to quit the study of useful legal norms and flee to the interdisciplinary approach or abstract theorising.[20]

---

[15]Goodhart CAE (1997).

[16]See Grundmann S, Micklitz HW, Renner M (eds) (2015); van Gestel R, Micklitz HW, Rubin EL (eds) (2016).

[17]Holmes OW (1897), p. 469; Posner RA (2002), p. 1317; LoPucki LM (2016), pp. 506 and 538.

[18]Sieber U (2010), p. 171.

[19]Maslow AH (1966), p. 15: "I suppose it is tempting, if the only tool you have is a hammer, to treat everything as if it were a nail." See also Hayek FA (1944); Glendon MA (1991); Epstein RA (1992); Teubner G (2012). For an alternative to mandatory law, see, for example, Thaler RH, Sunstein CR (2008).

[20]See Posner RA (2002), pp. 1315 and 1323.

What all this means is that you need an alternative to legal dogmatics, the interdisciplinary approach and law-and-something disciplines. Moreover, you should preferably focus on something else than legal norms.

The purpose of this short book is to study legal phenomena from the user's perspective and build a new platform for legal science. We call it User-Friendly Legal Science.[21] Like other scientific disciplines, it has its own theoretical base. It has its core assumptions, its own field, its own research interests that one can call its orientation or point of view, its own methods and ambitions of conceptual rigour. Other disciplines have their own core assumptions, fields, points of view and methods.[22]

The core assumption of this new discipline is that people use legal tools and practices to reach their objectives[23] and that one can describe societal reality through the lens of the use of legal tools and practices evidenced in legal texts.[24]

The point of view of User-Friendly Legal Science is how users can use legal tools and practices to reach their objectives in different contexts. One can build theories to describe this kind of user behaviour.

The overall goal of User-Friendly Legal Science is interpretive understanding (Verstehen)[25] combined with problem solving (constructive research, design knowledge).[26] It represents the pragmatical school of thought.

User-Friendly Legal Science chooses a holistic research approach. By describing patterns,[27] the holistic approach can facilitate better understanding of complex societal phenomena such as the use of law and legal tools for the purpose of reaching private or societal goals. The holistic approach means that User-Friendly Legal Science is an area of qualitative research.[28]

User-Friendly Legal Science is thus a fundamentally new approach to the study of law. If accepted by the scientific community, the four previous approaches—the traditional doctrinal study of law, the interdisciplinary approach with an internal point of view, the interdisciplinary approach with an external point of view and comparative law—can be complemented by User-Friendly Legal Science in the future.

---

[21] Mäntysaari P (2013).

[22] See, for example, Iggers GG (1988) on the paradigm of historical science. For the need to choose new reference points, see Latour B (2013) pp. 29–30.

[23] White JB (2002), p. 1397: "You learn the law in order to use it – in order to achieve a set of objectives, to establish and maintain a set of relations, to move yourself and others in a direction you wish to go, even to discover that direction." For examples of legal "framing devices" and "referencing devices", see Malloy RP (2004), pp. 6–8.

[24] Wittgenstein L (1953), § 1 and § 43.

[25] For sociology, see Weber M (1922). For other examples of the use of an interpretive approach in law, see Malloy RP (2004), pp. 56–57 and Grundmann S, Micklitz HW, Renner M (eds) (2015), p. 3.

[26] Simon HA (1967), pp. 14–15; van Aken JE (2004).

[27] For the pattern model of explanation, see Kaplan A (1964).

[28] In qualitative research, it is customary to use grounded theory. See Glaser BG, Strauss AL (1967), p. 18.

We can now turn to the benefits of theory building. Theory building can bring benefits in any discipline.[29] The choice of the point of view of User-Friendly Legal Science for legal theory building and research is no exception.

The theories of this new discipline seem to fill a gap as the 'middle term' between law and practice.[30] Generally, 'nothing is so practical as a good theory',[31] but some good theories are more practical than others.[32] As there is an immediate link between theory and practice in this new discipline, good user-friendly theories are useful for practitioners and predict behaviour to some extent.[33] They can predict behaviour because what is perceived as rational behaviour can work as a social norm. There is a social norm to want certain things in certain contexts and to do useful things to reach such objectives.[34]

Regulating society is a form of practice in the broad sense. User-friendly theories can help to see legal regulation and legal norms in a new light. It can be easier to assess the functions and quality of legal regulation and legal norms if the framework exists outside the normative system.[35]

We can list the societal and discipline-specific benefits of the new discipline. User-friendly theory building can make it possible to

- increase the relevance of legal science for a very large number of users of legal tools and practices[36];
- expand the area of legal science;
- build falsifiable theories that help to elevate legal science to a science;
- describe societal reality in the language of law and legal science[37];

---

[29]See, for example, Glaser BG, Strauss AL (1967), p. 3.

[30]Kant I (1793), p. 61: ". . . a middle term is required between theory and practice . . ." Edwards HT (1992–1993), p. 34: "While the schools are moving toward pure theory, the (law) firms are moving toward pure commerce, and the middle ground – ethical practice – has been deserted by both."

[31]Lewin K (1945), p. 129.

[32]van Aken JE (2004), p. 220.

[33]For economics, see Friedman M (1953), p. 15.

[34]Hydén H (2011), p. 122: "To put it in a nutshell, how does one get from 'is' to 'ought'? . . . Within the system under investigation, there is an in-built, taken for granted rationality that decides what is right and what is wrong." According to what is known as Hume's guillotine, it is not obvious how one can coherently move from descriptive statements to prescriptive ones. Hume D (1739), book III, part I, section I.

[35]Banakar R (2006), p. 78: "I argue, therefore, that legal scholars can break new grounds once they turn outwards, for only if they step outside law, they can view their undertaking in different, and perhaps new, lights."

[36]See also Hart HLA (1961/ 2012), p. 40 on the "puzzled man"; White JB (2002), p. 1397; Banakar R, Travers M (2005b), p. 134.

[37]For example, legal concepts can be regarded as "ideal-types" that can be made subject to an empirical investigation. Weber M (1949), p. 43 (a translation of Weber M 1913). For legal history, see Lobban M (2012), paragraph 29: "One of the tasks of the legal historian speaking to a wider historical audience is to remind them that the language which lawyers and legal officials use, and the operation of their institutions play a crucial part in the governance of society and in structuring private relations." For the traditional view, however, see Ross A (1958), p. 34.

- identify practical syllogisms that influence societal relationships[38];
- use legal science as a complement to economic sciences, sociology and other social sciences and as an alternative or better way to describe society;
- make legal science stronger in the battle for scientific hegemony[39];
- facilitate innovation[40];
- develop new areas of law that are functional and less path dependent than the traditional areas of law;
- improve the quality of regulation by giving information about the typical intentions of parties and the effect of different legal tools and practices[41];
- reduce the need for regulation as parties can be educated to use legal tools and practices themselves (self-regulation instead of regulation);
- improve the quality of the interpretation of norms and contracts by giving information about the parties' typical intentions in the relevant contexts and about the effect of different legal tools and practices[42];
- address the problem of legal pluralism by studying all relevant legal aspects from a well-defined user perspective (Sect. 3.4.3)[43];
- improve the scientificity of comparative law by providing a scientific way to study the functions of law;
- improve the quality of legal advice[44];
- increase the development of low-cost legal services for the public (by identifying the typical objectives of a particular classes of users in particular contexts and by describing how the objectives can be reached by legal tools and practices);
- create a more practice-ready curriculum[45];
- increase the shelf life of legal research; and

[38]von Wright GH (1971), p. 96. See, for example, Kusch N (2003), p. 350.

[39]Ross A (1958), pp. 331 and 328; Bourdieu P (1975), p. 19; Simon HA (1967), p. 15. Basedow J (2014): "What is often denounced as a wave of neo-liberalism that has flooded the world has in reality ensued from a mix of economic, political and comparative legal investigations."

[40]For innovation and the constructive approach, see Kasanen E, Lukka K, Siitonen A (1993), p. 246.

[41]Compare Ross A (1958), p. 334 on legal politics as a science: "... the principle of purity of science requires, that every political directive shall name the objectives and attitudes which are accepted as hypothetical premises guiding the theoretical researches and the practical conclusions ..." Critically on Ross' science Dalberg-Larsen J (2005), p. 47.

[42]Grundmann S, Micklitz HW, Renner M (eds) (2015), p. 4: "Von der Übersetzungsleistung der Rechtstheorie kann die Rechtsdogmatik profitieren: Sie kann sich mit Hilfe der Rechtstheorie ein genaueres Bild der gesellschaftlichen Kontexte Machen, in denen Rechtsregeln wirken."

[43]Dagan H (2011), p. xviii: "For legal realists, the profound and inescapable reason for doctrinal indeterminacy is the availability of multiple and potentially applicable doctrinal sources." Berman HJ (1983), p. 11: "The conventional concept of law as a body of rules derived from statutes and court decisions ... is wholly inadequate to support a study of a transnational legal culture."

[44]For management accounting theory, see Kasanen E, Lukka K, Siitonen A (1993), p. 252: "Truly functioning constructions have great commercial value."

[45]Dewey J (1938), Chapter 1; Saurama E, Julkunen I (2012), p. 61: "What Dewey wanted to do was to restore the value of the needs of practical life in the field of knowledge formation; although practice is uncertain, chaotic and volatile, it is nevertheless the reality within which people have to

- improve researchers' incentives to focus on legal research that fulfils the customary scientific requirements.

This leads us to methods. Theory and methods go hand in hand.[46] User-Friendly Legal Science has its own disciplinary requirements as regards methods. For example, its methods must reflect its point of view, and its primary sources must consist of the documentation of legal tools and practices.

Although User-friendly Legal Science has its own disciplinary requirements, the starting point is that one can use the customary methods of social sciences. This is necessary in order to ensure scientificity. Moreover, since User-Friendly Legal Science is a form of qualitative practice research, its methods can be influenced by the methods of other disciplines. The rich literature on the methodology of practice research is mainly interdisciplinary and can be shared by many different areas of social sciences.

This means that User-Friendly Legal Science can to some extent be eclectic in the use of theory and methods.[47] Eclecticism can be regarded as a good thing because it serves the pursuit of truth.[48]

While User-Friendly Legal Science is partly designed as a reaction to problems caused by the interdisciplinary approach (in addition to the lack of scientificity of doctrinal research), one can see that other social sciences play an important role in this new discipline as well. What is new is that the new point of view can lead to a more structured, rational and critical use of the theories of other social sciences.

User-Friendly Legal Science seems to be necessary. The use of legal tools and practices to reach private and societal objectives is a very large and important phenomenon that is part of everyday life. Studying it is a worthwhile research task in its own right. It does not really matter whether User-Friendly Legal Science is regarded as an example of the 'internal or external' view,[49] the study of 'law in action',[50] the study of 'the norms of law' or primarily the study of things that are not perceived as 'law'. It means primarily the study of behaviour. It does not matter whether user-friendly research fits in what is perceived as 'jurisprudential analysis', 'doctrinal study of law', 'sociology of law', 'legal politics' or something else. It is designed as a new legal discipline with its own point of view. Neither does it matter whether it is regarded as a 'true science' or 'a false science'.[51] This is of course provided that its ambitions are truly scientific and that it can comply with the

solve the problems they face." See also Simon HA (1967), p. 15 (on the organisational problem of professional schools); van Aken JE (2004), p. 219 (management research and business schools).

[46]See, for example, Banakar R, Travers M (2005a), p. 19.

[47]For interpretive management accounting research, see Elharidy AM, Nicholson B, Scapens RW (2008), p. 142. For legal history, see Duss V (2012), p. 989.

[48]See also Kaplan A (1964), § 1, p. 3.

[49]Hart HLA (1961/2012), pp. 88–90.

[50]Alf Ross divided the science of law into, first, legal dogmatics or jurisprudence that studies legal norms and, second, the sociology of law that studies law in action. See Ross A (1958), § 4; Dalberg-Larsen J (2005), p. 41.

[51]Bourdieu P (1975), pp. 38–39.

customary scientific requirements. The use of legal tools and practices to reach private and societal objectives should be studied because it makes sense to study what people do and help them in their lives.

Chapters 2–5 set out the general principles of User-Friendly Legal Science. Chapter 2 places User-Friendly Legal Science on the map of sciences by describing the nature of its theory building. Chapter 3 focuses on the choice of the research question, theories and methods. The choice of the research question is connected to the intended use of findings. The use of findings is discussed in Chap. 4. One of the ways to use findings is system building. Since system building is important for any science, it is discussed in Chap. 5.

Chapters 6–8 place User-Friendly Legal Science on the map of legal science. Chapter 6 discusses certain earlier attempts to make legal science more empirical. It explains how this new discipline differs from the earlier attempts and where its boundaries lie. In other words, Chap. 6 tells you what User-Friendly Legal Science is not. Chapter 7 focuses on anomalies[52] and applications. It provides examples of certain anomalies of normal legal science that could also be regarded as applications of the user perspective and redefined as disciplines of User-Friendly Legal Science. They include legal rhetoric, international law and commercial law. Moreover, Chap. 7 shows how several traditional legal disciplines could be upgraded into disciplines of User-Friendly Legal Science. In other words, Chap. 7 tells you what User-Friendly Legal Science might become. There is a summary of conclusions in Chap. 8.

References

Bacon F (1620) Novum Organum. Apud Joannem Billium, Typographum Regium, Londini

Banakar R (2006) How can sociology and jurisprudence learn from each other? A reply to Mauro Zamboni. Retfærd 29(2):75–84

Banakar R, Travers M (2005a) Law, sociology and method. In: Banakar R, Travers M (eds) Theory and method in socio-legal research. Hart Publishing, Oxford and Portland Oregon, pp 1–25

Banakar R, Travers M (2005b) Studying legal texts. In: Banakar R, Travers M (eds) Theory and method in socio-legal research. Hart Publishing, Oxford and Portland Oregon, pp 133–137

Basedow J (2014) Comparative law and its clients. Am J Comp Law 62(4):821–857

Berman HJ (1983) Law and revolution: the formation of the Western legal tradition. Harvard University Press, Cambridge

Bourdieu P (1975) The specificity of the scientific field and the social conditions of the progress of reason. Soc Sci Inf 14(6):19–47. doi:10.1177/053901847501400602

Dagan H (2011) Property: values and institutions. Oxford University Press, Oxford

Dalberg-Larsen J (2005) Alf Ross and the sociology of law. Scandinavian Stud Law 48:39–50

Dewey J (1938) Experience and education. Macmillan, New York

Duss V (2012) Chronik. Arbeitskreis "Augen der Rechtsgeschichte". Fünftes Symposium zur Methode der Rechtsgeschichte. Einsiedeln 20.-22. January 2011. Zeitschrift der Savigny-

[52]Kuhn TS (1970), Chapter 6.

Stiftung für Rechtsgeschichte. Germanistische Abteilung 129(1):986–990. doi:10.7767/zrgga.2012.129.1.986
Edwards HT (1992–1993) The growing disjunction between legal education and the legal profession. Mich Law Rev 34:34–70
Ehrlich E (1913) Grundlegung der Soziologie des Rechts. Duncker & Humblot, München and Leipzig
Elharidy AM, Nicholson B, Scapens RW (2008) Using grounded theory in interpretive management accounting research. Qual Res Accounting Manag 5(2):139–155. doi:10.1108/11766090810888935
Epstein RA (1992) Book review. Rights and 'Rights Talk'. Harv Law Rev 105:1106–1123
Friedman M (1953) The methodology of positive economics. In: Friedman M (ed) Essays in positive economics. University of Chicago Press, Chicago, pp 3–43
Gast W (2015) Juristische Rhetorik. 5., überarbeitete und erweiterte Auflage. C.F. Müller Verlag, Heidelberg
Glaser BG, Strauss AL (1967) The discovery of grounded theory: strategies for qualitative research. Aldine de Gruyter, New York
Glendon MA (1991) Rights and 'Rights Talk': the impoverishment of political discourse. The Free Press, New York
Goodhart CAE (1997) Economics and the law: too much one-way traffic? Mod Law Rev 60(1): 1–2
Grundmann S, Micklitz HW, Renner M (eds) (2015) Privatrechtstheorie. Mohr Siebeck, Tübingen
Hart HLA (2012) The concept of law, 3rd ed. With an introduction by Leslie Green. Oxford University Press, Oxford
Hayek FA (1944) The road to serfdom. George Routledge & Sons, London
Heck P (1914) Gesetzesauslegung und Interessenjurisprudenz. Archiv für die civilistische Pracis 112:1–318
Hegel GWF (1820/1821) Grundlinien der Philosophie des Rechts; oder Naturrecht und Staatswissenschaft im Grundrisse. Nicolaische Buchhandlung, Berlin
Holmes OW (1897) The path of the law. Harv Law Rev 10:457–490
Hume D (1739) A treatise of human nature. John Noon, London
Hydén H (2011) Looking at the world through the lenses of norms. Nine reasons for norms: a plea for norm science. In: Papendorf K, Machura S, Andenaes K (eds) Understanding law in society. Developments in socio-legal studies. LIT Verlag, Berlin, pp 120–159
Iggers GG (1988) The crisis of the Rankean paradigm in the nineteenth century. Syracuse Scholar (1979–1991) 9(1), Article 7
Jestaedt M (2006) Das mag in der Theorie richtig sein ... Vom Nutzen der Rechtstheorie für die Rechtspraxis. Mohr Siebeck, Tübingen
Kant I (1783) Prolegomena zu einer jeden künftigen Metaphysik die als Wissenschaft wird auftreten können. Johann Friedrich Hartknoch, Riga
Kant I (1793) Über den Gemeinspruch: Das mag in der Theorie richtig sein, taugt aber nicht für die Praxis. Berlinische Monatsschrift 22:201–284. English translation: On the common saying: 'this may be true in theory but it does not apply in practice'. In: Reiss H (ed) (1991) Kant: Political writings. Cambridge University Press, Cambridge, pp 61–92
Kaplan A (1964) The conduct of inquiry: methodology for behavioral science. Chandler Publishing Company, New York
Kasanen E, Lukka K, Siitonen A (1993) The constructive approach in management accounting research. J Manag Accounting Res 5:243–264
Kuhn TS (1970) The structure of scientific revolutions, Second edn. University of Chicago Press, Chicago
Kusch M (2003) Explanation and understanding: the debate over von Wright's philosophy of action revisited. In: Haaparanta L, Niiniluoto I (eds) Analytic philosophy in Finland. Poznań Studies in the Philosophy of the Sciences and the Humanities 80. Rodopi, Amsterdam New York, pp 327–356

Larenz K (1966) Über die Unentbehrlichkeit der Jurisprudenz als Wissenschaft. Vortrag gehalten vor der Berliner Juristischen Gesellschaft am 20. April 1966. Schriftenreihe der Juristischen Gesellschaft zu Berlin 26
Latour B (2013) An inquiry into modes of existence: an anthropology of the moderns. Harvard University Press, Cambridge
Lewin K (1945) The research center for group dynamics at Massachusetts Institute of Technology. Sociometry 8(2):126–136
Lobban M (2012) The varieties of legal history. Clio@Thémis 5:1–29
LoPucki LM (2016) Dawn of the discipline-based law faculty. J Leg Educ 65:506–542
Malloy RP (2004) Law in a market context: an introduction to market concepts in legal reasoning. Cambridge University Press, Cambridge
Mäntysaari P (2013) Was sollte man tun? Ein Plädoyer für anwenderfreundliche Rechtswissenschaft. Rechtstheorie 44(2):189–207. doi:10.3790/rth.44.2.189
Maslow AH (1966) The psychology of science: a reconnaissance. Harper & Row, New York
Novak M (2014) A typological reading of prevailing legal theories. Ratio Juris 27(2):218–235. doi:10.1111/raju.12042
Perelman C (1977) L'empire rhétorique. Rhétorique et argumentation. J. Vrin, Paris
Posner RA (2002) Legal scholarship today. Harv Law Rev 115(5):1314–1326
Ross A (1958) On law and justice. Stevens & Sons Limited, London
Saurama E, Julkunen I (2012) Approaching practice research in theory and practice. Soc Work Soc Sci Rev 15(2):57–75. doi:10.1921/095352211X636502
Sieber U (2010) Rechtliche Ordnung in einer globalen Welt. Die Entwicklung zu einem fragmentierten System von nationalen, internationalen und privaten Normen. Rechtstheorie 41(2): 151–198. doi:10.3790/rth.41.2.151
Simon HA (1967) The business school: a problem in organizational design. J Manag Stud 4(1): 1–16. doi:10.1111/j.1467-6486.1967.tb00569.x
Stigler GJ (1971) The theory of economic regulation. Bell J Econ Manag Sci 2(1):3–21
Teubner G (2012) Verfassungsfragmente. Gesellschaftlicher Konstitutionalismus in der Globalisierung. Suhrkamp, Berlin
Thaler RH, Sunstein CR (2008) Nudge: improving decisions about health, wealth, and happiness. Yale University Press, New Haven
Ulen TS (2002) A Nobel Prize in legal science: theory, empirical work, and the scientific method in the study of law. Univ Illinois Law Rev 4:875–920
van Aken JE (2004) Management research based on the paradigm of the design sciences: the quest for field-tested and grounded technological rules. J Manag Stud 41(2):219–246
van Gestel R, Micklitz HW, Rubin EL (eds) (2016) Rethinking legal scholarship: a transatlantic dialogue. Cambridge University Press, Cambridge
von Jhering R (1858) Geist des römischen Rechts auf den verschiedenen Stufen seiner Entwicklung. Druck und Verlag von Breitkopf und Härtel, Leipzig
von Kirchmann J (1848) Die Werthlosigkeit der Jurisprudenz als Wissenschaft. Verlage von Julius Springer, Berlin
von Savigny FC (1814) Vom Beruf unsrer Zeit für Gesetzgebung und Rechtswissenschaft. Mohr und Zimmer, Heidelberg
von Wright GH (1971) Explanation and understanding. Cornell University Press, Ithaca, New York
Weber M (1922) Wirtschaft und Gesellschaft – Grundriß der verstehenden Soziologie. J.C.B Mohr (Paul Siebeck), Tübingen
Weber M (1949) The methodology of the social sciences. The Free Press, Glencoe
White JB (2002) Legal knowledge. Harv Law Rev 115(5):1396–1431
Wittgenstein L (1953) Philosophische Untersuchungen. In: Anscombe GEM, von Wright GH, Rhees R (eds) Werkausgabe, Band 1. Suhrkamp, Frankfurt (1984), pp 224–485

Chapter 2
Core Concepts and Theory Building

2.1 General Remarks

In this book, User-Friendly Legal Science is defined as a scientific discipline. A scientific discipline has its own field, its own point of view (that is, research interests or orientation) and its own methods. Moreover, it has its own theories defining its characteristics. While theory building is free (Popper),[1] building theories is mandatory. The researcher should know how theories are generated (Glaser and Strauss)[2] and build the necessary theories. Theory building is not rocket science,[3] but you cannot build meaningful scientific theories without understanding their nature and function in scientific research.

Notions of Scientific Theories. All scientific research is theory based. The most important task of scientific disciplines is to produce new knowledge in the form of theories. Scientific theories describe external reality. There are different notions of scientific theories because there are different approaches to science. The most important approaches for our purposes include positivism, falsificationism and interpretive understanding. They will briefly be described below. One can say that a theory is a notion about why something is as it is (a cause-and-effect relationship) or how something is as it is (understanding).[4] A scientific theory (or model) must possess certain crucial characteristics.[5]

---

[1]Popper K (2005), number 30.

[2]Glaser BG, Strauss AL (1967), pp. 26–27 and 30.

[3]*Ibid*, p. viii: "Not everyone can be equally skilled at discovering theory, but neither do they need to be a genius to generate useful theory."

[4]For theory as a prognosis, see Popper K (2005) number 85. One can define even other goals for scientific research. Ronkainen S, Suikkanen A, Kunnari M (2014), p 98.

[5]For the assumptions crucial to the status of a model in financial research, see Ryan B, Scapens RW, Theobald M (1992), pp. 22–23.

P. Mäntysaari, *User-friendly Legal Science*, DOI 10.1007/978-3-319-53492-3_2

Generally, the different phases of the development of social sciences—the decline of positivism (logical empiricism) and the rise of qualitative and narrative research (understanding)—have equipped researchers with different methodological approaches and enabled them to design various kinds of useful scientific theories and disciplines.[6]

Positivism. Well-known early positivists include Sir Francis Bacon and David Hume (empiricism). In sociology, one can name August Comte (scientific sociology), Émile Durkheim (social facts), Paul Lazarsfeld (empirical sociology, mathematical sociology, multivariate analysis) and Robert K. Merton (middle-range theorising).[7] They are relevant as benchmarks for the purposes of this book.

Positivism looks to natural science for inspiration. For example, Durkheim argued that social facts can be studied as things by copying the methods of natural science.[8]

In practice, the forming and testing of hypotheses plays a big role in positivist research.[9] A hypothesis customarily is formed on the basis of existing theory. The hypothesis is then tested with data especially collected for the test.[10]

The purpose of middle-range theory was to integrate theory and empirical research. It was designed as a better alternative to both abstract theorising and too narrow empiricism that did not lead to successful theory building.

Falsificationism. Traditional positivism was criticised by Karl Popper,[11] who argued that scientific theories must be falsifiable. For example, statements that require value preferences are neither falsifiable nor scientific. Scientific theories can therefore be formed, applied, tested or falsified.

The conflict between positivism and falsificationism can be illustrated with neoclassical economics or 'mainstream economics'. Neoclassical economics is inspired by the positivism of natural science.[12] It has its own point of view. It rests on three assumptions: people are rational, individuals maximise utility and firms maximise profits, and people act independently on the basis of full and relevant information.[13] However, neoclassical economics has problems with falsifiability. First, although falsifiability is regarded as the defining characteristic of scientific theory, the confirmation of hypotheses seems to play a bigger role in

---

[6]Saurama E, Julkunen I (2012), p. 60.

[7]Merton RK (1968). See Boudon R (1991).

[8]Durkheim É (1894).

[9]Friedman M (1953), p. 7: "The ultimate goal of a positive science is the development of 'theory' or 'hypothesis' that yields valid and meaningful ... predictions about phenomena not yet observed." National Academy of Sciences, National Academy of Engineering, Institute of Medicine (1992), 2 Scientific Principles and Research Practices, pp. 36–39.

[10]Ragin CC (1994), pp. 14 and 25.

[11]Popper K (2005), number 4.

[12]See Friedman M (1953), p. 4.

[13]Weintraub ER (2002); Ryan B, Scapens RW, Theobald M (1992), p. 27.

economics.[14] Second, neoclassical economics does not explain individual behaviour.[15] Third, some general theories are related to values and impossible to falsify.[16] Fourth, some theories can have normative and prescriptive elements.[17]

Interpretive Understanding. The problem of the positivistic approach is that it produces plenty of small facts and is rather unable to explain complex societal phenomena.[18]

An alternative to positivism is phenomenology. In sociology, Max Weber assumed that the most appropriate way to gain knowledge about the social world is through interpretive understanding (Verstehen).[19] Traditional positivism is often replaced by a holistic research approach and interpretative understanding in disciplines that describe complex societal phenomena (see Sect. 2.4).

Disciplinary Cultures in Science. In addition to different notions of scientific theories, there are different disciplinary cultures in science. According to Tony Becher, the disciplinary cultures are connected to differences relating to the subject matter and knowledge form of research.[20]

Becher distinguishes between four kinds of disciplinary areas: (1) the hard-pure (natural sciences such as physics), (2) the soft-pure (humanities and social sciences such as history and anthropology), (3) the hard-applied (science-based professions such as clinical medicine or engineering) and (4) the soft-applied disciplinary areas (social professions such as education). In soft-applied disciplinary areas, knowledge is holistic and results in understanding or interpretation.

The existence of different kinds of disciplinary areas reflects the difference between two kinds of scientific ideals. Gerard Radnitzky distinguishes between the logical-empiricist and the hermeneutic-dialectic schools of contemporary 'metascience' (that is, philosophy of science).[21] (a) It is characteristic of logical empiricism to reduce scientific research to what is quantifiable according to the principles of the unity of science (see Sect. 6.1). Its notion of causality is the same as in classical physics.[22] However, the reduction of reality to what is quantifiable means that there is an inherent conflict between logical-empiricist research and

---

[14]Posner RA (1990), p. 363. See also Friedman M (1953), p. 9: "Factual evidence can never 'prove' a hypothesis; it can only fail to disprove it, which is what we generally mean when we say, somewhat inexactly, that the hypothesis has been 'confirmed' by experience."

[15]See Ryan B, Scapens RW, Theobald M (1992), p. 58. According to Friedman M (1953), it does not matter.

[16]See, for example, Siems MM (2008); Boland LA (2003).

[17]For the agency theory, see Ryan B, Scapens RW, Theobald M (1992), pp. 54–55.

[18]Berglund L, Ney A (2015), p. 154.

[19]Weber M (1922).

[20]Becher T (1994); Auranen O (2014), p. 66. Svein Kyvik suggests that cognitive and social differences among disciplines have implications for publication practices. Kyvik S (1991); Auranen O (2014), p. 67.

[21]Radnitzky G (1970).

[22]Bohr N (1948).

reality.[23] (b) In contrast, the hermeneutic-dialectic school is more holistic and focuses on understanding rather than mere causality.[24] There can nevertheless be different notions of understanding. For example, understanding was a task of causal explanations in the Annales tradition in historiography but is beyond causal explanation when the perspective is hermeneutical.[25]

Design Sciences. It is customary to distinguish between explanatory research with the positivist approach and descriptive research with the holistic approach (interpretive understanding).[26] Differences between sciences can also be connected to their techniques.

Herbert Simon distinguishes between the analytic techniques of the scientist and the synthetic techniques of the practitioner. According to Simon, the practitioner of any profession 'designs by organizing known principles and devices into larger systems'.[27]

Joan van Aken builds on this and distinguishes between formal sciences, explanatory sciences and design sciences. Philosophy and mathematics are examples of formal sciences. The explanatory sciences include natural sciences and some sections of social sciences. Design sciences include, for example, engineering sciences, medical sciences and management science.[28]

Mainstream Legal Science. These classifications can even be applied to legal science. Becher regards law as a soft-applied disciplinary area as it seems to produce functional and utilitarian knowledge aimed at enhancing professional practices.

However, one may ask whether legal dogmatics, the core of mainstream legal science, is a science at all. There is no serious search for any scientific identity in mainstream legal science.[29] Theory building and hypotheses of societal reality play a very different role in legal dogmatics. They are largely absent.[30] There have nevertheless been attempts to define propositions of valid law as falsifiable theories (Sect. 6.2), and there are new research areas called law and something (Sect. 6.3), each with its own scientific identity.

---

[23]See Husserl E (1962), §§ 2, 9(h) and 10.

[24]See *ibid*, §§ 14–15.

[25]Iggers GG (1984), p 45.

[26]See, for example, Ryan B, Scapens RW, Theobald M (1992), p. 119: "[F]rom a holistic perspective, generalizations and general laws do not explain, only the specific circumstances of the case can be used to explain."

[27]Simon HA (1967), p. 14.

[28]van Aken JE (2004), p. 224.

[29]See, for example, Siems MM (2008); von Holderstein Holtermann J, Madsen MR (2015); Bartrum IC (2013), p. 262. See nevertheless Mæhle SS (2015), pp. 131–132. There was a similar problem in management accounting in the past. See Kasanen E, Lukka K, Siitonen A (1993), p. 251.

[30]Sandgren C (2005), pp. 306 and 314; Engel C, Schön W (2007), p. IX.

User-Friendly Legal Science. It is possible to upgrade legal science from a non-science or a soft-applied disciplinary area to a soft-pure disciplinary area or a design science (Sects. 2.5 and 7.2). This can be achieved by applying generally accepted principles of scientific theory building. A theory defining a scientific discipline must lay down its core concepts (Sect. 2.2). It must also choose its research approach. The complex nature of society and law can best be captured by the holistic research approach (Sect. 2.3). The holistic research approach is connected with the way the relevant phenomena can be understood (Sect. 2.4). There are three basic forms of reasoning of which abduction is regarded as suitable for the holistic research approach (Sect. 2.5). User-friendly legal theories can be falsifiable, although there are problems caused by its holistic research approach (Sect. 2.6). The explanatory power of a theory depends on many things (Sect. 2.7).

2.2 Core Concepts

A scientific discipline must be based on a theory that defines its characteristics.[31] It must have a field, its own point of view (that is, knowledge interests or orientation) and methods. The theory must also define the necessary concepts (that is, the particular language of the scientific discipline).[32] The concepts should be sufficiently clear and unambiguous.[33] Obviously, the core concepts depend on the discipline and its prevailing preferences.[34] We can have a look at the core concepts of User-Friendly Legal Science.

Point of View. The point of view of User-Friendly Legal Science is how users can use legal tools and practices to reach their objectives in different contexts. This point of view is unique.[35] For example, the point of view of legal dogmatics is the interpretation and systematisation of law, the point of view of law and economics is the economic efficiency of law, and legal sociology has its own point of view (Sect. 6.3.2).

Field. There must be a field. A field is a social space. It is characteristic of User-Friendly Legal Science that the field consists of two or more overlapping and

[31]Kant I (1783), § 1.

[32]Kant I (1787), B XI–B XIII (on the language of geometry).

[33]Wittgenstein L (1922), Vorwort: "Man könnte den ganzen Sinn des Buches etwa in die Worte fassen: Was sich überhaupt sagen lässt, lässt sich klar sagen; und wovon man nicht reden kann, darüber muss man schweigen." This was originally limited to the propositions of natural science and the meaningfulness of propositions. *Ibid*, 6.53. However, it can act as inspiration even here.

[34]For legal history, see Duss V (2012), p. 987.

[35]See nevertheless Mæhle SS (2015), p. 142 and Wendehorst CC (2008), p. 602 distinguishing between different forms of legal reasoning: "Legal reasoning can take four different basic perspectives, which may be described as the internal, the external, the sovereign, and the subordinate perspective. Each of them has its own goals, its own patterns of argumentation, and its own tools for coping with plural and fragmented sources."

interacting fields. The legal field is one of them. An alternative way to put it is to say that the field of User-Friendly Legal Science consists of coupled systems with the legal system as one of them.[36]

For example, one could define 'municipal administration' as a particular field that consists of overlapping legal, political and economic fields or systems. The field of 'commercial law' consists of the overlapping fields of legal systems and markets.[37]

A bigger field can consist of sectors. A sector possesses the same general characteristics as other sectors in the same field. In addition, it has its own particular characteristics.

These fields and sectors are not the same thing as traditional fields of law. The latter are collections of legal norms. The fields of User-Friendly Legal Science consist of more elements and are not limited to things customarily known as 'pure law'[38] or the 'juridical field'[39] (for legal sociology, see Sect. 6.3.2).

Actors and Users. User-Friendly Legal Science focuses on the behaviour of users. Users are actors in a field. The choice of users means the choice of a perspective, that is, focusing on the general interests, context-specific objectives and means of a particular class.[40] Users can include people, organisations, public-sector entities such as the state or, under the actor-network theory, non-human actors (Sect. 7.2).

Actors that share the same interests and objectives in the same context customarily belong to the same class. Their interests and objectives coincide.[41] Neither their interests nor their objectives have to be connected or common,[42] but they can be connected or common depending on the context. Different classes of actors customarily have different interests or different objectives.

Actors have a smaller number of common denominators and a smaller number of shared goals (interests and objectives) where the class is less narrowly defined and less homogeneous. One can identify more common denominators and more detailed goals where the class is more narrowly defined and more homogeneous.

---

[36]Luhmann N (2004), Chapter 10, I, p 383.

[37]Mäntysaari P (2014).

[38]Kelsen H (1934).

[39]Compare Bourdieu P (1987), pp. 817 and 831: "The juridical field is the site of a competition for monopoly of the right to determine the law ... The juridical field is a social space organized around the conversion of direct conflict between directly concerned parties into juridically regulated debate between professionals acting by proxy. It is also the space in which such debate functions."

[40]See, for example, Mäntysaari P (2012), pp. 17–18.

[41]See, for example, Ross A (1958), p. 360: "Let us imagine two persons, A and B, both locked up in the same prison cell, both anxious to escape ... To that extent their interests may be said to coincide."

[42]For a definition, see Ross A (1958), p. 360.

The users and other actors in the field can be regarded as ideal types. The use of Weber's ideal types makes it easier to describe and understand complex societal phenomena. The use of ideal types facilitates the holistic approach of this discipline.[43] One can note that in economics, the use of ideal types facilitates a positivist approach and explanatory research.[44]

Ideal types make it possible to focus on representative users. One can say that there is normal behaviour (which includes the behaviour of both 'the bad man' and 'the good man') [45] and pathological behaviour (which might also be called outlier observations).[46] Central to the use of ideal types is what is regarded as normal or representative behaviour to the extent that one can describe societal mechanisms.[47]

The choice of a user, that is, an ideal type, makes it easier for real-life people and organisations to benefit from research findings. The researcher may choose a particular user class to give guidance to users belonging to that class, to give guidance to third parties that can adapt their own behaviour according to the expected behaviour of the ideal type/user or generally to increase the transparency of social mechanisms.

The researcher might even choose the ideal type/user for the purpose of influencing user behaviour. Obviously, a study of user behaviour does not create any legal obligations to behave the way ideal types are expected to behave. It might nevertheless be wise for users to act rationally or in ways perceived as rational (Sect. 6.3.2). Practical syllogisms[48] (see below) can thus become societal mechanisms, and a theory in social science can turn into a self-fulfilling prophecy.

Context. There are different contexts in the field. The choice of a context is connected to the choice of users and other actors. The context means a situation of interaction between the field's different actors.[49] In practice, one can define the context in various ways.

---

[43]Weber M (1904), II: "[Sie sind] von hohem heuristischen Wert für die Forschung und hohem systematischen Wert für die Darstellung, wenn sie lediglich als begriffliche Mittel zur Vergleichung und Messung der Wirklichkeit an ihnen verwendet werden. In dieser Funktion sind sie geradezu unentbehrlich." Weber M (1949), p. 43 (a translation of Weber M 1913): "Whatever the content of the ideal-type ... it has only one function in an empirical investigation. Its function is the comparison with empirical reality in order to establish its divergences or similarities, to describe them with the most unambiguously intelligible concepts, and to understand and explain them causally. Rational juridical concepts supply this need for the empirical history of law ..." See also Petersen J (2014), § 5 IV pp 120–121; Glaser BG, Strauss AL (1967), p. 23.

[44]Friedman M (1953), p. 36: "The ideal types are not intended to be descriptive; they are designed to isolate the features that are crucial for a particular problem."

[45]Holmes OW (1897).

[46]Durkheim É (1894), Chapter III.

[47]Weber M (1904), II: "Es handelt sich um die Konstruktion von Zusammenhängen, welche unserer Phantasie als zulänglich motiviert und also »objektiv möglich«, unserem nomologischen Wissen als adäquat erscheinen." Hydén H (2011), p. 121.

[48]von Wright GH (1971), p. 96.

[49]Compare Capra F, Mattei U (2015), p. 4: "In this book, we call for a profound change of legal paradigms, leading to a new 'ecology of law.' At the heart of this new ecological legal order lies a view of social reality not as being an aggregate of individual 'building blocks' but rather as being composed of social networks and communities. Law, in this view, is not an objective structure, but

One can start with a field or a sector (for example, logistics) and identify the relevant actors (for example, a supplier, the seller, the buyer, the freight forwarder, the carrier and so forth). One can define the context in greater detail by choosing the user (for example, the freight forwarder), as well as the type of the user's interaction (such as management of freight forwarding transactions) with other actors. The choice of the type of the user's interaction helps the researcher to define other relevant actors. One can further limit the context by choosing the form of the user's interaction with the other actors (for example, freight forwarding contracts and other contracts).

In other words, the context consists of many elements. The elements of the context include even its geographical scope. Since legal tools and practices are connected to one or more jurisdictions, the geographical scope of the context can influence the number of jurisdictions that can be relevant.

The context can be broad or narrow. For theory building, you need a sufficiently limited and particular context. The choice of a very broad context leads to a high level of generality. A narrow context helps the researcher to describe reality in a more detailed way.[50] The choice of the level of generality depends on the researcher's knowledge interests.

Objectives. The user's objectives depend on the context. One cannot focus on other than very general objectives where the chosen context is very broad. It is possible to identify more specific objectives where the context is narrow and well defined. For example, you could say that a firm manages cash flow, risk, principal–agency relationships and information in any transaction. On the other hand, a firm certainly has more specific goals in a particular context such as corporate governance or when a freight forwarding firm negotiates a contract for the provision of freight forwarding services to a customer.

Culture. User objectives, as well as legal tools and practices, may depend on culture. (a) It would be idealistic to assume that rational users have the same objectives in the same context worldwide. Even the contexts may be different in different societies because the actors in the field are not necessarily of the same kinds and because the forms of interaction can be different. There are similar problems in legal history[51] and comparative law.[52] (b) Moreover, the available legal tools and practices could have developed during a long period of time.[53] They are not necessarily the same across cultures, legal families or jurisdictions.

---

emerges from actively engaged citizen and legal communities as the legal embodiment of their self-organization."

[50]Glaser BG, Strauss AL (1967), pp. 32 and 79 distinguish between substantive and formal areas of sociological inquiry. While "patient care" is a substantive area of sociological inquiry, "social mobility" is a formal one.

[51]Wesel U (1974), p. 348.

[52]Different societies do not face similar needs and do not need similar institutions to meet the needs. Zweigert and Kötz represented the opposite view. See Michaels R (2008), p. 369.

[53]For the organic development of law, see Berman HJ (1983), p. 5.

Rationality. The existence of user objectives is a conditio sine qua non of rational decision-making (for rationality, see Sect. 2.4). Users have identifiable objectives as a class because users tend to be rational. The fact that users are assumed to act in rational ways means that rational behaviour is here used as an ideal type.

In reality, there are many ways for people to act in 'rational' ways[54] and people do not always act in ways that are perceived as 'rational'. Whether users that are perceived as acting 'rationally' at a certain point in time will prevail in the long run[55] remains to be seen in the future. In any case, it is reasonable to assume that well-informed users are more likely to prevail in the long term than poorly informed users.

In reality, people can also choose their objectives and the combination of legal tools and practices to reach them according to their preferences. For example, there is no one best way to organise a firm (contingency theory).[56]

Legal Tools and Practices. There can be several reasons to use legal tools and practices: the means can serve many ends. What can be regarded as legal tools and practices?

To begin with, one can distinguish between tools and practices. For example, a hammer is a tool and the customary ways to use hammers can be described as practices. A contract is without doubt one of the customary legal tools, and the ways to use contracts belong to the most popular legal practices. The same can be said of legal norms. They can be used in various ways for political or private purposes by the state, various entities or private individuals.[57]

The legal tools and practices must be 'legal'. Without this limitation, it would not be possible to regard User-Friendly Legal Science as a 'legal science' and draw a line between this new discipline and sociology. What makes legal tools and practices 'legal' is their direct or indirect legal effect, that is, connection to enforceability by state authorities.

While legal norms obviously belong to legal tools,[58] legal tools are not limited to legal norms and legal practices are not limited to mere compliance.

---

[54] Weber M (1922), First Part, Chapter I, § 1, I, 3, pp. 3–4; Williamson OE (1985), p. 44; Dewey J (1938), Chapter 6; Joas H (1996).

[55] For economics and finance, see Ryan B, Scapens RW, Theobald M (1992), p. 28.

[56] Woodward J (1958); Schoonhoven CB (1981).

[57] Andy Fastow, the former CFO of Enron, put it in the following way in a speech (Peter Elkind, The confessions of Andy Fastow, Fortune, July 1, 2013): "I thought: That's how the game is played. You have a complex set of rules, and the objective is to use the rules to your advantage."

[58] For a romantic view on the role of law, see Capra F, Mattei U (2015), p. 12: "The legal order is the most important vehicle through which a worldview is enforced and transformed into social action, and thus human law is also the agency through which we may implement new ideas and values."

The existence of a broad range of legal tools and practices is common knowledge in certain other legal disciplines. For example, it is customary to study a broad range of primary sources in legal history.[59] In comparative research, the existence of a broad range of legal tools and practices can help to explain differences in the laws of different countries.

Legal tools and practices can be made by the user or somebody else. The legal tools are thus not limited to legal norms made by somebody else, and the practices are not limited to mere regulatory compliance or compliance with other external norms.[60]

The legal tools and practices can be regulated or unregulated. This can be illustrated with compliance and the interpretation of laws. (a) Legal norms are normative, and people are expected to comply with them, but people are free to decide whether to actually do so. The actual process of compliance tends to be unregulated. Actual compliance is thus a choice and, apart from some exceptions,[61] an unregulated practice. (b) The interpretation of laws is a very important context in legal science. Most legal scholars would say that the interpretation of laws is at the core of normal legal science. The interpretation of laws requires legal argumentation. However, the practices of legal argumentation are, to a large extent, unregulated. This leaves plenty of room for legal rhetoric (Sect. 7.3).

At a more general level, legal tools and practices connect the overlapping fields (or coupled systems) of User-Friendly Legal Science. Depending on the user, legal tools can connect the fields (couple the systems) structurally or operationally. In the words of Niklas Luhmann, a German sociologist, 'the legal system is coupled with the political and the economic systems by highly specific devices'[62] and '[t]he structural coupling of economy and law achieved its modern ... form with the institutionalization of freedom of contract'.[63] While the state uses laws for structural couplings,[64] individuals and firms can use legal tools and practices for operative couplings[65] rather than structural couplings.

---

[59]See, for example, Maitland FW (1911), pp. 485–486: "Legal documents, documents of the most technical kind, are the best, often the only evidence that we have for social and economic history, for the history of morality, for the history of practical religion." See also Novak WJ (2000), p. 109 on Hurst's manuscript "Technology and the Law: The Automobile" (1949) and Hurst's list of 119 "Derivative Effects of the Auto Upon the Law".

[60]In contrast, Ehrlich and Pound focused on somebody else's norms. Likhovski A (2003), p. 628: "[T]here are intriguing similarities in Ehrlich's and Pound's thought: both were reacting against the excesses of late-nineteenth century formalist 'legal science.' Both wanted to expose the gap between formal and real-life 'living' law, and both saw law as the product of the people rather than the state. Both were, thus, interested in non-state norms of various sorts."

[61]See, for example, Mäntysaari P (2010a), Section 4.3.3.

[62]Luhmann N (2004), Chapter 10, I, p 383.

[63]See *ibid*, Chapter 10, III, p. 399.

[64]For legal norms, see Weber M (1922), Second Part, Chapter VII, § 1, p 394: "Andererseits werden wir immer erneut auch sehen, daß die von intern rechtstechnischen und politischen Momenten bedingten Eigenschaften des Rechts stark auf die Gestaltung der Wirtschaft zurückwirken."

[65]See Luhmann N (2004), Chapter 10, I, p 381.

Legal Norms, Law. Since behaviour is influenced by many kinds of norms, one may also ask where to draw the line between legal norms and other norms.[66] This could be a difficult question in legal sociology (Sect. 6.3.2). Moreover, one may ask about the connection between the legal tools and practices on one hand and legal norms on the other.

For the purposes of User-Friendly Legal Science, the exact definition of 'law' is a 'needless problem'.[67] The rule-maker can be a state or a non-state body. Things perceived as 'law' in legal science are customarily enforceable by state authorities.

We can have a closer look at this question in the light of Alf Ross. On one hand, Ross pointed out that legal practitioners are interested in whether there is a directive to the courts as to how they are to exercise their authority:[68] 'If it must be assumed of any statutory provision that it does not contain a directive to the courts it can be regarded only as a moral-ideological pronouncement without legal relevance.'[69] The legal tools and practices could therefore be regarded as instruments and purposeful behaviour that influence the application of such directives to the courts (norms). On the other hand, Ross assumed that 'the courts' are public authorities and that their judgments can be enforced by public exercise of force.[70] One can therefore say that it does not really matter whether 'the courts' are public authorities or not. There are bodies that can work as the functional equivalents of courts without being public authorities (such as arbitral tribunals and other non-state dispute resolution mechanisms), and there are public authorities that are the functional equivalents of courts without being courts (such as many regulatory authorities). What matters is the existence of a connection to enforceability by state authorities. Hence, the legal tools and practices can be defined as instruments and purposeful behaviour that are relevant when legal norms are enforced by state authorities.

One can thus define legal norms, legal tools and legal practices in the following way for the purposes of User-Friendly Legal Science:

Legal norms are norms that are enforceable by state authorities directly (by state authorities themselves) or indirectly (by non-state bodies recognised by state authorities as the proper bodies to enforce the norms).

Legal tools are facilitated by norms enforceable by state authorities directly or indirectly. Legal tools do not need to be enforceable as such.

Legal practices mean the particular ways the legal tools are used or taken into account.

---

[66]See Ehrlich E (1913), p. 31 and Berman HJ (1983), pp. 4–5 on "living law".

[67]Ross A (1958), p. 32.

[68]*Ibid*, p. 33.

[69]*Ibid*, p. 33.

[70]*Ibid*, p. 34.

This can be illustrated with the following examples:

- Legal norms: industry self-regulation often relies on the work of non-state bodies. From the user perspective, norms adopted by such non-state bodies can be perceived as the functional equivalents of norms adopted by the state. Whether the norms are legal norms depends on whether the norms ultimately rely on the enforcement powers of state authorities.[71]
- Legal tools: contract terms can be binding and enforceable under the applicable provisions of law, binding but not enforceable or neither binding nor enforceable. Non-binding or unenforceable contracts are often used as legal tools because of their de facto effect.
- Legal practices: the user can take legal norms into account by adapting its behaviour. It can avoid norms (opt out), submit to norms (opt in), mitigate legal risk (compliance) or accept legal risk (limited adaptation of behaviour, non-compliance).
- Legal norms, tools and practices: the provisions of criminal law contain directives to the judge. If a private individual wants to reduce the risk of being sentenced to prison for murder,[72] he will need to acquire information about the regulation of wrongful killings and adapt to this regulation before killing anyone. There may be important practices for the collection and management of such information. If caught after the act, prior compliance with the provisions of criminal law may enable the individual to be sentenced to prison for manslaughter rather than murder. Legal compliance is thus an important legal tool for potential killers. Moreover, the norms of criminal law are 'operative in the mind of the judge, because they are felt by him to be socially binding and therefore obeyed'.[73] The tricks of the trade that killers use to make the judge show leniency according to a social norm binding on judges and sentence the killer to prison for manslaughter instead of murder are legal practices for killers.

2.3 Holism, Ontology, Epistemology, Use of Findings, Transplants

User-Friendly Legal Science needs a holistic research approach because law is a complex societal phenomenon, societal or user objectives cannot be attained without taking into account all relevant aspects and the understanding of complex societal phenomena requires a holistic approach. The holistic research approach is

---

[71] Compare the more sociological approaches of Ehrlich E (1913), pp. 405–406 on living law and Capra F, Mattei U (2015), p. 13 on the systemic, ecological paradigm of the law: "Law emerges from actively engaged citizens in self-organizing communities . . . Law is what is deemed to be law by civic and legal communities . . ."

[72] Homicide was used as an example in Ross A (1958), p. 33.

[73] *Ibid*, p. 35.

even connected to certain ontological and epistemological assumptions. We will now have a look at these issues.

Law. The approach of law is holistic for various reasons. In order to be perceived as legitimate, legal norms generally must be justified as general rules. Legal norms tend to leave room for discretion to take into account a wide range of relevant facts because legal norms are designed to solve complex problems and conflicts of interest that exist in real life. Moreover, legal norms are embedded in legal and societal cultures, and legal norms are path dependent.

It is easy to find examples of how law facilitates a holistic approach. To name a few, they include the widespread use of general principles and other open norms, the openness of the interpretation of legal norms, the many alternative practices of legal rhetoric used in the context of the interpretation of legal norms, the discretion of the judge, the nature of evidence that may be taken into account in legal proceedings and the nature of evidence that may be taken into account when interpreting contracts.

Legal Science. The holistic approach of law is reflected in the holistic approach of legal dogmatics. In particular, the coherence of the legal system and the relative weight of the societal outcomes of different propositions belong to key factors influencing the interpretation of legal norms (for legal rhetoric, see Sect. 7.3). The holistic approach is represented in very different theories of law ranging from Kelsen's pure law and systematisation to the legal realism and pragmatism of Ross.[74]

Comparative law is an example of the connection between the holistic approach and a functional approach. The functional method is the most popular method in micro-comparison.[75] The functional method means the comparison of sets of legal things that share the same societal function.

Social Sciences. Each scientific discipline defines its own point of view and methods. Since research projects in other social sciences do not produce findings designed to be used normatively in the legal sense, they do not need to reflect real-life complexity as closely as law and legal science. Other disciplines can choose a narrower approach.

The research approach can be narrow in two main ways. One can distinguish between methodological collectivism and methodological individualism.[76] Methodological individualism means that social phenomena are explained by the

[74]*Ibid*, p. 338.

[75]Zweigert K, Kötz H (1996). For the functional method, see also Husa J (2003); Michaels R (2008); De Coninck J(2010).

[76]The term "methodological individualism" was first used by Schumpeter J (1908). See, for example, Blaug M (1992), pp. 44–48; Udehn L (2001), p. 104; Udehn L (2002).

motivations and actions of individual agents. Methodological collectivism means the opposite: the motivations and actions of individual agents are explained by external social forces.[77]

For example, the rational-actor model is an application of methodological individualism in economics.[78] In contrast, Marxists used to reject methodological individualism.

User-Friendly Legal Science. User-Friendly Legal Science chooses neither methodological individualism nor methodological collectivism. While methodological individualism and collectivism are attempts to explain facts causally, the new discipline focuses on interpretive understanding rather than causal relationships. This requires a pragmatic and holistic research approach in the sense that the relevance of facts depends on the context, and one should take into account all relevant facts.

By definition, User-Friendly Legal Science studies how users can use legal tools and practices to reach their objectives in different contexts. Users may be able to use a broad range of alternative and/or complementary legal things to reach one and the same objective in the same context. Moreover, each user may simultaneously have conflicting objectives in one and the same context, and a user may have objectives even in other contexts that the user takes into account in its decision-making. The actual choices of a particular user reflect the user's preferences and cannot be causally explained. Simplified causal explanations would not help to describe such complex reality.

Ontology. The holistic approach of User-Friendly Legal Science is connected with its ontological assumptions. In principle, there could be different assumptions about the nature of reality (ontology) such as realism ('there is a single truth'), internal realism ('truth exists, but is obscure'), relativism ('there are many truths') and nominalism ('there is no truth').[79] While the realist position is characteristic of legal dogmatics, User-Friendly Legal Science cannot represent realism. The use of ideal types and the fact that truth depends on the choice of the user and the context indicate the relativist position.[80] Moreover, the interpretation of language generally is subject to the 'indeterminacy of translation'.[81]

Epistemology. The holistic approach of User-Friendly Legal Science is even connected with its epistemology, that is, its ways of enquiring into the nature of the

[77]Johansson LG (2015), p. 160; Johansson LG (2015), p. 161.

[78]Arrow KJ (1994), p. 1.

[79]Eeasterby-Smith M, Thorpe R, Jackson PR (2015), Table 3.2, p 50.

[80]User-friendly Legal Science is thus not part of Scandinavian Legal Realism. See Leiter B (2009): "[O]ne of H.L.A. Hart's decisive achievements was to demonstrate the failure of the Scandinavian program to account for the perspective of actors within a legal system - such a perspective, Hart argued plausibly, being essential to account for the social phenomenon of law."

[81]Quine WV (1960), Chapter 2.

world. In principle, one could again choose between competing epistemological approaches.

The competing approaches include positivism, idealism and interpretive understanding. (a) Positivism is based on the assumption that the world has an existence independent of us. In this case, science describes things that exist independent of the mind. The positivist approach is that these external things can be empirically and objectively observed and measured. Positivism focuses on causal relationships. (b) Idealism means in this context that the world is regarded as a creation of the human mind and that one can obtain knowledge about reality by thinking, that is, without empirical observations. (c) While complex societal phenomena cannot be explained by simple causal relationships, they can be described by the holistic approach and interpretive understanding (Sect. 2.4).

User-Friendly Legal Science is not a positivist science. While societal reality obviously exists, the ideal types used in this new discipline do not 'exist'. Ideal types are just a means to describe societal reality.

Neither does User-Friendly Legal Science represent idealism. Idealism is based on the assumption that one can obtain knowledge about reality without empirical observations, but User-Friendly Legal Science is based on both theory and empirical findings.

The complex societal phenomena studied in User-Friendly Legal Science can be described better by the holistic approach and interpretive understanding. Understanding is increased by pragmatism and grounded theory (Sect. 2.5).

Use of Findings. The ontology and epistemology of User-Friendly Legal Science are connected to the use of its findings. The findings are designed to be used pragmatically (Chap. 4).

Transplants. The holistic nature of law, legal science and User-Friendly Legal Science plays a role when one uses (a) legal notions or theories from other jurisdictions or (b) theories from other social sciences.

One can learn from experiences in comparative law in this respect. The use of legal transplants is a well-known phenomenon in comparative law.[82] Transplants do not necessarily work well in the host legal system, although they might work well in the home legal system, that is, the legal system in which the transplants originate. They can become legal irritants in the host legal system.[83]

Theory transplants from other social sciences cannot be expected to work better than legal transplants in the host legal system. In fact, they are likely to be worse. This is because of the fundamental difference between law and theories from other social sciences. While law is normative and holistic (a system the contents of which are based on values), theories from other social sciences are not normative and may give a very simplified picture of societal mechanisms (especially when based on

[82] Watson A (1974).

[83] Teubner G (1998).

positivist and causal assumptions, the myth of unity of science, or methodological individualism or collectivism).[84]

Moreover, the use of theory transplants from other social sciences can become a threat to the values that laws are based on. Since law is normative, it must be applied to a wide range of people and organisations that exist in real life, and the legal system must take into account the complexity of society and reflect values that work in real life. Other social sciences can develop theories that do not need to reflect real-life complexity as closely as the legal system does. In the long run, theories in social sciences can become self-fulfilling prophecies if applied by many people. Those applying such theories can create the social mechanisms described by the theories and contribute to the outcome that the theories predict.[85] The choice of a theory is thus a political act.

The same problems could arise in User-Friendly Legal Science where theories from other social sciences are utilised as method theories (Sect. 3.3) in a research project. The researcher should be critical and understand the underlying values and what the employment of such imported theories really means. There is no reason to blindly import theories from other social sciences regardless of how well established they are in the scientific discipline in which they originate.

This means that there is room for more suitable theories in legal science. The new discipline can facilitate the building of theories that reflect both societal and legal reality and make it possible to replace theory irritants from other social sciences with tailor-made theories originating in legal science.

Theory Transplants and Irritants: Duties Owed to the Company. The problems that arise when you transplant a narrow theory from other social sciences into law can be illustrated with a company law question. To whom are the duties of board members owed in a limited liability company?

It is common knowledge that the company has several stakeholders such as employees, lenders, shareholders, contract parties and the state. According to one of the most basic company law rules, a limited liability company is a separate legal entity distinct from its stakeholders and board duties are owed to the company.

However, the neoclassical theory of the firm assumes that the firm is just a 'set of contracts', shareholders are 'owners' and the 'principal', and managers are 'agents' that should further the interests of shareholders.[86] Moreover, the shareholders of this theory are homogeneous and fictive shareholders with fictive preferences rather

[84]See, for example, Weber M (1949), pp. 43–44: "Economic theory is an axiomatic discipline in a way which is logically very different from that of the systematic science of law. Its relationship to economic reality is very different from the relationship of jurisprudence to the phenomena treated by the history and sociology of law." See also Grundmann S, Micklitz HW, Renner M (eds) (2015), p. 1.

[85]For a case showing how economic theories can influence legislation, see Ferraro F, Pfeffer J, Sutton RI (2005); Kieser A (2004); André T Jr (1998).

[86]Jensen MC, Meckling WH (1976); Fama EF (1980).

than the heterogeneous real-life shareholders each with the shareholder's own actual preferences.

In real life, board members cannot owe legal duties to fictions because the existence of such absurd duties would harm the firm and society as a whole. Neither can board members owe their general duties to actual shareholders. This is because real shareholders are heterogeneous rather than homogeneous and have conflicting interests. This explains why the rights of shareholders tend to be rather limited in company law[87] and why duties are owed to the company and not to shareholders.

The neoclassical theory of the firm is thus a theory irritant in the company law system (see Sect. 6.3.4). It is possible to replace the neoclassical theory of the firm with user-friendly legal theories of corporate governance and company law.[88]

2.4 Understanding and Rationality

The overall goal of User-Friendly Legal Science is interpretive understanding (Verstehen).[89] It is therefore necessary to define understanding. Understanding is connected with the notion of rationality.

Notions of Rationality. One can distinguish between various forms of rationality. Weber distinguished between (1) actions that are rational in a technical or mathematical way (Zweckrationalität, instrumental actions) and (2) actions that are rational because they are perceived as reasonable (Wertrationalität, value-rational actions). In addition, he identified (3) affective (emotional) actions and (4) traditional actions as alternatives to rational actions.[90] Human actions can be rational even in other ways.[91]

The choice of a notion of rationality can be illustrated with economics. The orientation of traditional economics is influenced by the positivist approach of natural sciences and the fact that natural events have causes (Humean causes). Traditional economics is thus based on the first form of rationality mentioned by Weber. It is customary to distinguish between three levels of instrumental rationality in economics: 'The strong form contemplates maximizing. Bounded rationality is the semistrong form. The weak form is organic rationality.'[92] For example,

[87]See, for example, Mäntysaari P (2005).

[88]Mäntysaari P (2010a); Mäntysaari P (2012). For similar problems in accounting caused by "the positive accounting cult", see Chambers RJ (1993).

[89]For sociology, see Weber M (1922).

[90]Weber M (1922), § 2.

[91]See, for example, Korobkin RB, Ulen TS (2000); Dewey J (2000); Dewey J (1938), Chapter 6 (purposeful action); Joas H (1996), pp. 4–6. Joas argues that "a third model of action should be added to the two predominant models of action", the two models being rational action and normatively oriented action. The third model "emphasizes the creative character of human action".

[92]Williamson OE (1985), p. 44.

neoclassical economics maintains a 'maximising orientation' and institutional economics (transaction cost economics) relies on the cognitive assumption of 'bounded rationality'.

Legal norms provide a different kind of example. Legal norms are obviously based on values. They exist for the purpose of balancing different kinds of interests according to the relevant political preferences.[93]

Turning to User-Friendly Legal Science, one might ask whether it would be possible to try to identify cause-and-effect relationships. Legal tools and practices are after all used for a reason. It might be tempting to talk about societal cause-and-effect relationships in the sense that the effect of the use of a particular legal tool or practice is the reason for its use and its cause.[94] Some have understood cause-and-effect relationships even in this way.[95]

However, cause-and-effect relationships belong to positivism. Human actions with which social sciences are concerned do not have Humean causes and should not be causally explained. Human actions can have multiple causes, and one cause can lead to various kinds of actions.[96] Moreover, focusing on cause-and-effect relationships would exclude the holistic approach. The identification of cause-and-effect relationships can thus not be the form of understanding in User-Friendly Legal Science. One could say that User-Friendly Legal Science shares a positivist approach only in a very broad sense as the opposite of metaphysics.[97]

If human actions can be rational in different ways, it would be wrong to assume that the actual preferences of users are limited to those based on just one form of rationality. One can try to understand human actions even in this respect.

Understanding, Practical Syllogisms. The form of understanding takes the form of practical syllogisms. An action is understood if and only if it is regarded as the conclusion of a suitable practical syllogism (von Wright).[98] Practical syllogisms seem to suit User-Friendly Legal Science very well because legal tools and

---

[93]Heck P (1914).

[94]Lamprecht K (1896), p. 5: "Sind nun aber Zweck und Kausalverknüpfung vollkommen voneinander geschiedene intellektuelle Vorgänge? Keineswegs! Sie sind nur verschiedene, unserem Denken gleich immanente Betrachtungsweisen eines und desselben Voganges. Denke ich mir die vorgestellte Wirkung irgend eines Geschehnisses als dessen Ursache, so wird dies Ursache zum Zweck." For the relevance of Lamprecht, see Iggers GG (1988).

[95]See, for example, Lamprecht K (1896), pp. 6 and 13: "Die kausale Methode kann nirgends leichter gehandhabt werden als auf dem Gebiete der sozialen und wirtschaftlichen Erscheinungen."

[96]See, for example, Kusch M (2003), p. 350: "Natural events do have (Humean) causes, unlike human actions with which social sciences are concerned. This is why human action (and anything manifesting it) should not be causally explained but understood in terms of the reasons of the actors ... Understanding is not dependent on reference to causes and general laws."

[97]Comte distinguished between the theological, the metaphysical, and the positive phase in the development of society.

[98]von Wright GH (1971), p. 96. For a summary of the central claims of von Wright GH (1971) and von Wright's modified position, see Kusch M (2003), p. 350.

practices are used for a reason. Understanding means here understanding the intentions of the parties and the function of the legal tools and practices.[99] Understanding does not mean the description of causal relationships.[100] What one tries to understand is a prescription: 'If you are A and you are in situation Z, you want to achieve Y and something like action X will help.'[101]

Ideal Types, Reasonable Explanations, Theory, Hermeneutical Circle. This kind of understanding is facilitated by the use of ideal types, reasonable explanations, theory and the hermeneutical circle.

The use of ideal types makes it possible to focus on representative users and representative phenomena (Sect. 2.2). During the course of the research process, the researcher can define and redefine the ideal types used in the project.

Reasonable explanations are related to notions of rationality. Actions can be regarded as rational if they are perceived as reasonable. The explanation of actions can be regarded as rational where the explanations are reasonable. There could be a long list of potential explanations, but some explanations are more probable than others.

Theory can help to describe behaviour. Due to the pluralism of sources, it can be difficult to take into account all potentially relevant materials. Theory can help to determine what is relevant.[102]

The hermeneutical circle[103] is regarded as a suitable process for the understanding of complex societal facts. The process is called a hermeneutical circle because the researcher's own prior knowledge (Vorverständnis) and understanding develop during the course of the research and the researcher can obtain better information when the researcher gets a better idea of what to look for.[104]

2.5 Reasoning

The main forms of reasoning in scientific research include deduction, induction and abduction. Scientific reasoning is subject to disciplinary requirements.

Theory building contains both deductive and inductive (empirical) elements.[105] However, deductive reasoning (which moves from the general rule to the specific

---

[99]Berglund L, Ney A (2015), p. 84.

[100]For the main differences between description-driven and prescription-driven research programmes, see van Aken JE (2004), p. 236.

[101]Compare van Aken JE (2004), p. 227: "[M]any prescriptions in a design science are of a heuristic nature. They can rather be described as 'if you want to achieve Y in situation Z, then something like action X will help'."

[102]Berglund L, Ney A (2015), p. 87.

[103]Ast DF (1808), pp. 179–180; Heidegger M (1926), § 63.

[104]Firat AF (1987); Berglund L, Ney A (2015), pp. 121–126.

[105]Popper K (2005), number 85.

application) and inductive reasoning (which means drawing generalised conclusions on the basis of specific observations) are not enough to describe the way reasoning works in social sciences. In particular, they do not describe the process of reasoning where the researcher chooses the holistic perspective, focuses on interpretive understanding and uses the hermeneutical circle.

Deduction and induction are complemented by abduction. Abductive reasoning is commonplace in social sciences: 'In fact, most of the qualitative research in social sciences could probably be included within the limits of the different degrees of abductive reasoning'.[106] Moreover, pure inductive research is 'impossible',[107] and pure deductive reasoning lacks empiricism. Abductive reasoning helps to understand complex phenomena[108] and generate new scientific knowledge.[109]

User-friendly legal theories benefit from abductive reasoning. User-friendly theories are theories of practice, and knowledge formation from practice 'means in effect the use of a methodological approach that is in accordance with abductive reasoning'.[110]

Abductive Reasoning. Abductive reasoning has long roots. Aristotle discussed it as apagōgē.[111] In 1597, Julius Pacius translated it to Latin as abductio. The present-day notion of abduction was coined by Charles S. Peirce, who used the term in 1867 in his article 'Abduction for the Dictionary of Logic'.[112]

Abductive reasoning can be defined as reasoning from given data to a hypothesis that explains the data.[113] It starts from the known facts and probes backwards into the reasons or explanations for them.[114]

---

[106]Saurama E, Julkunen I (2012), p. 61. See also Harman G (1965); Niiniluoto I (1984); Magnani L (2001); Lipton P (1991); Walton D (2014).

[107]Saurama E, Julkunen I (2012), p. 61. Induction was regarded as more important when the benchmark was positivism. See, for example, Lamprecht K (1896), p. 3: "Die Geschichtswissenschaft ist im Rahmen der für die Induktion geltenden erkenntnistheoretischen Kautelen und Ergänzungen eine induktive Wissenschaft; also kann nur der jeweilige Charakter des induktiven Beweisverfahrens und dessen verschiedenartige Auffassung wahrhaft wissenschaftliche Gegensätze und Strömungen in ihr begründen." See also Iggers GG (1984).

[108]Peirce CS (1931–1935), 5.145: "Abduction consists in studying facts and devising a theory to explain them. Its only justification is that if we are ever to understand things at all, it must be in that way."

[109]Peirce CS (1931–1935), 5.172: "A man must be downright crazy to deny that science has made many true discoveries. But every single item of scientific theory which stands established today has been due to Abduction."

[110]Saurama E, Julkunen I (2012), p. 65.

[111]Aristotle, Organon, Analytica priora, second book, chapter 25.

[112]Peirce CS (1883), p. 108.

[113]See Walton D (2014), p. xiii; Walton D (2001), p. 144.

[114]Walton D (2001), p. 145.

Abductive reasoning can also be called inference to the best explanation.[115] It is assumed to lead to just one hypothesis or a small number of hypotheses.[116] This brings one close to Ockham's injunction not to multiply entities beyond necessity.

Abductive reasoning means guessing the likely 'middle term'.[117] This is the fundamental difference that separates abduction from deduction and induction. The differences between these three forms of reasoning can be illustrated with the 'singular syllogism in Barbara' in Peirce's article about probable inference:[118]

> Rule: Every M is a P. Case: S is an M. Result: S is a P.

An ordinary syllogism proceeds from Rule and Case to Result. Induction proceeds from Case and Result to Rule. Abduction proceeds from Rule and Result to Case.[119]

It is characteristic of abduction that you use probable inference.[120] This is not to be mixed with probabilities. The validity of abduction designed to produce hypotheses does not depend on probabilities as such.[121] In 1903, Peirce gave the following schema for abductive inference:

> The surprising fact C is observed. But if A were true, C would be a matter of course. Hence, there is reason to suspect that A is true.[122]

Therefore, one could also say that abduction proceeds from Result (a known quantity, the surprising fact C) to Rule and Case (two unknowns):

> Something unintelligible is discovered in the data and, on the basis of the mental design of a new rule, the rule is discovered or invented and, simultaneously, it becomes clear what the case is.[123]

Grounded Theory. Abduction discourse leads to what is known as grounded theory. Grounded theory is a very important method in modern social research.

---

[115]Harman G (1965), pp. 88–89; Lipton P (1991).

[116]Peirce CS (1931–1935), 5.171: "Deduction proves that something must be; Induction shows that something actually is operative; Abduction merely suggests that something may be."

[117]Aristotle, Organon, Analytica posteriora, first book, Chapters 13 and 34; Analytica priora, second book, Chapter 25; Niiniluoto I (1984), p. 33; Woods J (2014), p. 32.

[118]Peirce CS (1883), pp. 127–128.

[119]Niiniluoto I (1984), p. 33.

[120]Peirce CS (1883), p. 127; Peirce CS (1931–1935), 2.712.

[121]Peirce CS (1931–1935), 2.102: "Upon this subject, my doctrine has been immensely improved since my essay 'A Theory of Probable Inference' was published in 1883 . . . When, after repeated attempts, I finally succeeded in clearing the matter up, the fact shone out that probability proper had nothing to do with the validity of Abduction, unless in a doubly indirect manner."

[122]Peirce CS (1931–1935), 5.189. See also 2.712. Discussed, for example, in Niiniluoto I (1984), p. 33; Woods J (2014), pp. 32–33.

[123]Reichertz J (2007), p. 219.

Some regard it as a methodology. In any case, it justifies the scientificity of much of qualitative research in social sciences.[124]

The original grounded theory was a method established by Barney Glaser and Anselm Strauss.[125] It was influenced by the distinction between inductive and abductive reasoning[126] and split into two directions.[127]

Glaser represents inductive reasoning. According to Glaser, theory building emerges directly from the collected data. Glaser also regards grounded theory as a methodology.[128]

In contrast, Anselm Strauss and Juliet Corbin represent abductive reasoning.[129] Strauss and Corbin think that the development of theory is theory guided[130] and that researchers must be in a position to modify or reject concepts during and due to observation. The grounded theory of Strauss and Corbin can thus combine the rational (reasonable) and innovative (the generation of better understanding and new knowledge) sides of abduction.[131] Moreover, Strauss and Corbin regard grounded theory as a method.[132]

In the light of the Strauss and Corbin model, the surprising facts mentioned by Peirce can pop up in the event that prior studies do not provide any appropriate explanation for the collected data. The surprise leads one to search for a new explanation. Since the explanation is new, it must be invented or discovered by means of a mental process.[133] Peirce regarded abduction as the only way to originate new ideas in science.[134]

Constructive Research. Understanding a problem with the help of abduction and grounded theory is only halfway to solving it.[135] One can also provide a solution.

---

[124]See, for example, Dubois A, Gadde LE (2014) and Dubois A, Gadde LE (2002) on business research.

[125]Glaser BG, Strauss AL (1967).

[126]Reichertz J (2007), p. 215: "[T]he Glaser–Strauss controversy can be characterized, at least in part, as one between induction and abduction."

[127]Glaser BG (1992); Strauss AL, Corbin JM (1990); Corbin J, Strauss AL (1990); Strauss AL, Corbin JM (1994).

[128]Glaser BG (1992), p. 16.

[129]Reichertz J (2007), p. 215: "Neither Strauss nor Strauss and Corbin have systematized this logic of abductive discovery, nor have they linked it to the considerations of Charles S. Peirce, the founder of abduction."

[130]Strauss AL, Corbin JM (1990), p. 73: "Every type of inquiry rests on the asking of effective questions."

[131]Reichertz J (2007), p. 216.

[132]Strauss AL, Corbin JM (1990), p. 24.

[133]Reichertz J (2007), p. 219.

[134]Peirce CS (1931–1935), 5.145: "All the ideas of science come to it by the way of Abduction."

[135]van Aken JE (2004), p. 220.

The constructive approach is a research procedure for producing 'constructions'. Constructions refer to things that provide solutions to explicit problems.[136] There are examples of the constructive research approach in various kinds of disciplines such as technical sciences, clinical medicine, option pricing and management research.[137] It is customary in 'design sciences'.[138]

The constructive approach is intended to be scientific.[139] It uses abductive reasoning, grounded theory and the hermeneutical circle. Moreover, the constructions can be described as practical syllogisms: if you want A but you think you are currently in situation B, you should use construction X.[140]

The particular aspects of the constructive approach have their roots in its knowledge interests or point of view:

- The research question should be relevant for practitioners who apply scientific knowledge when solving practical problems.
- The answer to the research question should provide an innovative solution to the practical problem.
- Abduction is complemented by deduction. Because of the knowledge interests of the constructive approach, the researcher should demonstrate that the solution works.[141] The researcher should also examine the scope of the solution's applicability. The actual usefulness cannot be proved without a practical test.[142]
- Abduction is complemented by induction. The researcher should show the theoretical connections and the research contribution of the solution concept.[143]

---

136 Kasanen E, Lukka K, Siitonen A (1993), p. 244. See Elharidy AM, Nicholson B, Scapens RW (2008), p. 141: "[Interpretive management accounting research] is interested in studying real world practices, decisions and settings, with the objective of analysing, interpreting and understanding them: thereby identifying solutions to pragmatic problems."

137 van Aken JE (2004), p. 221 (design sciences); Kasanen E, Lukka K, Siitonen A (1993), p. 245. For option pricing, see Black F, Scholes M (1973).

138 van Aken JE (2004), p. 224. Compare Sterling RR (1975). Sterling's article shows how difficult it was to define accounting as a science before the constructive approach and the notion of a design science. There were traces of what became the constructive approach already in Chambers RJ (1956).

139 Kasanen E, Lukka K, Siitonen A (1993), p. 258.

140 von Wright GH (1971), p. 96.

141 Kasanen E, Lukka K, Siitonen A (1993), p. 258: "The possibility of checking the steps of a construction … linked with the criteria of objectivity, criticalness and autonomy, contributes to the issue that anybody can try out the construction and obtain results similar to the person who has made the original construction."

142 *Ibid,* p. 253.

143 *Ibid,* p. 246: "The constructive approach may be characterized by dividing the research process into phases, the order of which may, of course, vary from case to case: 1. Find a practically relevant problem which also has research potential. 2. Obtain a general and comprehensive understanding of the topic. 3. Innovate, i.e., construct a solution idea. 4. Demonstrate that the solution works. 5. Show the theoretical connections and the research contribution of the solution concept. 6. Examine the scope of applicability of the solution."

Constructive research can be either quantitative or qualitative or both. Customarily, it applies the case method.[144] Innovation is a core element of a successful constructive study.[145]

Although the constructive approach should be relevant for practitioners, it is not designed as a form of applied science.[146] It is based on the assumption that one can draw theoretical conclusions from the usability of constructions.[147] This means that all problem solving is not regarded as constructive research: 'an essential part of the constructive approach is to tie the problem and its solution with accumulated theoretical knowledge'.[148]

Abductive Reasoning, Grounded Theory, the Constructive Approach and User-Friendly Legal Science. Abduction is no stranger in law. Abduction is customarily used in assessing evidence. For example, when you find a dead man A with a knife in his back, the prosecutor may connect the dots between A being dead and the knife sticking in his back by forming a hypothesis that it was the injury caused by the knife that killed A. Moreover, if there are fingerprints of B on the knife, the prosecutor may form the hypothesis that the knife sticks in the back of A because B put it there. The hypothesis will then be subject to testing. Such evidence can be enough for a conviction if it is 'beyond reasonable doubt'[149] that B is guilty of killing A with the knife.

Abductive reasoning is useful in User-Friendly Legal Science as well. It is part of a path that even contains deductive and inductive elements. First, abductive reasoning leads to a 'hypothesis', that is, a preliminary understanding that is a synthesis from theory and empirical facts about the phenomenon under investigation. This preliminary understanding provides the preliminary theoretical framework. Second, the 'hypothesis' can be tested by means of deductive reasoning (examples, case studies). Third, the results can be generalised back to the theoretical framework through induction. This improves the understanding and the theoretical framework. The researcher may need to repeat the process several times.

In User-Friendly Legal Science, there are many ways to test a theory that describes the objectives of the chosen user in a certain context and the legal tools and practices that can be employed to reach them. For example, the researcher may find out what the documentation of legal tools says about the objectives and practices. The researcher may also interview people who can give information about the relevant objectives and practices. There is plenty of room for methodological creativity.

---

[144]*Ibid*, p. 255.

[145]*Ibid*, pp. 246–247.

[146]van Aken JE (2004), p. 225.

[147]Kasanen E, Lukka K, Siitonen A (1993), p. 259, referring to Peirce CS (1931–1935), 1.54.

[148]Kasanen E, Lukka K, Siitonen A (1993), p. 246.

[149]This applies to Anglo-American countries. For German law, see § 261 and § 244 StPO (penal law cases) and § 286 ZPO (civil law cases).

Both grounded theory and the constructive research approach seem to be feasible in user-friendly legal research. This implies that User-Friendly Legal Science is a design science (Sect. 2.1).

The similarities between this new discipline and the design sciences are evident even in its knowledge interests. Obviously, it has its own knowledge interests (its point of view). However, one can distinguish between different forms of knowledge in the same way as in other design sciences.

The forms of knowledge are object knowledge, realisation knowledge and process knowledge.[150] Object knowledge can here mean knowledge about the law and legal tools, as well as knowledge about their effects in the relevant contexts (legal and other contexts). Realisation knowledge could relate to legal practices, that is, the way the legal tools can be used. Process knowledge is knowledge about the design process, that is, knowledge about the objectives of users, how they obtain relevant information and how they manage to end up using the legal tools and practices in the relevant context.

2.6 Falsifiability

The falsifiability of user-friendly legal theories is made more difficult by the holistic perspective, the goal of interpretive understanding and the use of ideal types. Moreover, the phenomena described by user-friendly legal theories have a connection to legal norms in one or more jurisdictions, one or more legal and societal cultures, and values.

However, user-friendly legal theories can describe user behaviour. They can be 'sufficiently good approximations'.[151] The falsifiability of user-friendly legal theories depends on the theory in question and is not impossible as such (Sect. 2.7).

In practice, the researcher repeats the hermeneutical circle many times. The researcher should test the draft theory against prior theory and societal facts (Strauss and Corbin) and modify the draft theory to make sure that it would not be too easy for others to falsify it.[152] When doing so, the researcher increases the explanatory power of the draft theory. We will therefore continue to discuss the question of falsifiability in the context of explanatory power.

---

[150]van Aken JE (2004), pp. 226–227.

[151]Economics faces similar challenges in this respect. Friedman M (1953), p. 15: "To put this point less paradoxically, the relevant question to ask about the 'assumptions' of a theory is not whether they are descriptively 'realistic,' for they never are, but whether they are sufficiently good approximations for the purpose in hand. And this question can be answered only by seeing whether the theory works, which means whether it yields sufficiently accurate predictions."

[152]See also Sandgren C (2005), pp. 310–311.

2.7 Explanatory Power

The value of a theory lies in its 'explanatory power'.[153] One may ask how to build a theory with high explanatory power.

Falsifiability and Testability. According to Popper, the answer lies in the easiness of falsification.[154] The explanatory power of a theory and the easiness of falsification are two sides of the same coin. A theory is more useful if it has a wide explanatory range. However, a theory with a wide explanatory range is easier to falsify and less likely to be true. Very general and simple theories are even easier to falsify. In contrast, banal theories and theories that have minimal content are not very powerful. At the same time, they are more difficult to falsify and more likely to be true.

Therefore, the explanatory power of a theory depends on two main things. First, it depends on its 'empirical content' (the range of things that can be falsified) and testability. The greater is the theory's empirical content and the easier it is to test it, the greater is the explanatory power of the theory (and the easier it is to falsify it).[155] Second, the explanatory power of a theory depends on the range of facts that it seeks to explain and the number of explanatory concepts used to explain them (simplicity). The wider is the range of facts and the smaller the number of concepts, the larger is its explanatory power (and the easier it is to falsify it).[156]

Nicholas Aroney gives an example of the application of these principles in legal research. He argues that the explanatory power of a theory is 'a function of four paired qualities, each pair expressing an irreducible tension between two desirable but contrasting features'. These paired qualities are '(1) the simplicity and intricacy of the theory, (2) the range and complexity of the phenomena that the theory seeks to explain, (3) the specificity and generality of the theory's explanations in relation to those phenomena, and (4) the capacity of the theory to be integrated with other theories or to unify the explanations provided by them'.[157]

Theories possessing a high level of explanatory power are thus relatively simple (number 1) rather than intricate.[158] They have also a higher pedagogical value.[159] In addition, the explanatory power is higher when the theory is ambitious and explains phenomena over a relatively wide range or a relatively complex set of phenomena

[153]Popper K (2005), number 35; Popper K (2002), pp. 77, 189, 259–260 and 319; Aroney N (2013), p. 6.

[154]Popper K (2005), number 43.

[155]Popper K (2005), number 35; Popper K (2002), pp. 77, 189, 259–60, 319; Glaser BG, Strauss AL (1967), p. 24; Aroney N (2013), p. 6.

[156]Popper K (2005), numbers 36, 38 and 43.

[157]Aroney N (2013), p. 2.

[158]*Ibid,* p. 10.

[159]Mæhle SS (2015), p. 148: "En enkel teori vil derfor ja flere åpenbare pedagogiske kvaliteter enn en utførlig og intrikat modell . . .".

in a detailed way (number 2). Moreover, the explanatory power of a theory is higher when it can be made part of a system of theories (number 4).[160]

However, both specificity and generality can contribute to the explanatory power of a theory since general explanations explain a wide range of things and specific explanations explain things with a high level of detail and precision (number 3).

Understanding and Explanatory Power. The picture is slightly different when the overall goal is interpretive understanding and one chooses the holistic approach with ideal types.

While the explanatory approach is applied in positivist research, the holistic approach is applied in descriptive research. One may ask whether it is meaningful to talk about 'explanatory' power in research that does not choose the explanatory approach in the first place. The answer is yes. When one talks about 'explanatory power', the emphasis is on the power to explain or describe rather than the research project representing the explanatory approach. For the purposes of this book, 'explanatory power' means the same as 'descriptive power'.[161]

The problems lie somewhere else. First, theories based on ideal types are not as easy to falsify because real-life things do not match the ideal type perfectly.[162] For example, the general understanding of the social phenomena under investigation might not be hampered by the existence of a pathological case.[163] Second, contingency theory[164] makes it even more difficult to falsify user-friendly theories. While user-friendly theories can tell you about the objectives of ideal types and the pool of legal tools and practices that they can use in order to reach their objectives, real-life people have their actual objectives and choose a combination of legal tools and practices according to their own preferences in the circumstances. Third, the hermeneutical circle (the process of understanding) or a narrative cannot be falsifiable in the same sense as theories of natural sciences.

However, even these theories can be falsifiable in the broad sense. When the evidence mounts, there may come a point when the description of the societal phenomena under investigation can be regarded as falsified.[165] It is interesting to

[160] Aroney N (2013). p. 10.

[161] For the terminology, see Ryan B, Scapens RW, Theobald M (1992), p. 119. The "pattern model of explanation" and description seem to be the same thing.

[162] According to Friedman M (1953), p. 36, theories based on ideal types cannot even be descriptive: "The ideal types are not intended to be descriptive; they are designed to isolate the features that are crucial for a particular problem."

[163] Durkheim É (1894), Chapter III (on normal and pathological behaviour).

[164] Woodward J (1958), Schoonhoven CB (1981). According to the contingency theory, there is no one right way to organise a firm.

[165] Friedman M (1953), p. 9: "The hypothesis is rejected if its predictions are contradicted ('frequently' or more often than predictions from an alternative hypothesis); it is accepted if its predictions are not contradicted; great confidence is attached to it if it has survived many opportunities for contradiction. Factual evidence can never 'prove' a hypothesis; it can only fail to disprove it . . ." Glaser BG, Strauss AL (1967), p. 24: "In short, the discovered theoretical category lives on until proven theoretically defunct for any class of data, while the life of the accurate evidence that indicated the category may be short." Compare van Aken JE (2004), p. 235:

note that the problem of falsifiability is not limited to research that chooses interpretive understanding and the holistic perspective. It is the same in positivist sciences.[166] For example, 'research programmes' are generally protected against falsification by theories that form the 'protective belt' surrounding the 'hard core' of the programme (Imre Lakatos).[167] This can be illustrated with the efficient market hypothesis. Numerous research findings have contradicted the hypothesis that markets are efficient, but the mounting anomalies were not immediately accepted as the falsification of the hypothesis.

While easiness of falsification is positively correlated with explanatory power, the theory has little explanatory power after it has been falsified. The researcher should therefore ensure that the theory is sufficiently reliable. The researcher can do this by repeating the hermeneutical circle such as the process of abduction (Peirce) or the process of grounded theory (Strauss and Corbin).

Repeating the Hermeneutical Circle. In the light of Peirce, the researcher should use many rounds of abductive, deductive and inductive reasoning[168] to minimise surprises (unexplainable facts) in the event that the theory is applied.[169] In other words, unexplained findings lead us to look for an explanation. Finding an explanation results in a hypothesis by means of abduction. The hypothesis is checked by means of deduction (the derivation of predictions from the hypothesis) and induction (the search for facts that will 'verify' the assumptions). If the hypothesis is not in compliance with the facts, the process starts again.[170]

"The effectivenes for distinguishing academic research results from the prescriptions found in 'Heathrow-literature', is justification. The effectiveness of an algorithmic technological rule (applied as recipe) can be proven in deterministic or stochastic terms. But the indeterminate nature of heuristic rules—and most tehnological rules in the field of management will be heuristic—makes it impossible to provide such proof. However, through multiple case-studies one can accumulate supporting evidence which can continue until 'theoretical saturation' [Eisenhardt KM (1989a] has been obtained." For legal history, see Stolleis M (2008), pp. 31–32.

[166] Friedman M (1953), p. 9; National Academy of Sciences, National Academy of Engineering, Institute of Medicine (1992) 2 Scientific Principles and Research Practices, p 38: "But as theories survive more tests, they are regarded with higher levels of confidence."

[167] Lakatos I (1970).

[168] Peirce CS (1931–1935), 5.145, 5.162 and 5.171 (about abduction): "Its only justification is that from its suggestion deduction can draw a prediction which can be tested by induction, and that, if we are ever to learn anything or to understand phenomena at all, it must be by abduction that this is to be brought about."

[169] *Ibid*, 5.197.

[170] Reichertz J (2007), p. 222: "When faced with surprising facts, abduction leads us to look for meaning-creating rules, for a possibly valid or fitting explanation that eliminates what is surprising about the facts. The end-point of this search is a (verbal) hypothesis. Once this is found, a multi-stage process of checking begins. If the first step in the process of scientific discovery consists of the finding of a hypothesis by means of abduction, then the second step consists of the derivation of predictions from the hypothesis, which is deduction, and the third step consists of the search for facts that will 'verify' the assumptions, which is induction. If the facts cannot be found the process begins again, and this is repeated as often as necessary until 'fitting' facts are reached."

Repeating the hermeneutical circle means more than just aligning the hypothesis with the facts (that is, it means more than what Glaser proposes). Existing theory is very much part of the hermeneutical circle (Strauss and Corbin). The point of view and the method depend on the discipline and the domain theory. The theoretical framework helps to understand the facts.

User-Friendly Legal Science and Explanatory Power. These principles can be applied even in user-friendly legal research.

Like in any scientific discipline in social sciences, it is possible to build user-friendly legal theories that have high explanatory power, that is, theories that (a) are simple rather than intricate, (b) explain phenomena over a relatively wide range or a relatively complex set of phenomena in a detailed way and (c) can be made part of a system of theories. The explanatory power of the draft theory obviously depends on the researcher's preferences.

Since abductive reasoning is complemented by deductive and inductive reasoning, there are some simple ways to improve the reliability of the findings of a user-friendly legal study and make it more difficult to falsify a user-friendly theory.

Where the researcher has built the draft theory deductively, there is an increased risk that the user-friendly theory does not reflect empirical observations. The researcher can reduce this risk by adding empirical content.

For example, a qualitative empirical study can take the form of a case study (Sect. 3.4.5). Systematic in-depth case studies have been called 'a natural complement to mainstream deductive research'.[171] The researcher can also benefit from easier empirical alternatives. The researcher can, for example, try to falsify the draft theory by analysing whether an untenable or absurd result would follow from its acceptance (argumentum ad absurdum) or by applying it to suitable cases (exemplum in contrarium).

Where the researcher has built the draft theory inductively, there is a risk that the theory does not cover all relevant observations from societal reality and that it would again be too easy to falsify it. The researcher can therefore test the draft theory against existing theory and take into account deductive elements. The researcher needs earlier theory also in order to be able to use the appropriate terms and language to describe and explain phenomena.

Such a circle should result in a theory that describes societal reality better. One can find an example in the field of company law where one can distinguish between deductive theories of corporate law and inductive theories of corporations.[172] The problem with the deductive theories is that they do not describe the existing regulation of corporations very well. The inductive theories tend to focus on particular details and fail to explain the regulation of corporations as a whole. Both are easy to falsify. It is possible to build a general company law theory by combining both deductive and inductive elements.[173]

---

[171]Eisenhardt KM, Graebner ME (2007), p. 26.

[172]Mäntysaari P (2012), Chapter 5.

[173]*Ibid*, Chapter 10.

Choice of the Research Question. The explanatory power and the level of difficulty may depend on the range of things that the theory seeks to explain, that is, the level of abstraction (generality or simplicity). This is important to keep in mind when choosing the research question.

It can be more difficult to identify common denominators where the level of generality is very high. The researcher may need plenty of analysis to build a general theory of commercial law, a general theory of corporate law or a general theory of contract law. But it can be easier for the researcher to build on existing general theories and identify particular objectives and particular tools and practices in a narrow and well-defined context. This does not always have to mean that the findings are limited to the particular case. It may be possible to generalise the findings and apply them in a more general context.

In the light of the point of view of User-Friendly Legal Science, the researcher should pay attention to the potential legal tools and practices when choosing the research question and the potential scope of the draft theory. The relevance of legal tools and practices depends on the choice of the field, the user and the context.

It can be difficult to take into account all thinkable legal tools and practices if the context is very general. There are, of course, several tools and practices that can be used even where the context is very general: virtually everybody benefits from the existence of a legal framework and rule of law directly or indirectly, one of the most important legal tools in any transaction is legal and regulatory compliance, the most important legal tool in market economy is the contract[174] and so forth. However, the characteristic legal tools and practices should be identified even in a general context.

It is easier to identify the relevant legal tools and practices where the user and the context have been defined narrowly. The researcher may then benefit from relatively simple observations. The downside is that this reduces the explanatory power of the theory.

What applies to theory building and the choice of context applies mutatis mutandis to the choice of the research question: the researcher's choices should preferably be sufficiently well defined and narrow (Chap. 3). Similar issues on choosing the research question can arise in comparative law when you apply the functional method (Sect. 6.4). It is difficult to cover all relevant legal things that share the same function unless the research question is narrow.

References

André T Jr (1998) Cultural hegemony: the exportation of Anglo-Saxon corporate governance ideologies to Germany. Tulane Law Rev 73:69–171

Aristotle, Organon

[174]See, for example, Williamson OE (1985).

Aroney N (2013) Explanatory power, theory formation and constitutional interpretation: some preliminaries. Aust J Leg Philos 38:1–31

Arrow KJ (1994) Methodological individualism and social knowledge. Am Econ Rev 84(2):1–9

Ast DF (1808) Grundlinien der Grammatik, Hermeneutik und Kritik. Bei Jos. Thomann, Buchdrucker und Buchhändler, Landshut

Auranen O (2014) University Research Performance: Influence of funding competition, policy steering and micro-level factors. Dissertation. Acta Universitatis Tamperensis 1910, Tampere University Press, Tampere

Bartrum IC (2013) Constitutional value judgments and interpretive theory choice. Florida State Univ Law Rev 40(2):259–304

Becher T (1994) The significance of disciplinary differences. Stud High Educ 19(2):151–161

Berglund L, Ney A (2015) Historikerns hantverk: Om historieskrivning, teori och metod. Studentlitteratur, Lund

Berman HJ (1983) Law and revolution: the formation of the Western legal tradition. Harvard University Press, Cambridge

Black F, Scholes M (1973) The pricing of options and corporate liabilities. J Polit Econ 81(3): 637–654

Blaug M (1992) The methodology of economics: or, how economists explain. Cambridge University Press, Cambridge

Bohr N (1948) On the notions of causality and complementarity. Dialectica 2:312–319. doi:10.1111/j.1746-8361.1948.tb00703.x

Boland LA (2003) Dealing with Popper in economic methodology. Philos Soc Sci 33:477–498

Boudon R (1991) What middle-range theories are. Contemp Sociol (American Sociological Association) 20(4):519–522

Bourdieu P (1987) The force of law: toward a sociology of the juridical field. Hastings Law J 38: 814–853

Capra F, Mattei U (2015) The ecology of law: toward a legal system in tune with nature and community. Berrett-Koehler Publishers, Oakland

Chambers RJ (1956) Some observations on "Structure of Accounting Theory". Account Rev 31(4):584–592

Chambers RJ (1993) Positive accounting theory and the PA cult. Abacus 29(1):1–26. doi:10.1111/j.1467-6281.1993.tb00419.x

Corbin J, Strauss AL (1990) Grounded theory research: procedures, canons, and evaluative criteria. Qual Sociol 13(1):3–21. doi:10.1007/BF00988593

De Coninck J (2010) The functional method of comparative law: Quo vadis? Rabels Zeitschrift für ausländisches und internationales Privatrecht 74:318–350

Dewey J (1938) Experience and education. Macmillan, New York

Dubois A, Gadde LE (2002) Systematic combining: an abductive approach to case research. J Bus Res 55:553–560

Dubois A, Gadde LE (2014) "Systematic combining"–A decade later. J Bus Res 67:1277–1284

Durkheim É (1894) Les régles de la méthode sociologique. Revue philosophique

Duss V (2012) Chronik. Arbeitskreis "Augen der Rechtsgeschichte". Fünftes Symposium zur Methode der Rechtsgeschichte. Einsiedeln 20.-22. Januar 2011. Zeitschrift der Savigny-Stiftung für Rechtsgeschichte. Germanistische Abteilung 129(1):986–990. doi:10.7767/zrgga.2012.129.1.986

Eeasterby-Smith M, Thorpe R, Jackson PR (2015) Management and business research, 5th edn. SAGE Publications Ltd, London

Ehrlich E (1913) Grundlegung der Soziologie des Rechts. Duncker & Humblot, München and Leipzig

Eisenhardt KM, Graebner ME (2007) Theory building from cases: opportunities and challenges. Acad Manag J 50(1):25–32

Elharidy AM, Nicholson B, Scapens RW (2008) Using grounded theory in interpretive management accounting research. Qual Res Account Manage 5(2):139–155. doi:10.1108/11766090810888935
Engel C, Schön W (2007) Vorwort. In: Engel C, Schön W (eds) Das Proprium der Rechtswissenschaft. Recht–Wissenschaft–Theorie. Mohr Siebeck, Tübingen, pp IX–XIV
Fama EF (1980) Agency problems and the theory of the firm. J Polit Econ 88(2):288–307
Ferraro F, Pfeffer J, Sutton RI (2005) Economics language and assumptions: How theories can become self-fulfilling. Acad Manag Rev 30(1):8–24. doi:10.5465/AMR.2005.15281412
Firat AF (1987) Historiography, scientific method, and exceptional historical events. In: Wallendorf M, Anderson P (eds) Advances in consumer research, vol 14. Association for consumer research, Provo, Utah, pp 435–438
Friedman M (1953) The methodology of positive economics. In: Friedman M (ed) Essays in positive economics. University of Chicago Press, Chicago, pp 3–43
Glaser BG (1992) Emergence vs forcing: basics of grounded theory. Sociology Press, Mill Valley
Glaser BG, Strauss AL (1967) The discovery of grounded theory: strategies for qualitative research. Aldine de Gruyter, New York
Grundmann S, Micklitz HW, Renner M (eds) (2015) Privatrechtstheorie. Mohr Siebeck, Tübingen
Harman G (1965) The inference to the best explanation. Philos Rev 74:88–95
Heck P (1914) Gesetzesauslegung und Interessenjurisprudenz. Archiv für die civilistische Pracis 112:1–318
Heidegger M (1926) Sein und Zeit. Max Niemeyer Verlag, Tübingen
Holmes OW (1897) The path of the law. Harv Law Rev 10:457–490
Husa J (2003) Farewell to functionalism or methodological tolerance? Rabels Zeitschrift für ausländisches und internationales Privatrecht 67:419–447
Husserl E (1962) Die Krisis der europäischen Wissenschaften und die transzendentale Phänomenologie. Eine Einleitung in die phänomenologische Philosophie. Herausgegeben von Walter Biemel. 2. Auflage. Husserliana Band VI. Martinus Nijhoff, Haag
Hydén H (2011) Looking at the world through the lenses of norms. Nine reasons for norms: a plea for norm science. In: Papendorf K, Machura S, Andenaes K (eds) Understanding law in society. Developments in socio-legal studies. LIT Verlag, Berlin, pp 120–159
Iggers GG (1984) New directions in European historiography. Wesleyan University Press, Middletown
Iggers GG (1988) The crisis of the Rankean paradigm in the nineteenth century. Syracuse Sch (1979–1991) 9(1), Article 7
Jensen MC, Meckling WH (1976) Theory of the firm: managerial behavior, agency costs and ownership structure. J Financ Econ 3(4):305–360
Joas H (1996) The creativity of action. University of Chicago Press, Chicago
Johansson LG (2015) Introduktion till vetenskapsteorin. Tredje upplagan, andra tryckningen. Bokförlaget Thales, Stockholm
Kant I (1783) Prolegomena zu einer jeden künftigen Metaphysik die als Wissenschaft wird auftreten können. Johann Friedrich Hartknoch, Riga
Kant I (1787) Kritik der reinen Vernunft. Zweite hin und wieder verbesserte Auflage. Johann Friedrich Hartknoch, Riga
Kasanen E, Lukka K, Siitonen A (1993) The constructive approach in management accounting research. J Manag Account Res 5:243–264
Kelsen H (1934) Reine Rechtslehre: Einleitung in die rechtswissenschaftliche Problematik, 1. Aufl. Deuticke, Leipzig Wien. / Jestaedt M (ed) (2008) Studienausgabe. Mohr Siebeck, Tübingen
Kieser A (2004) The Americanization of academic management education in Germany. J Manag Inq 13(2):90–97. doi:10.1177/1056492604265301
Korobkin RB, Ulen TS (2000) Law and behavioral science: removing the rationality assumption from law and economics. Calif Law Rev 88(4):1051–1144. doi:10.15779/Z38GB0N

Kusch M (2003) Explanation and understanding: the debate over von Wright's philosophy of action revisited. In: Haaparanta L, Niiniluoto I (eds) Analytic philosophy in Finland. Poznań studies in the philosophy of the sciences and the humanities 80. Rodopi, Amsterdam New York, pp 327–356

Kyvik S (1991) Productivity in academia: Scientific publishing at Norwegian universities. Norwegian University Press, Oslo

Lakatos I (1970) Falsification and the methodology of scientific research programmes. In: Lakatos I, Musgrave AW (eds) Criticism and the growth of knowledge. Cambridge University Press, Cambridge, pp 91–195

Lamprecht K (1896) Alte und neue Richtungen in der Geschichtewissenschaft. R. Gartners Verlagsbuchhandlung, Berlin

Leiter B (2009) Naturalizing jurisprudence: three approaches. In: Shook J, Kurtz P (eds) The future of naturalism. Prometheus Books, Amherst, pp 197–207

Likhovski A (2003) Czernowitz, Lincoln, Jerusalem, and the comparative history of American jurisprudence. Theor Inq Law 4:621–657

Lipton P (1991) Inference to the Best Explanation. Routledge, London

Luhmann N (2004) Law as a social system. Translated by Klaus A. Ziegert. Oxford University Press, Oxford. First published as Luhmann N (1993) Das Recht der Gesellschaft. Suhrkamp, Frankfurt am Main

Mæhle SS (2015) Rettsvitenskapelig forskningsmetodikk – i lys av grunnleggende forskningsverdier. Tidsskrift for Rettsvitenskap 128(2):125–157

Magnani L (2001) Abduction, reason, and science. Processes of discovery and explanation. Kluwer Academic/Plenum Publishers, New York

Maitland FW (1911) Why the history of English law is not written. In: Fisher HAL (ed) The collected papers of Frederick William Maitland, vol I. University Press, Cambridge, pp 480–497

Mäntysaari P (2005) Comparative corporate governance: shareholders as a rule-maker. Springer, Berlin Heidelberg

Mäntysaari P (2010a) The law of corporate finance: general principles and EU law. Volume I: Cash flow, risk, agency, information. Springer, Berlin Heidelberg

Mäntysaari P (2012) Organising the firm: theories of commercial law, corporate governance and corporate law. Springer, Berlin Heidelberg

Mäntysaari P (2014) Kauppaoikeuden teoriasta. Lakimies 112(3):347–367

Merton RK (1968) Social theory and social structure. Free Press, New York

Michaels R (2008) The functional method of comparative law. In: Reimann M, Zimmermann R (eds) The Oxford handbook of comparative law. Oxford handbooks in law. Oxford University Press, Oxford, Chapter 10, pp 339–382

National Academy of Sciences, National Academy of Engineering, Institute of Medicine (1992) Responsible science: ensuring the integrity of the research process, vol I. The National Academies Press, Washington. doi:10.17226/1864

Niiniluoto I (1984) Is science progressive? Reidel, Dordrecht

Novak WJ (2000) Law, capitalism, and the liberal state: the historical sociology of James Willard Hurst. Law Hist Rev 18:97–145

Peirce CS (1883) A theory of probable inference. In: Peirce CS (ed) Studies in logic by members of the Johns Hopkins University. Little, Brown and Co, New York, pp 126–181

Peirce CS (1931–1935) The collected papers of Charles Sanders Peirce, vols. I–VI. Hartshorne C, Weiss P (eds), Harvard University Press, Cambridge

Petersen J (2014) Max Webers Rechtssoziologie und die juristische Methodenlehre, 2. Auflage. Mohr Siebeck, Tübingen

Popper K (2002) Conjectures and refutations: the growth of scientific knowledge, Revised edn. Routledge, London

Popper K (2005) Logik der Forschung, 11. Auflage. Mohr Siebeck, Tübingen

Posner RA (1990) The problems of jurisprudence. Harvard University Press, Cambridge

Quine WV (1960) Word and object. Cambridge, M.I.T. Press
Radnitzky G (1970) Contemporary schools of metascience, 2nd edn. Akademiförlaget, Göteborg
Ragin CC (1994) Constructing social research. Pine Forge/Sage, Thousand Oaks
Reichertz J (2007) Abduction: the logic of discovery of grounded theory. In: Bryant A, Charmaz K (eds) The Sage handbook of grounded theory. Sage, London
Ronkainen S, Suikkanen A, Kunnari M (2014) Tieteellinen tieto ja tutkimuksen yhteiskunnallinen tehtävä. In: Muhonen R, Puuska HM (eds) Tutkimuksen kansallinen tehtävä. Vastapaino, Tampere
Ross A (1958) On law and justice. Stevens & Sons, London
Ryan B, Scapens RW, Theobald M (1992) Research method and methodology in finance and accounting. Academic Press, London
Sandgren C (2005) Om teoribildning och rättsvetenskap. Juridisk Tidskrift 16(2):297–333
Saurama E, Julkunen I (2012) Approaching practice research in theory and practice. Soc Work Soc Sci Rev 15(2):57–75. doi:10.1921/095352211X636502
Schoonhoven CB (1981) Problems with contingency theory: testing assumptions hidden within the language of contingency "Theory". Adm Sci Q 26(3):349–377
Schumpeter J (1908) Das Wesen und der Hauptinhalt der theoretischen Nationalökonomie. Duncker & Humblot, Leipzig
Siems M (2008) Legal originality. Oxf J Leg Stud 28(1):147–164
Simon HA (1967) The business school: a problem in organizational design. J Manag Stud 4(1): 1–16. doi:10.1111/j.1467-6486.1967.tb00569.x
Sterling RR (1975) Toward a science of accounting. Financ Anal J 31(5):28–36
Stolleis M (2008) Rechtsgeschichte schreiben. Rekonstruktion, Erzählung, Fiktion? Jacob Burckhardt-Gespräche auf Castelen 21. Schwabe, Basel
Strauss AL, Corbin JM (1990) Basics of qualitative research: grounded theory procedures and techniques. Sage, London
Strauss AL, Corbin JM (1994) Grounded theory methodology: an overview. In: Denzin NK (ed) Handbook of qualitative research. Sage, London, pp 273–285
Teubner G (1998) Legal irritants: good faith in British law or how unifying law ends up in new divergences. Mod Law Rev 61(1):11–32. doi:10.1111/1468-2230.00125
Udehn L (2001) Methodological Individualism: background, history and meaning. Routledge, London and New York
Udehn L (2002) The changing face of methodological individualism. Annu Rev Sociol 28: 479–507
van Aken JE (2004) Management research based on the paradigm of the design sciences: the quest for field-tested and grounded technological rules. J Manag Stud 41(2):219–246
von Holderstein HJ, Madsen MR (2015) European new legal realism and international law: how to make international law intelligible. Leiden J Int Law 28(2):211–230
von Wright GH (1971) Explanation and understanding. Cornell University Press, Ithaca, New York
Walton D (2001) Abductive, presumptive and plausible arguments. Inf Log 21(2):141–169
Walton D (2014) Abductive reasoning. Project Muse. The University of Alabama Press, Tuscaloosa
Watson A (1974) Legal transplants: an approach to comparative law. Scottish Academic Press, Edinburgh
Weber M (1904) Die "Objektivität" sozialwissenschaftlicher und sozialpolitischer Erkenntnis. Archiv für Sozialwissenschaft und Sozialpolitik 19(1):22–87
Weber M (1913) Der Sinn der Wertfreiheit der soziologischen und ökonomischen Wissenschaften. Verein für Sozialpolitik 83–120; rev. in (1918) Logos 7(1):40–88; transl. in Weber M (1949) pp 1–47
Weber M (1922) Wirtschaft und Gesellschaft – Grundriß der verstehenden Soziologie. J.C.B Mohr (Paul Siebeck), Tübingen
Weber M (1949) The methodology of the social sciences. The Free Press, Glencoe

Weintraub ER (2002) Neoclassical economics. In: Henderson DR (ed). Concise encyclopedia of economics, 1st edn. Library of Economics and Liberty

Wendehorst CC (2008) The state as a foundation of private law reasoning. Am J Comp Law 56(3): 567–604

Wesel U (1974) Zur Methode der Rechtsgeschichte. Kritische Justiz 7(4):337–368

Williamson OE (1985) The economic institutions of capitalism. The Free Press, New York

Wittgenstein L (1922) Tractatus Logico-Philosophicus: Logisch-philosophische Abhandlung. Kegan Paul, London

Woods J (2014) Against Fictionalism. In: Magnani L (ed) Model-based reasoning in science and technology, Studies in applied philosophy, epistemelogy and rational ethics, vol 8. Springer, Berlin Heidelberg, pp 9–42. doi:10.1007/978-3-642-37428-9

Woodward J (1958) Management and technology. Her Majesty's Stationary Office, London

Zweigert K, Kötz H (1996) Einführung in die Rechtsvergleichung auf dem Gebiete des Privatrechts, 3. neubearbeitete Auflage. Mohr Siebeck, Tübingen

Chapter 3
The Research Question, Theories and Methods

3.1 General Remarks

The research process consists of several steps. In social science, these steps customarily include stating the problem, defining the research question, choosing the research method, data collection, data analysis, interpretation of data and writing the research report.[1]

Moreover, scientific research is theory based in each discipline. There are various kinds of requirements relating to the research question, theories and methods.

These requirements can be general and not related to any particular discipline. For example, the basic general requirements include the clarity of language, the internal coherence of the study, the transparency of research methods and findings, falsifiability, the novelty of findings, compliance with ethical standards and compliance with requirements as to form.[2] There can be general requirements for natural sciences[3] and social sciences.[4]

In addition to such general requirements, there are discipline-specific requirements. You need theory to define the discipline, to find out what is prior knowledge and to get access to the necessary language.[5] Generally, theory has been described

---

[1]Strydom H (2014), p. 149.

[2]For a review of ethical standards, see Glerup C, Horst M (2014). For the minimum requirements, see, for example, Torstendahl R (2005), p. 214.

[3]National Academy of Sciences, National Academy of Engineering, Institute of Medicine (1992) 2 Scientific Principles and Research Practices, pp. 36–39.

[4]See, for example, Mæhle S (2015); Sandgren C (2005); Graver HP (2008); Berglund L, Ney A (2015), pp. 127–128 and 152.

[5]Quine WV (1975), pp. 75–76: "The channels by which, having learned observation sentences, we acquire theoretical language, are the very same channels by which observation lends evidence to scientific theory ... We see, then, a strategy for investigating the relation of evidential support, between observation and scientific theory."

P. Mäntysaari, *User-friendly Legal Science*, DOI 10.1007/978-3-319-53492-3_3

as 'a strategy for handling data in research'.[6] The research question must reflect the point of view (knowledge interests) of the discipline.[7] The method is the way to obtain information on the basis of which the research question can be answered. There can be discipline-specific requirements setting out the acceptable methods.[8]

There is plenty of room for the researcher's subjective preferences and values in spite of the existence of general and discipline-specific requirements. At the end of the day, the researcher does research because it serves the researcher's personal interests.[9]

Research design is the result of several choices. The choice of the discipline, research question, theories and methods reflects the researcher's personal preferences. These choices are not fully explained by compliance with disciplinary requirements.

For example, the choice of the research question and the research methods is influenced by other circumstances such as the researcher's beliefs about disciplinary expectations and career prospects,[10] the researcher's beliefs about policy or funding expectations[11] and the researcher's methodological skills and methodological commitments.[12] The choice of the method to combine theory and empirical data may influence both the research question and the findings of the research.

In this sense, neither legal science[13] nor any other social science can be value free.[14] Research design is not value free.

User-Friendly Legal Science is no exception. However, while the choice of the field, the context, the research question, the method and generally the objects of study is not value free, answering the research question on the basis of information

---

[6]Glaser BG, Strauss AL (1967), p. 3. See also *ibid.*

[7]For socio-legal research, see Banakar R, Travers M (2005b), p. 2.

[8]Kaplan A (1964) § 1 p 4. For historiography, see Torstendahl R (2005), pp. 214–215.

[9]Bourdieu P (1975), p. 21.

[10]For the drawbacks of interdisciplinary research in this respect, see Banakar R, Travers M (2005b), p. 6.

[11]Bryman A (2007), p. 16.

[12]*Ibid.*

[13]See, for example, Wesel U (1974), p. 353 on the illusions of legal positivism.

[14]For economics, see Friedman M (1953), p. 6: "Agreement about the economic consequences of the legislation might not produce complete agreement about its desirability, for differences might still remain about its political or social consequences; but, given agreement on objectives, it would certainly go a long way toward producing consensus." For legal history, see Duss V (2012), p. 988: "Zunächst ist ein Konsens dahingehend zu konstatieren, dass sich eine Kritik der Methode ohne Kritik am Textinhalt als Unmöglichkeit darstellt. Die Frage danach, welche Funktion der Text erfülle, welcher Textgattung er angehöre, welchen Adressaten er im Auge habe, seien zwingend mitbestimmend für die Methodenwahl - eine Tatsache zu nennende Eigenheit von Texten, die sich nur schwerlich bis gar nicht von der Hand weisen lässt, wenn man die Performanz und die Funktion von Text im Auge behält." For practice research, see Saurama E, Julkunen I (2012), p. 67: "In other words, practice research is value-laden."

obtained by using the chosen method should preferably be value free in the same way as in comparative law, sociology or other social sciences.[15]

In User-Friendly Legal Science, the choice of the research question (Sect. 3.2), the theoretical framework (Sect. 3.3) and the method (Sect. 3.4) must reflect the discipline's particular characteristics. There are fundamental differences between User-Friendly Legal Science and other areas of legal science in this respect. What is not different is that the researcher should choose a sufficiently narrow research question in order to be able to answer it.

3.2 The Research Question

3.2.1 General Remarks

The researcher chooses to find new or deeper knowledge about a certain thing defined in the research question. Research questions are expected to be theory based. 'Theory-based' means here that they are designed to build on prior knowledge (that is, theory and literature) and add something new.[16] A research question can be theory based in two main ways. In applied research, the researcher adds something new by applying existing theory to solve practical problems. In basic research, the researcher adds something to existing theory. In both cases, the research question is meaningful only in the context of the chosen theoretical framework. In contrast, studies that are not theory based cannot be regarded as scientific research.[17] Many traditional doctrinal studies fall, by definition, outside the scope of scientific research in the absence of a proper theoretical framework.

The fact that research questions are expected to be theory based might give the false impression that one must always start with a thorough analysis of existing theory before formulating the research question (Sect. 3.2.3). This is not always the case, and the impression is wrong. The choice of the research question is part of the hermeneutical circle.

The researcher might start with a vague idea. When the researcher learns more about the matter, the researcher can develop the initial ideas into more specific questions.[18] The same can be said of the theoretical framework. Alternative

[15]Saurama E, Julkunen I (2012), p. 70: "The Mertonian norms of science say that a researcher needs to seclude him or herself from the subject matter and neutralize her own influence on the field of study. We have identified this problem realizing that a researcher needs to be able to perform different kinds of mental transformations during the research. When gathering the research material, discussing, perceiving and interviewing, he or she might well identify him or herself with the work group and users, but the analysis of the material, must be based upon tried research methods."

[16]See, for example, Graver HP (2008), pp. 164–166; Berglund L, Ney A (2015), p. 152.

[17]See, for example, Patel R, Davidson B (2012), p. 15.

[18]See Gilbert N (2008), section 3.5 pp. 57–58.

disciplines and theoretical frameworks might be relevant in the context. The initial vague ideas may develop into a deeper understanding after an analysis of existing theory. This can help to modify the theoretical framework.

In practice, the choice of the theoretical framework can thus depend on the research question. This is the case, for example, when the researcher chooses a particular discipline in order to find a suitable theoretical framework for the study or where the researcher chooses a suitable method theory (Sect. 3.3) for the study to complement the chosen domain theory.

In any case, the research question plays a key role in the research project. The choice of the research question should reflect the choice of the theoretical framework, and the choice of a theoretical framework should reflect the research question. The methods should reflect the research question and make it possible to answer it.[19]

There are disciplinary requirements for the choice of research questions in User-Friendly Legal Science (Sect. 3.2.2) but many alternative ways to generate them (Sect. 3.2.3).

3.2.2 *Characteristic Questions*

The research question is expected to reflect the discipline's point of view. There are thus characteristic questions that are part of the disciplinary requirements.

The underlying assumption in User-Friendly Legal Science is that users use legal tools and practices to reach their objectives in particular contexts. One can thus identify the following three characteristic questions that can be used separately or combined:

1. What objectives do the users have in the context? (In this case, the legal tools and practices and how they are used may be studied in later research.)
2. What legal tools and practices can the users use to reach their objectives in the context? (The objectives are already known. How the legal tools and practices are used can be studied in later research.)
3. How do the users use legal tools and practices to reach their objectives in the context? (The objectives and the legal tools and practices are already known.)
4. The researcher may combine alternatives 1 and 2 or alternatives 1, 2 and 3.

The point of view of User-Friendly Legal Science will thus influence the choice of the research question. The research question relates to societal reality and focuses on user behaviour.

Since other areas of legal science do not share this point of view but have other knowledge interests, their characteristic questions are different. For example, the point of view of legal dogmatics is the interpretation and systematisation of legal

[19] Bryman A (2007), p. 6.

norms. Therefore, the research questions of doctrinal research would not fulfil the disciplinary requirements of User-Friendly Legal Science.

3.2.3 Generating Research Questions

Research questions are meaningful only in the context of prior theory. Findings are new only in relation to prior theory. Therefore, you need to study prior theory in order to choose meaningful research questions that may be able to lead to new findings.[20]

The research question can address the characteristic questions of User-Friendly Legal Science in many ways (Sect. 3.2.2). First, the research question depends on the purpose of the research project. The research question can be designed to provide findings suitable for their intended use. Second, the study should preferably have a worthy topic. The research question can be ambitious or less ambitious. Third, there are different ways to address prior theory in research design.

Purpose of Study, Intended Use of Findings. The choice of the research question can depend on the purpose of the research project.[21]

Generally, the purpose of a research project consists of three main elements. One can distinguish between the ulterior motive of the researcher (subjective purpose), the express goal of the research project (objective purpose) and the way the express goal is to be reached (research design). Each of them is a way to motivate the research question.

The ulterior motive of the researcher may remain hidden. It explains why the researcher chooses a particular discipline and carries out research in the first place, why the researcher chooses a particular field and a particular context and why the researcher has particular knowledge interests in that context.

Obviously, these choices influence the express goal of the research project as well. The express goal of the research project is a way to justify the research question and relates to the intended use of findings in two ways. First, the express goal has a connection to theory. Scientific theories can be formed, applied, tested or falsified (Sect. 2.1). Second, it has a connection to the intended societal effects of the research project. In User-Friendly Legal Science, the fact that there are many ways to use the findings of the research project (Chaps. 1 and 4) means that there are many ways to justify the research question.

Research design depends on the express goal of the research project. The express goal can be reached in various ways, and one may need to take specific steps to reach it. The researcher may focus on one or more of them when formulating the

[20] Berglund L, Ney A (2015), p. 152 on historical research.

[21] Strydom H (2014), p. 150: "The purposes of research have been described differently by different authors … The terms research designs, strategies, purposes, objectives, goals or aims are … used interchangeably by various authors."

research question.[22] In social science generally, this can lead to different kinds of research questions and different kinds of research (exploratory, descriptive, explanatory, correlational, evaluation, intervention and action research).[23] One can again see a connection to theory or the intended societal effects. One can distinguish between different kinds of research on the basis of connection to theory and how deep understanding one is aiming at (exploratory, descriptive, explanatory, evaluation research) or connection to the intended societal effects and the form of applied research (intervention research, participatory action research). Exploration, description and explanation are regarded as the most common purposes of research in social sciences.[24]

Worthy Topic. The choice of the research question should generally contribute to high research quality.[25] In addition, research should preferably have a worthy topic, that is, a topic that is relevant, timely, significant and interesting.[26]

Research in social science tends to be interesting when it challenges prior theory.[27] One of the contributing factors is explanatory power. Since the explanatory power of the findings depends on the level of generality (high v low), the choice of a context (broad v narrow) and users (heterogenic of homogenic) can depend on the researcher's ambitions (Sect. 2.7).

Gap Spotting and Problematisation in Social Sciences. Research questions are generally expected to be formulated as a reaction to existing theory and literature (Sect. 5.1). In social science, the two major ways to generate research questions are gap spotting and problematisation. We can have a look at them before turning to how they can be applied in User-Friendly Legal Science.

Gap spotting is the prevalent way of generating research questions in social science. One can distinguish between confusion spotting, neglect spotting and application spotting.[28] In other words, there can be different reasons for the existence of a gap. First, there can competing explanations (confusion spotting). Second, the area can be overlooked or under-researched, existing theory can lack empirical support or the empirical phenomenon can be a new one (neglect spotting). Third, the gap can relate to applications. One can then extend the scope of existing theory by complementing existing literature (application spotting).

---

[22]Strydom H (2014), p. 151 on the basis of a literature review: "More than one purpose can be delineated for the same study, but one will normally dominate a particular study . . .".

[23]Fouché CB, De Vos AS (2011), pp. 94–99.

[24]Babbie E (2016), p. 90. See also Strydom H (2014).

[25]Tracy SJ (2010), pp. 839: ". . . high quality qualitative methodological research is marked by (a) worthy topic, (b) rich rigor, (c) sincerity, (d) credibility, (e) resonance, (f) significant contribution, (g) ethics, and (h) meaningful coherence."

[26]*Ibid*, pp. 840–841.

[27]Davis MS (1971); Bartunek JM, Rynes SL, Ireland RD (2006), p. 11.

[28]Sandberg J, Alvesson M (2011), pp. 28–29.

Not only is gap spotting relatively easy and uncontroversial; it is also encouraged by research and publication traditions and the personal incentives of researchers in social science. However, gap spotting and gap filling do not question the fundamental assumptions of existing literature.[29]

The alternative to gap spotting in social science is problematisation. Generating research questions through problematisation can be defined as identifying and challenging the assumptions underlying existing theories.[30]

Problematisation is more difficult than gap spotting. It means questioning the received wisdom. Since a theory is more likely to receive attention and become famous if it challenges the assumptions underlying existing theories, research can have a bigger impact where it is based on the problematisation route.[31]

There are two preliminary questions relating to these assumptions. What types of assumptions are relevant? How can they be identified, articulated and challenged in an interesting way?[32]

One can distinguish between five sets of assumptions: in-house, root metaphor, paradigm, ideology and field assumptions.[33] An in-house assumption is 'shared and accepted as unproblematic' by its advocates within a school of thought. Root metaphor assumptions are 'associated with broader images of a particular subject matter'. Paradigmatic assumptions can be defined as the 'ontological, epistemological, and methodological assumptions that underlie a specific literature'. Ideology assumptions include 'various political-, moral-, and gender-related assumptions held about the subject matter'. Finally, field assumptions are 'a broader set of assumptions about a specific subject matter that are shared by several different schools of thought within a paradigm, and sometimes even across paradigms and disciplines'.[34]

As regards the manner of problematisation, the researcher can try to choose a worthy topic (see above). In other words, the research can try to identify, articulate and challenge existing assumptions in a way that can be expected to lead to the development of an interesting theory.[35]

User-Friendly Legal Science, Original Theory Building, the Constructive Approach, Gap Spotting and Problematisation. In User-Friendly Legal Science, the four main routes to generate research questions can be defined as original theory building, the constructive approach, gap spotting and problematisation.

[29] Alvesson M, Sandberg J (2011), p. 249.

[30] *Ibid*, p. 247.

[31] See Davis MS (1971); Davis MS (1986); Alvesson M, Sandberg J (2011), p. 247.

[32] Alvesson M, Sandberg J (2011), p. 254. For the methodological principles for identifying, articulating, and challenging assumptions, see p. 256.

[33] *Ibid*, p. 254.

[34] *Ibid*, pp. 254–255.

[35] See *ibid*, pp. 254 and 256.

The fact that User-Friendly Legal Science presents a novel way to do legal research means that gap spotting and problematisation can be replaced by original theory building. Original theory building can be the result of the constructive approach or consist of exploratory or descriptive research.

The constructive approach is relevant in the light of the point of view of this new discipline. Legal tools and practices are used for the purpose of reaching objectives, that is, to solve practically relevant problems. The researcher may be able to find a practically relevant problem that has research potential.[36] Since legal tools and practices have been used to reach objectives in many contexts for hundreds or thousands of years, practitioners may have plenty of useful knowledge that has not yet been made part of a scientific framework.[37]

Gap spotting can be relevant in two important situations even before the emergence of a larger body of user-friendly research.

First, gap spotting is an alternative where user-friendly legal research is chosen for the purpose of helping to solve problems in other areas of legal research or areas of non-legal research. For example, let us assume that there is a doctrinal problem of the interpretation of norms in a certain context. User-friendly legal research can be employed to provide information about (a) the normal intentions of the relevant actors and (b) the expected societal outcomes of different interpretation alternatives.

Second, gap spotting is an alternative when the prevailing research approach in another area of legal science bears a close resemblance to the research approach of User-Friendly Legal Science. Gaps in the existing literature of the other area can then be exploited in the new discipline. For example, prior literature on legal rhetoric can provide a basis for the study of legal argumentation as a user-friendly discipline, and literature on international law with its state perspective can provide a basis for a user-friendly study focusing on the same context (Chap. 7).

Gap spotting is complemented by problematisation. In principle, problematisation can be used to question the assumptions of research in User-Friendly Legal Science. However, the problematisation route is affected by the present absence of a large enough body of research in this area. One can nevertheless question the assumptions of method theories (Sect. 3.3) that complement the main or domain theories of the study.

For example, there is a canon of economic theories customarily discussed in corporate law and corporate governance contexts. Such an economic theory can be used as a method theory in a user-friendly legal study focusing on the same context. The more holistic approach of user-friendly legal research and its different point of view can help to falsify economic theories that are narrower and based on fictions.[38]

---

[36]For management accounting, see Kasanen E, Lukka K, Siitonen A (1993), p. 246.

[37]Peirce CS (1931–1935), 1.54.

[38]See, for example, Mäntysaari P (2012), pp. 69–74.

3.3 Choice of Theory

3.3.1 General Remarks

Since scientific research is theory based, the researcher must choose the necessary theories. Different theories can have different functions.

First, a scientific study must belong to a scientific discipline. At least one of the theories must be a main theory (that is, a domain theory) that defines the scientific discipline, as well as its fundamental concepts. Different main theories can lead to different paths of research with different research questions and methods. The researcher is thus expected to understand what the choice of a particular main theory means.[39]

Second, the research question is a reaction to prior theory (Sect. 3.2). The researcher must choose these theories as well. They are necessary for gap spotting and problematisation, which belong to the traditional ways to generate research questions (Sect. 3.2.3). One may need original theory building in the absence of existing theories.

Third, prior theories can help to understand the phenomena under investigation by providing useful concepts and a framework for interpreting data.[40] Main theories can thus be complemented by so-called method theories.

The research question and the findings may depend on the choice of the theoretical framework. The choice of a theoretical framework reflects the values of the researcher.

For these reasons, there is no such thing as 'the best' theory or theoretical framework for the study. The chosen theoretical framework should nevertheless be relevant in the light of the discipline, the research question and the intended use of findings, and the choice should facilitate the internal coherence of the study.[41] What can be regarded as 'the best' theory from the researcher's subjective perspective depends on the researcher's knowledge interests and general intellectual profile.[42]

In User-Friendly Legal Science, there are characteristic issues relating to the choice of the main theories and the method theories (Sects. 3.3.2 and 3.4.5), and the role of theories on legal argumentation and interpretation (Sect. 3.3.3).

[39]See Berglund L, Ney A (2015), p. 121 on historical research.

[40]*Ibid*, p. 119.

[41]See, for example, Fallon RH Jr. (1999), p. 562: "... I have argued that the selection of a constitutional theory should be based largely on instrumental grounds. Among theories satisfying a fit requirement, the best will be that which most optimally promotes mixed, weighted interests in the rule of law, political democracy, and appropriately specified substantive rights."

[42]Mæhle SS (2015), p. 157.

3.3.2 Main Theories and Method Theories

In User-Friendly Legal Science, one of the main theories (domain theories) can be the theory of User-Friendly Legal Science presented in this book.[43] There can also be more specific theories that are applications of the user-friendly research approach in the chosen context. For example, where the context is corporate governance, the main theories could consist of the theory of User-Friendly Legal Science and a legal theory applying it in the particular context of corporate governance.[44]

The main theory or theories can be complemented by method theories.[45] Method theories are not the same thing as the method. Method theories can explain relevant phenomena in the language of another scientific discipline and provide useful concepts.[46] However, it is meaningful to call these theories *method* theories. The method is a systematic way to collect evidence, and a method theory is one of the ways to collect necessary information.

Method theories are used for the purpose of providing a better understanding of the phenomena under investigation. There can be alternative method theories. In the long run, the diversity of method theories can improve understanding. The choice of the method theory or theories depends on what is useful. For example, it can depend on (a) the field, the user and the context; (b) the research question; and (c) doctrinal and other external expectations. The choice of these theories can thus be eclectic.[47]

By definition, the field of User-Friendly Legal Science and each of the fields of its specific areas consist of two or more overlapping and interacting fields (or coupled systems). You need a method theory to describe each such field (for the legal field, see Sect. 3.3.3). Method theories can also provide information about the context, as well as the particular objectives of users in the chosen context.

The research question is the result of subjective choices that reflect the researcher's knowledge interests, preferences and values. It is complemented by the choice of a theory that seeks to describe the relevant phenomena from a certain perspective and provides useful concepts. In the light of the plurality in sciences (Sect. 5.1), there is a large toolbox of scientific theories each providing a slightly different view of societal reality. For example, in the context of

[43]Mäntysaari P (2013); Mäntysaari (2015); Mäntysaari P (2016b).

[44]See Mäntysaari P (2010a); Mäntysaari P (2012).

[45]For method theories, see Lukka K, Vinnari E (2014); Kaplan A (1964), § 1 p. 4.

[46]See, for example, Olsen L (2004), pp. 130–131.

[47]For interpretive management accounting research, see Elharidy AM, Nicholson B, Scapens RW (2008), p. 142: "... IMAR is eclectic, as it draws on various research methods, theoretical frameworks and perspectives to provide better understandings or explanations of the substantive research phenomena. To achieve understanding, interpretive researchers study diversity ..." For legal history, see Duss V (2012), p. 989: "Weiter wurde die Frage nach dem theoriegeleiteten Arbeiten erneut diskutiert, also der Übernahme fachfremder (?) theoretischer Konzepte. Es scheint mittlerweile als Geschmacksache empfunden zu werden, ob und welche Theorien (Luhmann, Derrida, Bourdieu, Foucault u. a.) man den anverwandten Disziplinen entleiht, solange man über Theorieapplikation, Umfang des sowie Gründe für den Eklektizismus Rechenschaft ablegt."

corporate governance, the researcher may choose between various perspectives. On one hand, the researcher might choose the perspective of employees because of the researcher's own values. The method theories could then consist of theories of corporate social responsibility and stakeholder theories. On the other hand, the researcher might also choose the perspective of shareholders reflecting the values of economic elites and most economists. In practice, the researcher would then end up applying a canon of economic theories.[48]

Doctrinal and other external expectations can obviously play a role. There are theories that facilitate platforms that enable researchers to communicate across scientific disciplines. These theories are well known and are often regarded as relevant by the relevant members of the 'audience' (for rhetoric, see Sect. 7.3). The acceptance of a research article for publication can depend on whether the author has addressed the theories that the reviewers and editors regard as relevant. Depending on the discipline, there can be a canon of theories that researchers are expected to address.

One can illustrate these expectations with legal research at business schools. Many business schools have departments of law. In principle, one can choose different method theories in legal research even at a business school. In practice, however, the researcher has incentives to choose method theories from the relevant areas of business economics because it would increase the usefulness or acceptance of the legal study across disciplinary boundaries at the researcher's business school.

Generally, User-Friendly Legal Science should develop its own body of main theories and be careful about the use of method theories. The development of the discipline's core concepts and own language can be hampered by the use of other disciplines' theories that happen to be 'en vogue'. You need to ignore noise in order to develop a discipline.[49] Moreover, the theories of other social sciences do not necessarily reflect the holistic nature of User-Friendly Legal Science and law.[50]

3.3.3 Theories on Legal Argumentation and Interpretation as Method Theories

Doctrinal theories on legal argumentation and interpretation play a particular role as method theories because one can neither describe nor use legal tools and practices in a reliable way without taking into account the legal norms that they are based on and how the relevant norms might be interpreted.[51]

---

48 See Whaples R, Morris AP, Moorhouse JC (1998); Fleischer H (2001).

49 See, for example, Duss V (2012), p. 989.

50 See already Augustine of Hippo, De doctrina christiana, Third Book, XXX.

51 See also Ross A (1958), p. 20: "The social phenomena which are the subject of sociology of law do not acquire their specific legal character until they are placed in relation to the norms of the law in force."

The researcher should focus on what is relevant. The relevance of aspects relating to legal argumentation and interpretation depends again on the choice of the user, the context and the research question.

At one end of the scale, the context is the interpretation of legal norms, and the user is anyone interpreting legal norms. In order to reach unspecified objectives outside the legal system in this context, the user will use legal rhetoric (Sect. 7.3). In this case, useful method theories can be found in rhetorics, legal theory and legal dogmatics.

At the other end of the scale, the researcher chooses particular users that have particular objectives in a certain context, and the legal tools to reach them are legal norms (Sect. 7.2). In this case, answering the research question may require (a) systematisation of legal norms on the basis of their function from the user perspective (there are similarities with the functional method of comparative law in this respect), (b) analysing how they would be interpreted in the context and the legal risk inherent in interpretation and (c) analysing what the user should do in order to reach objectives with legal norms (such as adoption of new legal norms and management of legal risk inherent in interpretation).

In all cases, it is important for the user to understand the contents of the relevant legal framework. The user may also need to understand how the risk inherent in the interpretation of the legal framework can be managed.[52]

3.4 Method

3.4.1 General Remarks

There should be a method. Generally, the method is a systematic way to collect information (evidence, empirical data) and analyse it for the purpose of answering the research question.[53] The method is thus an important part of the research process.[54] One can distinguish between the method and methodology. Methodology means the study of methods.[55]

[52]See Mäntysaari P (2010b).

[53]Bryman A (2008), p. 160: "'Methods' might be instruments of data collection like questionnaires, interviews or observation; they might refer to the tools used for analysing data, which might be statistical techniques or extracting themes from unstructured data; or the term might refer to aspects of the research process like sampling."

[54]Mæhle SS (2015), p. 127 on the legal research process generally.

[55]Bryman A (2008), p. 160: "It is concerned with uncovering the practices and assumptions of those who use methods of different kinds." Mæhle SS (2015), p. 127: "Sett i dette perspektivet er forskningsmetodikk det teoretiske grunnlaget og de refleksjonene som ligger til grunn for valg av metode(r) som trengs for å gjennomføre forskningsarbeidet."

Elements of the Method. The method means four things in particular: one has to obtain information about things that are relevant in the light of the point of view ('about what', Sect. 3.4.2); one has to obtain information from sources of some kind ('where from', Sect. 3.4.3); one has to obtain information one way or another ('how', Sect. 3.4.4), for example by cases studies (Sect. 3.4.5); and one has to give information a meaning by interpreting it ('what content', Sect. 3.4.6). It is characteristic of abduction that the researcher chooses these elements both ex ante and during the research process. The quality of the method can be scrutinised ex post.[56] The method should ensure that one can count on the study and its conclusions (Sect. 3.4.7).

Basically, a method is just a combination of these elements. There are thus a very large number of potential methods.[57] The existence of many alternative methods can increase the overall quality of the findings of the research area,[58] and science can progress best if all available methods are used.[59] The researcher may choose the appropriate methods for the study, but the researcher should be able to justify the choice.[60]

Theory and Method. Theory and method are two sides of the same coin for three reasons. First, what is perceived as a scientific method depends on the definition of science. For example, one can distinguish between positivism and phenomenology. A representative of phenomenology, Weber assumed that the most appropriate way to gain knowledge about the social world is through interpretive understanding (Verstehen).[61] Positivists consider interpretation to be outside the boundaries of scientific enquiry. Second, you cannot build meaningful theories about society without empirical evidence. Theory building should thus be based on both deductive and inductive elements.[62] Third, the choice of the method is influenced by the theoretical framework. You should find information about things that are relevant in the light of the point of view of the discipline. In addition to the point of view, the domain theory can define the nature of the primary sources. The theoretical framework influences even the choice of the research question, and the method is the way to obtain the information you need to answer the research question.

Values. The choice of the method may influence the findings of the research. The choice may depend on the discipline, the theoretical framework, the research question and the skills and preferences of the researcher. The choice of the method is thus not completely value free in social sciences. One should nevertheless

[56]In linear and positivist research, however, it is assumed that one can both choose the method and scuritinise it ex ante.

[57]Torstendahl R (2005), p. 215.

[58]See also Kaplan A (1964), § 4 p. 28.

[59]Feyerabend PK (1975).

[60]Berglund L, Ney A (2015), p. 163.

[61]Weber M (1922).

[62]Popper K (2005), number 85.

distinguish between the preliminary choices necessary for research design on one hand and the actual conclusions made on the basis of the method and the data on the other. While the researcher reveals his preferences by the choice of the research question, the theories and the method,[63] the conclusions based on them should ideally not be dependent on the values of the researcher.[64]

Discipline-Specific Requirements. There are discipline-specific requirements in User-Friendly Legal Science. They are partly caused by the fact that it is defined as a legal discipline. One can assume that a legal discipline must share its field with legal disciplines, that knowledge of the field must be based on normative materials and that the language must be the language of legal science (Sect. 5.3).[65] The discipline-specific requirements are also connected to the point of view of User-Friendly Legal Science.

3.4.2 Relevant Information

You need information about something. What is perceived as relevant depends on disciplinary requirements and the theoretical framework.

In User-Friendly Legal Science, the method is an organised way to obtain information about facts that are relevant in the light of the point of view of this discipline. The relevant facts relate, in particular, to the field, the user, the context, the user's objectives in the context and the relevant legal tools and practices. The exact nature of these facts depends on the research question. In any case, you need information about both legal and societal things. This is due to the existence of two or more overlapping fields or coupled systems. Consequently, lawyers may need to leave their traditional comfort zone. It is not enough to focus on legal norms. Non-lawyers that are well acquainted with the context may be in a good position to identify the central objectives of the parties.[66] In user-friendly research, they should not forget to describe the phenomena under investigation in the language of law and legal science, identify legal tools and practices and connect the tools and practices with the legal system.

In contrast, the use of quantitative methods in economics would not be possible without reducing complex societal phenomena to a relatively small number of quantifiable factors. Since the true motivations of individual agents are complex

---

[63]There is a similar distinction even in natural sciences. Ross A (1958), pp. 319–320.

[64]Weber M (1904), p. 148: "… denn wir sind der Meinung, daß es niemals Aufgabe einer Erfahrungswissenschaft sein kann, bindende Normen und Ideale zu ermitteln, um daraus für die Praxis Rezepte ableiten zu können."

[65]Ross A (1958), p. 20: "The social phenomena which are the subject of sociology of law do not acquire their specific legal character until they are placed in relation to the norms of the law in force."

[66]Moorhead R (2010).

and unclear, economic models can be based on several assumptions and fictions. In a similar way, the quantitative study of law can mean that legal phenomena are reduced to a small number of variables that are given a numeric value.[67] The relevance of information can thus depend on the choice of the discipline. There are differences between the quantitative study of law and User-friendly Legal Science in this respect.

3.4.3 Relevant Sources

You need sources of information. The question of the relevant facts (Sect. 3.4.2) obviously influences the choice of the relevant sources.[68] One can distinguish between primary sources and secondary sources. The primary sources are discipline specific. The secondary sources give information about the primary sources.

The primary and secondary sources have different functions. The secondary sources help to choose a research question, put the primary sources in a context, interpret the primary sources in the context and increase understanding. The primary sources are used for the purpose of producing findings that are new.[69]

The role of primary and secondary sources can be illustrated with the different characteristics of historical science and sociology. If there is a difference[70] between these two disciplines, it can at least partly be explained by their respective primary sources. According to Leopold von Ranke, historical research should tell you how things actually were ('wie es eigentlich gewesen').[71] Ranke introduced the ideas of reliance on primary sources (empiricism) and an emphasis on narrative history. In historical science, historical facts are inferred from what remains, that is, 'relics' such as natural objects, artefacts or written documents.[72] Sociology is different. Information about social facts is based on a broad range of sources, but information about historical facts tends to be based on secondary sources. Historical sociologists draw their information from literature written by historians. One can also mention that von Savigny, the legal scholar, used legal materials as primary sources.[73]

---

[67]La Porta R, Lopez-de-Silanes F, Shleifer A, Vishny RW(1998). See also Djankov S, La Porta R, Lopez-de-Silanes F, Shleifer A (2008); Djankov S, Glaeser E, La Porta R, Lopez-de-Silanes F, Shleifer A (2003).

[68]See, for example, Banakar R (2006), p. 76 on a study in legal sociology: "Why is he focusing on the discourses of legal theory, if his intention is to examine the 'standpoint of legal actors' and legal processes through which political values are transformed into legal concepts."

[69]Berglund L, Ney A (2015), p. 129.

[70]Giddens A (1979), p. 230; Giddens A (1988), p. 416. See also Subrt J (2012), pp. 403–404.

[71]von Ranke L (1885), p. VII: "Man hat der Historie das Amt, die Vergangenheit zu richten, die Mitwelt zum Nutzen zukünftiger Jahre zu belehren, beigemessen: so hoher Ämter unterbindet sich gegenwärtiger Versuch nicht: er will blos zeigen, wie es eigentlich gewesen."

[72]Goldthorpe JH (1991), p. 212.

[73]Posner RA (2002), p. 1314.

Primary Sources in User-Friendly Legal Science. One can distinguish between primary sources and secondary sources even in User-Friendly Legal Science. There are disciplinary requirements as to the primary sources.

The question of primary sources is important. If User-Friendly Legal Science has its own primary sources, it can provide a new view of societal reality and compete against other scientific disciplines for interpretation hegemony.[74]

The underlying assumption is that one can obtain information about societal mechanisms by studying the use of legal tools and practices. Moreover, the primary sources of this new discipline should reflect the fact that we are talking about a legal science rather than sociology, history or other non-legal areas of social science. The researcher should therefore use the legally relevant documentation of legal tools and practices as the primary source. The choice of such legal documents as primary sources is meaningful. Documentation can give information about the context, party objectives and the relevant practices. Documentation can provide information about society outside the legal system because legal tools and practices are widely used in various kinds of transactions and when societal structures are formalised.

Since there is a wide range of potential legal tools and practices depending on the context, there is a wide range of potential primary sources depending on the context, and the classification of sources as primary or secondary sources depends on the context.

The primary sources can be internal/private and generated by the user. For example, internal or private materials include contracts, wills, protocols, internal guidelines, company documentation or similar evidence of how users actually use legal tools and practices and what their objectives are.[75]

The primary sources can also be external and generated by external rule-makers. External materials include normative materials such as legal regulation, case law or sectoral self-regulation.

Pluralism. The fact that there is a wide range of potential primary sources contributes to source pluralism in User-Friendly Legal Science.[76] One of the problems inherent in the pluralism of sources is how to define the relevant sources and reduce the number of sources that should be taken into account in the research project.[77]

---

[74]See even Mäntysaari P (2013).

[75]Zweigert K, Kötz H (1996), § 3 II: "Grundsätzlich ist bei der Durchforschung ausländischer Rechte jegliche Beschränkung zu meiden. Das gilt namentlich für die Frage, was alles als 'Rechtsquelle' heranzuziehen ist. Rechtsquelle im Sinne rechtsvergleichender Forschung ist alles, was das Rechtsleben der herangezogenen Ordnung gestaltet oder mitgestaltet."

[76]For source pluralism generally, see Ehrlich E (1912/1967); Teubner G (1997); Myrdal J (2007).

[77]Compare Dagan H (2011), p. xviii: "For legal realists, the profound and inescapable reason for doctrinal indeterminacy is the availability of multiple and potentially applicable doctrinal sources." For legal history, see Berman HJ (1983), p. 8: "... the law includes not only legal institutions, legal commands, legal decisions, and the like, but also what legal scholes ... say about those legal institutions, commands, and decisions. The law contains within itself a legal science, a meta-law, by which it can be both analyzed and evaluated."

The problem of source pluralism can be mitigated by choosing a narrow context, a narrow user class and a narrow research question. User-Friendly Legal Science can provide a way to cope with source pluralism because a potential source may have its own scope of application and is not necessarily relevant in the narrow context of the user-friendly study, and many potential sources may not be relevant in the light of the study's point of view and user objectives.

Secondary Sources. One can find information about the users' objectives and their legal tools and practices even in secondary sources.

The secondary sources consist of literature (prior research and prior theories), sectoral recommendations and models (such as model documents, standard contracts and model articles of association), as well as case law and legal science.

For example, case law can sometimes provide information about the actual use of legal tools and practices.[78] Model contracts can provide evidence of user objectives and practices.

In principle, the secondary sources could include prior studies in User-Friendly Legal Science. However, their number is still small.

The secondary sources can nevertheless include studies in other areas of legal science. For example, comparative studies (Sect. 6.4) can be a useful source of information in this new discipline. If a comparative study is based on the use of the functional method and focuses on the interests of the same class of users, it can reveal the same objectives[79] and part—but, due to the fact that the focus is on legal norms rather than behaviour, perhaps not all—of the legal tools and practices. Moreover, many comparative lawyers are legal practitioners or study legal practice in their research.[80]

The secondary sources can even include studies in other social sciences. For example, prior studies in business economics can provide information about the use of legal tools and practices in particular business contexts.

Many Sources. Many kinds of sources can contribute to a better understanding. The line between primary and secondary sources might be written on water. For example, the researcher may have drafted a hypothesis or a theory about the parties' objectives and practices on the basis of the available primary and secondary sources. The researcher can test the hypothesis or theory by using interviews (empirically) or by studying non-legal literature. According to our definition, interviews are a secondary source that gives information about documentation.

---

[78]Cases are relevant regardless of connections to a certain legal family and the civil law or common law traditions. See, for example, Guével D (2012), p. 34, Introduction, III, 2, no 47: "Comme toutes les autres branches du droit francais, conformément à notre tradition romaniste, le droit commercial et des affaires a pour source principale les textes. C'est une source officielle et le support privilégié d'un droit, non pas fait de "cases" à l'anglo-saxonne, mais de règles de principe, éventuellement assorties de temperaments et d'exceptions. Les textes sont traditionellement classes hiérarchiquement."

[79]You can find an example in Mäntysaari P (2005), section 2.3 and Mäntysaari P (2010a), section 8.2.

[80]Husa J (2009), p. 477.

However, interviews would be regarded as a primary source in other social sciences.

3.4.4 Collecting Information

You need to collect information from sources in one way or another. Generally, the researcher can obtain information about the users' objectives and the use of legal tools and practices by methods customarily used in social science.

Data collection can be haphazard or systematic. In social science, the positivist view is that it should be a systematic process and based on a clearly stated method.[81] There are alternative methods. While it can be relatively easy to describe the data collection method in linear research that chooses the positivist approach, it would be difficult to describe it in detail in holistic research that chooses interpretive understanding and uses abduction (Sects. 2.5 and 2.7).

User-Friendly Legal Science has its own disciplinary requirements. The methods of data collection can be the same as in social science in general, but their application is influenced by the particular characteristics of User-Friendly Legal Science and the research question.

First, there are particular methods to collect information about the contents of law. (a) The methods to collect published legislative materials and case law are obvious in most cases and do not need to be discussed. There can be exceptions. For example, the researcher may lack the necessary language skills and knowledge of foreign law. (b) Finding out about the contents of law requires some interpretation and the use of the data collection methods of legal dogmatics. (c) Where the researcher needs information about the contents of the legal framework in different jurisdictions, the functional method of comparative law can help.

Second, the study should always be based on a sufficient review of existing research (literature). The study can be a literature study or a literature study combined with an empirical study. In the absence of prior research and theories, an empirical study can provide information about facts that are relevant in the light of the point of view and research question.

Third, where the study is an empirical study, one can distinguish between qualitative and quantitative methods. (a) Interpretive understanding requires a qualitative method of some kind.[82] Qualitative methods facilitate a more holistic approach. In practice, they can help the researcher to identify more aspects that are relevant for the chosen users compared with quantitative methods. (b) Quantitative methods can be useful where the aspects that potentially are

[81] See, for example, Bryman A (2011); Lundahl U, Skärvad PH (1999).

[82] Berglund L, Ney A (2015), p. 159: "När vi tolkar skriftliga källor ägnar vi oss oftast åt någon form av kvalitativ metod. Här handlar det om att uttolka textens mening eller djupare innebörd."

relevant have already been identified.[83] The choice of these aspects can nevertheless be influenced by the researcher's bias[84] (for reliability, see Sect. 3.4.7).

Fourth, there are case studies and survey studies. In a case study, the researcher focuses on one or a small number of cases in order to obtain more detailed information and a deeper understanding (an empirical and qualitative study).[85] A survey study is a literature study of many previous studies.

3.4.5 Cases and Examples

Scientific theory building is based on data. There must be a connection between theory, empirical observations and sources (Sect. 3.4.3). Cases and examples play an important role in User-Friendly Legal Science that primarily focuses on behaviour rather than legal norms.

The researcher can use various kinds of cases ranging from systematic case studies to more or less random examples.[86] Since theory can be generated inductively from a broad range of studies and examples, there is no fundamental difference between them in this respect. In contrast, there is a fundamental difference between them in positivist research as regards the verification of theory.

Examples. Examples can be used in various ways to generate theory, to increase understanding or opportunistically as a rhetorical tool.

First, the researcher can use more or less random cases inductively at an early stage of theory building provided that the context is relevant and the cases seem to reflect the chosen point of view. The researcher can then try to find a pattern.[87] The researcher can also try to falsify the draft theory deductively by applying it to suitable cases and analysing the findings. Moreover, the researcher can apply the draft theory deductively to various kinds of cases and find out whether an untenable or absurd result would follow from its acceptance (argumentum ad absurdum, exemplum in contrarium). In these situations, the findings may indicate that there is reason to modify the draft theory: 'Both implicitly and explicitly, the analyst continually checks out his theory as the data pour in.'[88]

Second, examples can be used for the purpose of increasing understanding. The overall goal of the research—interpretive understanding—should be reflected in its

[83] See also Sandgren C (2005), pp. 316–317.

[84] See, for example, La Porta R, Lopez-de-Silanes F, Shleifer A, Vishny RW (1998) in which the authors focused on particular issues according to their own preferences.

[85] Eisenhardt KM, Graebner ME (2007), Pratt MG (2009).

[86] Generally, see Scapens RW (1990); Ryan B, Scapens RW, Theobald M (1992).

[87] Kaplan A (1964), § 2 p. 14.

[88] Glaser BG, Strauss AL (1967), p. 26.

form. The text should preferably be both analytic and useful.[89] Examples can be used to illustrate the facts and the theory and to make them easier to understand.[90]

Third, examples can be used opportunistically as a rhetorical tool. It is possible to find examples to support any view[91]: 'A researcher can easily find examples for dreamed-up, speculative, or logically deduced theory after the idea has occurred.'[92]

Case Studies. A qualitative empirical study can take the form of a case study. Systematic in-depth case studies have been called 'a natural complement to mainstream deductive research' that focuses on verification.[93] However, case studies are particularly useful in holistic research such as research in User-Friendly Legal Science.

The suitability of cases depends on the context and the research design. Case research design depends (a) on the research approach and overall method (a positivist approach with a linear method or a holistic approach with a non-linear method) and (b) on the purpose of the use of case studies.

Positivist Approach, Linear Method, Deductive Model. A linear method is a deductive model of explanation. It can be used when there are relatively clear causal relationships between variables. The deductive model of explanation provides predictions of occurrences at the empirical level, based on more abstract general laws or theories. However, the deductive model of explanation does not provide explanations of those occurrences, and case studies are not regarded as the best research method to use in such a context.[94] The value of case studies is limited to exploratory work, such as hypothesis generation and theory development. Hypothesis testing must be carried out in other ways because of the limited number of observations.[95]

Holistic Approach, Non-Linear Method, Pattern Model. The pattern model (Abraham Kaplan)[96] is the opposite of the deductive model. The pattern model is regarded as 'probably the only satisfactory method available' for the study of 'dynamic systems in which relations between variables are subject to a process of constant change'.[97] It is also useful for interpretive understanding, abductive reasoning and theory building.[98] Under the pattern model, 'the researcher seeks to identify a pattern in the case and uses theories to explain the observed relations.

[89]According to Glaser and Strauss, concepts should be analytic and sensitizing. *Ibid*, pp. 38–39.

[90]*Ibid*, p. 5: "[G]rounded theory is derived from data and then illustrated by characteristic examples of data." *Ibid*, p. 23: "In discovering theory, one generates conceptual categories or their properties from evidence; then the evidence from which the category emerged is used to illustrate the concept."

[91]See already Augustine of Hippo, De doctrina christiana, Third Book, XXV.

[92]Glaser BG, Strauss AL (1967), p. 5 on "exampling".

[93]Eisenhardt KM, Graebner ME (2007), p. 26.

[94]Ryan B, Scapens RW, Theobald M (1992), pp. 119–120.

[95]*Ibid,* p. 120.

[96]Kaplan A (1964), § 38 p. 332.

[97]Ryan B, Scapens RW, Theobald M (1992), p. 120.

[98]Kaplan A (1964), § 41 p. 351; Ryan B, Scapens RW, Theobald M (1992), p. 120.

Where existing theories do not provide convincing explanations, the new theories may have to be developed or existing theories modified.'[99] Therefore, '[t]heories will be used to explain empirical observations, and empirical observations will be used to modify theory'.[100]

Choice of Cases for the Pattern Model. Case study design and the choice of cases depend on the case study's purpose. The researcher can choose an exploratory case, a critical case, an extreme case or a multiple case study.

An exploratory case can be used to begin the process of theory development in situations where there is little available theory. The selection of the particular case is relatively unimportant[101] other than for rhetorical and the researcher's own subjective purposes provided that the context is right and the case seems to be useful in the light of the point of view of the study.

A critical case is useful where there is a well-formulated theory and the major research issues are clearly defined. A critical case is a case that directly addresses these issues: 'The objective of such a case study would be to determine whether the theory provides good explanations, or whether alternative explanations need to be developed.'[102]

An extreme case can be used for three purposes. It can be used in situations where the researcher wants to extend a theory to cover a wider range of circumstances, find out to what extent the scope of existing theory can be extended to provide explanations in widely differing circumstances or identify any areas in which the theory needs to be modified.[103]

Multiple case studies can be used for two purposes. The first is replication: 'A number of similar cases might be selected to replicate the theoretical explanations.' The second is theory development: '[D]issimilar cases may be selected to extend the theory to a wider set of circumstances.'[104]

3.4.6 Interpreting Information

Part of the method is to collect information about relevant facts (Sect. 3.4.2) from primary and other sources (Sect. 3.4.3) in certain ways (Sect. 3.4.4). However, the facts should also be interpreted and given a relevant meaning. They will obviously need to be interpreted in a qualitative study. You need interpretation even in a

[99]Ryan B, Scapens RW, Theobald M (1992), p. 120.

[100]*Ibid*, p. 120.

[101]*Ibid*, p. 121.

[102]*Ibid.*

[103]*Ibid.*

[104]*Ibid.*

quantitative study.[105] Therefore, one can distinguish between reporting and interpretation.[106]

The question of interpretation is at the core of what is regarded as the scientific method. Traditional positivists consider interpretation to be outside the boundaries of scientific enquiry. In phenomenology, Weber nevertheless assumed that the most appropriate way to gain knowledge about the social world is through interpretive understanding.[107]

In User-Friendly Legal Science, the facts that should be interpreted relate to two things.

The first is its point of view (the field, the user, the context, the user's objectives in the context and the relevant legal tools and practices). These facts can be interpreted in the same way as any facts in social sciences. It is worth noting that the primary research orientation of User-Friendly Legal Science is neither the interpretation nor the systematisation of 'pure law'[108] and that the interpretation of legal norms says very little about the user's objectives and practices in the context.

The second to be interpreted is the legal framework. Obviously, you cannot understand the use of legal tools and practices without information about the applicable legal framework, and you cannot understand the legal framework without the interpretation of laws (for the theory of legal dogmatics as a method theory, see Sect. 3.3.3). The contents of the legal framework cannot be interpreted without taking into account the methods of legal dogmatics or comparative law.

While interpretive understanding is the overall goal of User-Friendly Legal Science, the goal of interpretation and understanding is 'truth'.

Truth is one of the largest issues in philosophy, and there is no room to discuss it in detail in this book.[109] There are several philosophical theories concerning truth. The existence of different truth theories is even connected to the existence of different perceptions of reality in idealism and realism, as well as to the existence of different notions of scientific theories (Sect. 2.1).

The most famous theories about truth are the correspondence theory, the coherence theory and the pragmatist theory. They belong to the neoclassical theories of truth that try to answer the question about the nature of truth.

---

[105] See, for example, La Porta R, Lopez-de-Silanes F, Shleifer A, Vishny RW (1998) in which the authors gave particular facts a numerical value according to their own preferences.

[106] Bryant JM (1994), pp. 13–14: "[A]ll works of historiography are woven from two distinguishable strands: what might be called reportage on the one hand, and interpretation on the other. Reportage consists of information that pertains to basic questions of what, where, when, who, how many, etc. ... Interpretation involves establishing the meaning and the significance of these historical 'facts', i.e., the materials that constitute reportage ... Historical sociologists ... thus encounter primary materials in the reportage of historians ..." See also Subrt J (2012), p. 405.

[107] Weber M (1922).

[108] Kelsen H (1934).

[109] Compare White JB (2002), p. 1398: "Truth has a place in the law, a crucially important place, but it is hard to see and explain what this is."

The correspondence theory is regarded as the most important of the neoclassical theories. It is a realist theory. One of its core sources is Ludwig Wittgenstein's Tractatus.[110] The correspondence theory is based on the assumption that facts are entities that exist in their own right. A belief is true if and only if it corresponds to a fact.

Pragmatist theories of truth seem to reflect notions of the scientific method. According to Peirce, the pragmatist, abduction is a process and there is no final truth. Truth would therefore be the end of enquiry, but there will be no such thing according to Peirce.[111] Ludwik Fleck pointed out that scientific truths are preliminary and the result of the historical development of research techniques.[112] Thomas S. Kuhn's influential work The Structure of Scientific Revolutions[113] is to some extent based on Fleck. Pragmatist theories are compatible with Popper's idea of falsification. They seem to reflect the ontological assumptions of User-Friendly Legal Science (Sect. 2.1).

3.4.7 Assessing Methodological Rigour and Practical Aspects

Where it is difficult to assess research quality and methodological rigour, the long-term success of the findings in describing the phenomena under investigation might be used as a proxy.[114] But this is not always enough due to the researcher's own short-term interests and the interests of the research project's stakeholders.

Since the quality of the method of a scientific research project is likely to be assessed ex post, the researcher has an incentive to pay attention to the relevant principles for the assessment of the quality of the method during the research process ex ante. However, there is a conflict between methodological rationalism (empiricism, positivist approach) and relativism (hermeneutical approach) in this respect.[115]

---

[110]Wittgenstein L (1922), 1.13: "Die Tatsachen im logischen Raum sind die Welt." 2.1: "Wir machen uns Bilder der Tatsachen." 2.14: "Das Bild besteht darin, dass sich seine Elemente in bestimmter Art und Weise zu einander verhalten." 2.12: "Das Bild ist ein Modell der Wirklichkeit." 2.21: "Das Bild stimmt mit der Wirklichkeit überein oder nicht; es ist richtig oder unrichtig, wahr oder falsch." 2.06: "Das Bestehen und Nichtbestehen von Sachverhalten ist die Wirklichkeit. (Das Bestehen von Sachverhalten nennen wir auch eine positive, das Nichtbestehen eine negative Tatsache.)" 2.063: "Die gesamte Wirklichkeit ist die Welt."

[111]Glaser BG, Strauss AL (1967), p. 32 (theory as process); Peirce CS (1931–1935), 3.432.

[112]Fleck L (1979) Chapter 2, Section 1. Originally published in 1935.

[113]Kuhn TS (1962).

[114]Johansson LG (2015), p. 103.

[115]See Ryan B, Scapens RW, Theobald M (1992), pp. 8–9.

Many of the principles for the evaluation of the method have originally been developed for quantitative and positivist research.[116] Some of the tests customarily used to establish the quality of any empirical social research include construct validity, internal validity, external validity and reliability.[117]

Since these principles and tests have been designed for quantitative and positivist studies, they make qualitative and hermeneutic studies look rather bad. For example, abduction is not compatible with the linear research method of positivist studies.[118] Interpretive understanding and the holistic approach are not compatible with the notion of 'construct validity',[119] the notion of 'internal validity'[120] and the notion of 'reliability'.[121] Moreover, the use of interpretive understanding and the holistic approach makes it difficult to compare the findings of different studies and make generalisations on the basis of different studies.[122]

Obviously, these principles and tests cannot be as relevant in qualitative research as they are in positivist research. They have not been designed for qualitative and hermeneutical studies in the first place. However, there is no consensus on how to analyse and present qualitative data.[123] A consensus is unlikely to be reached because the analysis and presentation of qualitative data is a question of rhetoric.

Rhetoric. The attainment of the researcher's subjective objectives (Sect. 3.1) depends on the perceived quality of the method and the credibility of the findings. The researcher needs to use rhetoric to increase credibility and perceived quality.[124]

When choosing the rhetoric, the researcher will need to pay attention to general research-related requirements, discipline-specific requirements and method-specific requirements. These requirements apply to all aspects of the method such as the description of the method underlying the study, the presentation of the study and the presentation of its relation to theoretical concepts.[125]

---

[116]See Glaser BG, Strauss AL (1967), p. 16.

[117]Yin RK (2014), Chapter 2; Dubois A, Gadde LE (2014), p. 1281.

[118]For the linear model, see Piekkari R, Plakoyiannaki E, Welch C (2010), p. 110.

[119]Yin defines "construct validity" as "establishing correct operational measures for the concepts being studied". Yin RK (2014), Chapter 2.

[120]Yin defines "internal validity" as something limited to explanatory or causal studies. It means "establishing a causal relationship". *Ibid,* Chapter 2.

[121]Yin defines "reliability" as "demonstrating that the operations of a study - such as the data collection procedures - can be repeated, with the same results". *Ibid,* Chapter 2.

[122]See Miles MB (1979); Dubois A, Gadde LE (2014), pp. 1281–1282.

[123]See Dubois A, Gadde LE (2014), p. 1282.

[124]See *ibid*, p. 1282 on qualitative case research: "These conditions result in uncertainty about how to conduct 'good' case research and how to convince reviewers, editors, and the broader audience of readers of the real value of qualitative research and single case studies. There are certain problems in persuading advocates of the positivist school about the benefits of a research process in which frameworks evolve during the course of the study . . . Therefore, in order to convince the scientific community, qualitative researchers have to fight 'an uphill battle to persuade their readers' . . .".

[125]*Ibid*, p. 1282 on qualitative case research.

Moreover, the researcher should argue in a manner that makes it easier for readers to understand the study. This includes clarity,[126] the use of illustrations and comparisons and other ways to facilitate comprehension.[127]

General Research-Related Requirements. General research-related requirements relate to research ethics and coherence in the broad sense.[128]

Research ethics can mean many things. It is an idea of what research should be. It is also a particular discipline. Moreover, many different entities have adopted specific codes, rules and policies relating to research ethics. These normative standards can list the principles of research integrity[129] and examples of misconduct.[130]

Coherence is at the core of rhetoric in general. For example, ethos builds on the coherence of the matter and the person, and logos on the coherence of argumentation; argumentum ad personam and argumentum ad rem are counterarguments against the other party's ethos or logos, respectively; and exemplum in contrarium and argumentum ad absurdum are ways to highlight the lack of coherence in the other party's logos.

Coherence is also at the core of scientific rhetoric. There would be no scientific theory building and system building without the ideal of coherence (Sect. 5.1), and coherence is the cornerstone of legal dogmatics (for legal rhetoric, see Sect. 7.3).

As regards the research method, one can distinguish between external and internal coherence. External coherence can be defined as the method's coherence with facts and existing theory (the objective side of coherence) and the expectations of the audience (the subjective side of coherence). The internal coherence of the method means its coherence with the research question and the chosen theoretical framework, and the internal coherence of the text.

This is not new to researchers. Obviously, the method should provide a suitable way to produce the necessary information so that the research question can be and is answered in the study. The study should have a connection to theory in order to be regarded as a scientific study. Coherence has also been qualified in this context as 'meaningful coherence'.[131]

Discipline-Specific Requirements. The discipline-specific requirements reflect each discipline's point of view (Sect. 3.4.1). The method should enable the

[126]Wittgenstein L (1922), Vorwort.

[127]Glaser BG, Strauss AL (1967), pp. 228–233.

[128]See also Tracy SJ (2010), p. 839 on the characteristics of "high quality qualitative methodological research".

[129]See European Commission (2010, 2013). See also European Science Foundation, ALLEA (2011), Section 1.2.

[130]European Science Foundation, ALLEA (2011), Section 1.3.

[131]According to Tracy SJ (2010), p. 848, "meaningful coherence" means that qualitative studies should "(a) achieve their stated purpose; (b) accomplish what they espouse to be about; (c) use methods and representations practices that partner well with espoused theories and paradigms; and (d) attentively interconnect literature reviewed with research foci, methods, and findings".

researcher to produce information about things that are relevant in the light of the point of view. Moreover, these requirements reflect the discipline's research approach. For example, a qualitative method may not be regarded as convincing in a quantitative discipline regardless of the method's merits, and a narrow quantitative method may not be regarded as convincing in a holistic discipline that focuses on interpretive understanding.

Method-Specific Requirements. There are also method-specific requirements. For example, a quantitative study should comply with certain requirements, and there are requirements for qualitative case studies. Many of the principles for the evaluation of the method have originally been developed for quantitative research.

Particular Aspects of Interpretive Understanding and Abduction. In a holistic study, interpretive understanding is facilitated by a qualitative method. The researcher will again need to pay attention to general research-related, discipline-specific and method-specific aspects. We can focus on method-specific aspects because the starting point is that User-Friendly Legal Science—with the exception of some particular characteristics relating to primary sources and the role of legal dogmatics (Sect. 3.4.3)—shares its methods with other disciplines that choose interpretative understanding, the holistic approach, qualitative methods and abduction.

The method-specific aspects of a holistic and abductive enquiry in social sciences include description of the method, reliability, selectivity, representation, validity, operationalisation, the choice of variables and generalisation.[132]

Description of the Method. It is customary to describe the method in a scientific study. One can nevertheless distinguish between perceived methodological rigour and methodological rigour as such.

Since we are also talking about perceived rigour, the researcher may be able to signal high research quality in various ways depending on the context. In practice, perceived methodological rigour can sometimes be high even in the absence of a detailed account of the method.

At one end of the scale is a doctoral thesis that should contain a detailed account of the method because of the customary standards that the thesis is expected to comply with. Where the study is based on abductive inference, the researcher can signal methodological rigour ex post by describing the following:

- why abduction was chosen for the study, the nature of abduction and how it was used in the study;
- the choice of a method theory (Sect. 5.5.2);
- the choice of primary and secondary sources; and
- the choice, nature and use of the particular empirical methods complementing abductive inference.

[132]Torstendahl R (2005); Berglund L, Ney A (2015), pp. 150–151.

The nature of abductive inference makes it difficult to describe the process in detail ex ante. Since the method is not linear,[133] the researcher cannot say, in advance, what exactly the researcher will find out during the course of the research process and how exactly the preliminary findings will influence the method.

Generally, it can be difficult to describe the method in detail in qualitative and abductive studies even ex post. It would hardly be meaningful to ask the researcher to describe the complex intellectual path that led the researcher to see the light and understand the phenomena under investigation.

Since the overall goal of the study is interpretive understanding, the researcher obviously should not reduce perceived understanding by making the study very difficult to read. The researcher should not describe the researcher's own thought processes in detail.[134]

At the other end of the scale is a study that signals methodological rigour without a detailed account of the method. A knowledgeable reader can work backwards and identify evidence of methodological rigour from the text of the study. In other words, a reader may convince himself that the study as a whole signals methodological rigour.[135] For example, a narrative can be convincing because of its apparent quality, or the reader may put his faith on the apparent quality of the study and the researcher's personal authority.[136]

We have discussed perceived methodological rigour. The researcher will obviously have an incentive to do what it takes to convince the chosen audience. What about methodological rigour as such? Can one define methodological rigour in its own right?

It is clear that you cannot separate the method from the findings in abductive and non-linear studies. Findings are always preliminary and part of a 'loop' that will be repeated several times. Each abductive loop is closed by adjusting the text in the light of the preliminary findings and current theory. The closing of an abductive loop should improve understanding. This understanding is just preliminary, however, as the preliminary understanding will give a reason to search for new inputs. Adding new theory, new facts and new complementary methods will contribute to new findings. The abductive loop can again be closed by adjusting the text. There will not be any final truth about the matter (Sect. 3.4.6).[137] Neither can one identify the exact method. In abduction, the method is part of the loop. It will be influenced by the findings and the current understanding of theory and adjusted perhaps several times during the course of the study in the light of the level of understanding at different stages of the process. It would be futile to try to describe the method in great detail.

[133]See Dubois A, Gadde LE (2014), p. 1282.

[134]For thought processes, see James Joyce's Ulysses.

[135]See Bourdieu P (1992), Part II, I.

[136]A Bourdieu is a Bourdieu.

[137]Peirce CS (1931–1935), 3.432.

The understanding produced by the method can be used as evidence of methodological rigour. Gradually, it can become more and more difficult for the researcher to falsify the preliminary understanding. Adding new theory, new facts and new methods might not increase understanding other than marginally.[138] At this point, it can be more difficult even for readers to falsify the understanding. Where the reader cannot work backwards to find evidence of methodological rigour or lacks the means to try to falsify the findings, the researcher can signal methodological rigour by using a wide range of sources reflecting different kinds of methods and points of view. The personal authority of the researcher should not be regarded as sufficiently convincing.[139]

Reliability. The notion of reliability plays a central role in positivist studies that use a linear method. Reliability means that 'the operations of a study – such as the data collection procedures – can be repeated, with the same results'.[140] Such reliability depends on questions relating to representation, validity, operationalisation and generalisation.

However, the notion of reliability can depend on whether the research perspective is positivist (and focuses on causal explanations) or hermeneutical (interpretive understanding). Notions of reliability can thus be context specific and discipline specific.[141]

Interpretive understanding is based on abductive reasoning and a non-linear method. Abductive reasoning does not produce reliable results in the same sense as the linear research methods of positivist studies. When the researcher closes one abductive loop and produces a preliminary understanding, the researcher will start a new loop and search for new theories, facts and methods to improve the preliminary understanding. The closing of each loop is followed by the researcher's subjective choices. The 'operations' of an abductive study can thus not be described in any meaningful sense because the thought processes of a human being cannot be described exactly in any meaningful sense, and the operations of an abductive study cannot be 'repeated, with the same results' in any meaningful sense because the researcher's subjective choices are part of the abductive loop.

The 'reliability' of an abductive study must therefore be assessed on the basis of the findings rather than on the basis of whether the results can be repeated. Reliability can be connected to actual failure of falsification. The study is 'reliable'

---

[138]See also Glaser BG, Strauss AL (1967), pp. 224–225.

[139]A couple of examples: Saint Augustine (Augustine of Hippo) referred to Virgil several times in his major work De civitate Dei. Saint Thomas Aquinas referred to Augustine (Saint Augustine), Damascene (Saint John Damascene), Philosopher (Aristoteles), and Apostle (Paul) when discussing the existence of God in his work Summa Theologica. Pope Benedict XVI (Joseph Ratzinger) referred to prior theory in his biography of Jesus of Nazareth. This was regardless of the dogma of papal infallibility.

[140]Yin RK (2014), Chapter 2.

[141]See, for example, Kasanen E, Lukka K, Siitonen A (1993), p. 258: "The main condition of validity of constructions is clearly that they work (i.e., solve the problems in question)."

to the extent that it is falsifiable, but readers cannot falsify it. In the long run, the fate of the study is to be falsified and be replaced by studies that produce better understanding.

The hermeneutical circle (Sect. 2.4) and the abductive loop are ways to improve the understanding of complex phenomena and increase reliability. Higher reliability can require (a) the use of a wide range of sources, (b) studying the phenomena under investigation through the lens of theories that reflect different knowledge interests and different points of view and (c) the definition and redefinition of ideal types so that they reflect the patterns of behaviour that one can read in the sources.[142]

In order to limit the scope of source materials to what can reasonably be regarded as sufficient, it is necessary to pay attention to the research question. It should be sufficiently narrow and clearly defined (Sect. 3.2).

Signalling Reliability and Methodological Rigour. Since notions of reliability are context specific and discipline specific, the factors that contribute to reliability are context specific and discipline specific as well. In User-Friendly Legal Science (and other disciplines that are holistic, have interpretive understanding as the overall goal of research and use abductive inference), the researcher can both increase understanding and signal methodological rigour by paying attention to selectivity, representation, validity and generalisation. However, these notions do not mean the same things as in positivist research. Operationalisation is not a meaningful concept in User-Friendly Legal Science.

Selectivity. One of the key questions relating to the presentation of the study is selectivity. On one hand, understanding can be improved, and perceived methodological rigour can be increased, by increasing information about facts and theory. On the other, increasing information can also obstruct understanding and raise questions about methodological rigour. Therefore, '[t]he researcher's duty is to make available sufficient contextual information to facilitate the reader's evaluation of the research'.[143]

As regards the theoretical framework, three things stand out. First, there is neither abduction nor constructive reasoning (Sect. 2.5) without connection to prior theory. Second, the theoretical framework should be relevant in the sense that it is useful for the purposes of the study. Third, there should be conceptual clarity. The clarity and relevance (usefulness) of the theoretical framework require selectivity.

Representation. Representation means here that the sources should represent the chosen point of view. In User-Friendly Legal Science, the researcher needs information about the context, the users, the users' objectives, their legal tools and practices, and the ways users use legal tools and practices to reach their objectives.

[142] See, for example, Berglund L, Ney A (2015), pp. 121–126.

[143] Dubois A, Gadde LE (2014), p. 1282, citing Ruddin LP (2006).

What this means in practice is that the researcher needs to critically assess the sources and their relevance and usefulness for the study.[144] Defining the context, parties that have homogeneous objectives (interests) in the context and their objectives may require the use of a wide range of sources. Secondary sources can be from other social sciences. For example, legal norms are not enough since they say very little about the objectives of people and organisations, and just as little about the context.

Validity. There is a distinction between representation and validity. While representation is a question of the relevance of the information in the light of the chosen point of view, validity is a question of the truthfulness of the information in the light of what is being described. In other words, validity can be defined as a question of whether the data being collected measure the thing under investigation, and representation as a question of whether it is relevant to collect information about that particular thing in the first place.

Validity is different in positivist research. Yin distinguishes between 'construct validity', 'internal validity' and 'external validity'.[145] Internal validity focuses on causal relationships. It is intended 'for explanatory or causal studies only, and not for descriptive or exploratory studies'. In other words, it cannot be used when the overall goal of the study is interpretive understanding. External validity seems to be the functional equivalent of representation (see above). This leaves construct validity, that is, 'establishing correct operational measures for the concepts being studied'. Such construct validity might be meaningful when using linear research methods but cannot be applied in any meaningful sense in holistic and abductive studies. Construct validity seems to be the functional equivalent of operationalisation (see below).

Validity is required even in hermeneutics. However, it must be defined in other ways to reflect the holistic research approach. First, one can say that information is not valid unless it is reasonable to use it after the source criticism test.[146] Probably the most common test is that the sources should exhibit proximity, independence and absence of bias.[147] Second, information is not valid unless relevant sources have been used to the extent that it is reasonable.[148]

In User-Friendly Legal Science, the question of validity has a close connection to the chosen context. For example, it is not enough to say what users generally want. It is necessary to say what users want in the particular context. The sources

[144]Torstendahl R (2005); Berglund L, Ney A (2015), pp. 150–151.

[145]Yin RK (2014), Chapter 2, defining "construct validity" as "establishing correct operational measures for the concepts being studied", "internal validity" as "establishing a causal relationship", and "external validity" as "establishing the domain to which a study's findings can be generalized".

[146]See, for example, Torstendahl R (2005); Berglund L, Ney A (2015), p. 149; Johansson LG (2015) section 4.5.

[147]Berglund L, Ney A (2015), p. 149.

[148]*Ibid*, pp. 151–152.

should exhibit proximity to the chosen users in the chosen context in order for the information to be regarded as 'valid'.

Moreover, since the question of validity must reflect the holistic nature of User-Friendly Legal Science and the overall goal of interpretive understanding, information is not sufficiently 'valid' unless it is based on different kinds of sources.

General information about the regulation of certain activities is clearly not enough to ensure the representativeness and validity of information in User-Friendly Legal Science. The users' objectives and the means to reach them can only be identified by studying actual behaviour in the context.

One may ask whether it would be reasonable to require qualified validity in the sense that the sources should be 'the best' or 'the most useful' for the analysis or have 'the highest relative weight'.[149] The answer is no. In the light of the plurality of science, no particular sources can be 'the best' (for theories, see Sect. 3.3.1). Moreover, the holistic nature of User-Friendly Legal Science and the overall goal of interpretive understanding can require the use of many sources and various kinds of sources.

In practice, the researcher may understand the phenomena under investigation better if the researcher uses sources with different points of view and sources at different levels of abstraction. For example, the researcher may study dogmatic textbooks in a broad area of law, scientific articles about the particular context, professional articles containing tips for the practice, the legal documentation of transactions in the context and so forth. The different perspectives can melt into a better understanding.

Operationalisation, Choice of Variables. Operationalisation works in different ways depending on the research approach. Operationalisation is not a meaningful concept in User-Friendly Legal Science.

Operationalisation is customarily discussed in the context of positivist studies and quantitative methods. First, one must decide how the issue to be measured can be changed into a measurable variable. What can be used as a proxy for the issue? Second, one must also find out about the relationship between the different variables. The direction of the causal link should be from cause to effect. There are dependent variables (output or effect) and independent variables (inputs or causes).

Such operationalisation is not meaningful when the researcher chooses a qualitative method and a holistic research approach and focuses on interpretive understanding rather than causal relationships. In this case, it may be unclear what the relevant issues are.

The use of abduction, theory, ideal types and empirical data can help to identify and understand the relevant issues and to fill the dots between already known things. For example, it might be that the users' objectives in particular kinds of transactions are not clearly set out in the available documentation. The researcher might nevertheless be able to interpret existing documentation in the light of prior theory and literature and identify the users' typical objectives.

[149] See, for example, *ibid*, p. 151.

Generalisation. The last component of reliability discussed here is generalisation. The starting point is that one should integrate empirical research and theory (middle-range theorising).[150] There is a fundamental problem, though. The findings are based on a limited number of observations of cases of a certain type. One may ask whether the findings permit the researcher to make conclusions that cover even other cases of the same type.

One can probably draw different kinds of generalised conclusions.[151] The question is again not limited to qualitative research or User-Friendly Legal Science. It applies even to positivist science.[152] It would certainly be easier to make generalisations in classical physics with its notion of causality. In social sciences, one must deal with complex social reality and the fact that it is difficult to predict human behaviour. The problem of making generalisations is partly addressed by the use of ideal types (since the goal of research is to understand societal phenomena[153]) and abduction (since scientific research is a process and there is no end of enquiry[154]).

As regards User-Friendly Legal Science, the researcher studies primary and secondary sources that give information about user behaviour. The sources are limited to a sample of things: a sample of users, a sample of legal tools and practices and a sample of other things in one or more transactions and contexts. One may ask whether one can make wider claims about all users that belong to the same category or the use of legal tools and practices in all transactions that belong to the same category or their use in other contexts.

What is true at the level of one user can be true at the aggregate level (at least in research that chooses methodological individualism). In User-Friendly Legal Science, generalisation is a question of the quality of ideal types. Ideal types are designed to reflect normal cases and will not be falsified by the existence of pathological cases (Sect. 2.2).[155] For example, all users belonging to the same user category cannot be expected to behave in the same way because there can be users that

[150]Merton RK (1968); Boudon R (1991).

[151]For management accounting, see Lukka K, Kasanen E (1995), p. 72: "These generalized conclusions may be of several types: – conceptual frameworks, which offer us the possibility to discuss the subject area in general; – descriptive models, attempting to show 'how things are' in the problem field, covering more objects than the studied ones; – explanatory models, which attempt to capture the significant general relationships in the subject area; – prescriptive models, offering solutions to practical problems and guidance for further decision making in other similar, or corresponding, organizations."

[152]MacIntyre A (2007), p. 121 (generally): "They will be prefaced not by universal quantifiers but by some such phrase as 'characteristically and for the most part. . .' But just these . . . turned out to be the characteristics of the generalizations which actual empirical social scientists claim with good reason to have discovered." Lukka K, Kasanen E (1995), p. 73 (management accounting).

[153]Weber M (1904), II.

[154]Peirce CS (1931–1935), 3.432.

[155]Durkheim É (1894), Chapter III.

do not match the ideal type perfectly, but most users belonging to the same category can be expected to behave in roughly the same ways.

Generalisability rests on the quality of the ideal types, and the quality of the ideal types rests on the relevant theoretical knowledge, the empirical findings and their interpretation.[156]

The quality of ideal types and theory can be improved by repeating the hermeneutical circle or the abductive loop (Sects. 2.4 and 2.5). For example, the researcher may try to falsify the draft theory or test the generalisation of findings by using various kinds of examples (exemplum in contrarium) and extreme cases (argumentum ad absurdum). The researcher can also increase the number and variety of relevant sources. The researcher can dig deeper in a single case study or add more cases.[157]

Practical Aspects. In User-Friendly Legal Science, the goal of research is to merge theory and empirical findings so that theories about the behaviour of the users of legal tools and practices are connected to observable experiences. There should thus be a balance between data and theory.

Where the research question is very abstract, that is, where the theory is very general and covers a large number of different kinds of phenomena, it is more difficult to collect empirical data covering all phenomena. At the same time, it is easier to falsify the findings.[158] It is easier to collect empirical data at a fairly low level of generality when the research question is very concrete, that is, when it only covers a smaller number of homogeneous phenomena.[159] Moreover, such a study is easier for readers to understand and apply.[160] However, this will reduce the explanatory power of the findings (Sects. 2.5 and 2.6).

Since the purpose of the method is connected to theory and the research question, the choice of the method depends on the state of theory building in the context and the way the researcher wants to address the theory. Does the researcher want to apply an existing theory, test or falsify an existing theory or hypothesis, or build a theory? For example, in the absence of existing literature and theory, you may need to acquire information in various complementary ways in order to build a theory that possesses sufficiently high explanatory power without being too easy to falsify. However, it can be easier to apply an existing theory or test it in a narrowly defined context. It is sometimes possible to falsify an existing theory by finding examples of situations that seem to contradict the theory. In such cases, it may be enough to acquire information about a very narrow context.

---

[156]Lukka K, Kasanen E (1995), p. 82.

[157]*Ibid,* p. 76.

[158]Popper K (2005), numbers 36, 38 and 43.

[159]Yates SJ (2004), p. 15: "Theories in social sciences can vary between abstract general approaches (such as functionalism) and fairly low-level theories to explain specific phenomena (such as voting behaviour, delinquency, aggressiveness). By and large, the theories that are most likely to receive empirical attention are those which are at a fairly low level of generality."

[160]Glaser BG, Strauss AL (1967), p. 242.

References

Alvesson M, Sandberg J (2011) Generating research questions through problematization. Acad Manag Rev 36(2):247–271

Augustine of Hippo (426–427) De doctrina christiana

Babbie E (2016) The practice of social research, 14th edn. Cengage Learning, Boston

Banakar R (2006) How can sociology and jurisprudence learn from each other? A reply to Mauro Zamboni. Retfærd 29(2):75–84

Banakar R, Travers M (2005b) Law, sociology and method. In: Banakar R, Travers M (eds) Theory and method in socio-legal research. Hart Publishing, Oxford and Portland Oregon, pp 1–25

Bartunek JM, Rynes SL, Ireland RD (2006) What makes management research interesting, and why does it matter? Acad Manag J 49(1):9–15

Berglund L, Ney A (2015) Historikerns hantverk: Om historieskrivning, teori och metod. Studentlitteratur, Lund

Berman HJ (1983) Law and revolution: the formation of the Western legal tradition. Harvard University Press, Cambridge

Boudon R (1991) What middle-range theories are. Contemp Sociol (Am Sociol Assoc) 20 (4):519–522

Bourdieu P (1975) The specificity of the scientific field and the social conditions of the progress of reason. Soc Sci Inf 14(6):19–47. doi:10.1177/053901847501400602

Bourdieu P (1992) Les règles de l'art: genèse et structure du champ littéraire. Seuil, Paris

Bryant JM (1994) Evidence and explanation in history and sociology: critical reflections on goldthorpe's critique of historical sociology. Br J Sociol 45(1):3–19

Bryman A (2007) The research question in social research: what is its role? Int J Soc Res Methodol 10:5–20

Bryman A (2008) Of methods and methodology. Qual Res Organ Manage Int J 3(2):159–168

Bryman A (2011) Samhällsvetenskapliga metoder. Liber, Malmö

Dagan H (2011) Property: values and institutions. Oxford University Press, Oxford

Davis MS (1971) That's interesting! Towards a phenomenology of sociology and a sociology of phenomenology. Philos Soc Sci 1(4):309–344

Davis MS (1986) That's classic! The phenomenology and rhetoric of successful social theories. Philos Soc Sci 16(3):285–301

Djankov S, Glaeser E, La Porta R, Lopez-de-Silanes F, Shleifer A (2003) The new comparative economics. J Comp Econ 31:595–619

Djankov S, La Porta R, Lopez-de-Silanes F, Shleifer A (2008) The law and economics of self-dealing. J Financ Econ 88:430–465

Dubois A, Gadde LE (2014) "Systematic combining"–A decade later. J Bus Res 67:1277–1284

Durkheim É (1894) Les régles de la méthode sociologique. Revue philosophique

Duss V (2012) Chronik. Arbeitskreis "Augen der Rechtsgeschichte". Fünftes Symposium zur Methode der Rechtsgeschichte. Einsiedeln 20.–22. Januar 2011. Zeitschrift der Savigny-Stiftung für Rechtsgeschichte. Germanistische Abteilung 129(1):986–990. doi:10.7767/zrgga.2012.129.1.986

Ehrlich E (1912/1967) Das lebende Recht der Völker der Bukowina. Reprinted In: Rehbinder M (ed) Eugen Ehrlich, Recht und Leben, Duncker & Humblot, Berlin, pp 43–60

Eisenhardt KM, Graebner ME (2007) Theory building from cases: opportunities and challenges. Acad Manag J 50(1):25–32

Elharidy AM, Nicholson B, Scapens RW (2008) Using grounded theory in interpretive management accounting research. Qual Res Acc Manage 5(2):139–155. doi:10.1108/11766090810888935

European Commission (2010) European textbook on ethics in research. Publications Office of the European Union, Luxembourg. doi:10.2777/17442

European Commission (2013) Ethics for researchers: facilitating research excellence in FP7. Publications Office of the European Union, Luxembourg. doi:10.2777/7491

European Science Foundation, ALLEA (2011) The European Code of Conduct for Research Integrity. Strasbourg

Fallon RH Jr (1999) How to choose a constitutional theory. Calif Law Rev 87(3):535–579

Feyerabend PK (1975) Against method: outline of an anarchistic theory of knowledge. Humanities Press, London

Fleck L (1979) Genesis and development of a scientific fact. The University of Chicago Press, Chicago. Originally published in German as Fleck L (1935) Entstehung und Entwicklung einer wissenschaftlichen Tatsache. Einführung in die Lehre vom Denkstil und Denkkollektiv. Schwabe, Basel

Fleischer H (2001) Grundfragen der ökonomischen Theorie im Gesellschafts- und Kapitalmarktrecht. Zeitschrift für Unternehmens- und Gesellschaftsrecht 30(1):1–32

Fouché CB, De Vos AS (2011) Formal formulations. In: De Vos AS, Strydom H, Fouché CB, Delport CSL (eds) Research at grass roots: for the social sciences and human service professions. Van Schaik Publishers, Pretoria, pp 89–100

Friedman M (1953) The methodology of positive economics. In: Friedman M (ed) Essays in positive economics. University of Chicago Press, Chicago, pp 3–43

Giddens A (1979) Central problems in social theory. Macmillan, London

Giddens A (1984) The constitution of society: outline of the theory of structuration. Polity Press, Oxford, and University of California Press, Berkeley and Los Angeles

Giddens A (1988) Die Konstitution der Gesellschaft: Grundzüge einer Theorie der Strukturierung. Campus-Verlag, Frankfurt am Main [German translation of Giddens A (1984)]

Gilbert N (ed) (2008) Researching social life, 3rd edn. Sage, Thousand Oaks

Glaser BG, Strauss AL (1967) The discovery of grounded theory: strategies for qualitative research. Aldine de Gruyter, New York

Glerup C, Horst M (2014) Mapping 'social responsibility' in science. J Responsible Innov 1 (1):31–50. doi:10.1080/23299460.2014.882077

Goldthorpe JH (1991) The uses of history in sociology: reflections on some recent tendencies. Br J Sociol 42:211–230

Graver HP (2008) Vanlig juridisk metode? Om rettsdogmatikken som juridisk sjanger. Tidsskrift for Rettsvitenskap 121(2):149–178

Guével D (2012) Droit de commerce et des affaires, 4e edn. LGDJ, Paris

Husa J (2009) Theorie der Rechtsvergleichung als Rechtsphilosophie. Rechtstheorie 40:473–492

Johansson LG (2015) Introduktion till vetenskapsteorin. Tredje upplagan, andra tryckningen. Bokförlaget Thales, Stockholm

Kaplan A (1964) The conduct of inquiry: methodology for behavioral science. Chandler Publishing Company, New York

Kasanen E, Lukka K, Siitonen A (1993) The constructive approach in management accounting research. J Manag Account Res 5:243–264

Kelsen H (1934) Reine Rechtslehre: Einleitung in die rechtswissenschaftliche Problematik, 1. Aufl. Deuticke, Leipzig Wien. Jestaedt M (ed) (2008) Studienausgabe. Mohr Siebeck, Tübingen

Kuhn TS (1962) The structure of scientific revolutions. University of Chicago Press, Chicago

La Porta R, Lopez-de-Silanes F, Shleifer A, Vishny RW (1998) Law and finance. J Polit Econ 106 (6):1113–1155

Lukka K, Kasanen E (1995) The problem of generalizability: anecdotes and evidence in accounting research. Acc Audit Account J 8(5):71–90 doi:10.1108/09513579510147733

Lukka K, Vinnari E (2014) Domain theory and method theory in management accounting research. Account Audit Account J 27(8):1308–1338

Lundahl U, Skärvad PH (1999) Utredningsmetodik för samhällsvetare och ekonomer. Studentlitteratur, Lund

MacIntyre A (2007) After virtue. A study in moral theory, 3rd edn. University of Notre Dame Press, Notre Dame, Indiana
Mæhle SS (2015) Rettsvitenskapelig forskningsmetodikk – i lys av grunnleggende forskningsverdier. Tidsskrift for Rettsvitenskap 128(2):125–157
Mäntysaari P (2005) Comparative corporate governance: shareholders as a rule-maker. Springer, Berlin Heidelberg
Mäntysaari P (2010a) The law of corporate finance: general principles and EU law. Volume I: cash flow, risk, agency, information. Springer, Berlin Heidelberg
Mäntysaari P (2010b) The law of corporate finance: general principles and EU law. Volume II: contracts in general. Springer, Berlin Heidelberg
Mäntysaari P (2012) Organising the firm: theories of commercial law, corporate governance and corporate law. Springer, Berlin Heidelberg
Mäntysaari P (2013) Was sollte man tun? Ein Plädoyer für anwenderfreundliche Rechtswissenschaft. Rechtstheorie 44(2):189–207. doi:10.3790/rth.44.2.189
Mäntysaari P (2015) EU electricity trade law: the legal tools of electricity producers in the internal electricity market. Springer International Publishing, Cham. doi:10.1007/978-3-319-16513-4
Mäntysaari P (2016) Oikeudenaloista tieteenaloihin. Lakimies 114(2):297–304
Merton RK (1968) Social theory and social structure. Free Press, New York
Miles MB (1979) Qualitative data as an attractive nuisance: the problem of analysis. Adm Sci Q 24 (4):590–601. doi:10.2307/2392365
Moorhead R (2010) Lawyer specialization – managing the professional paradox. Law Policy 32 (2):226–259
Myrdal J (2007) Källpluralismen och dess inkluderande metodpaket. Historisk tidskrift 127 (3):495–504
National Academy of Sciences, National Academy of Engineering, Institute of Medicine (1992) Responsible science: ensuring the integrity of the research process, vol I. The National Academies Press, Washington. doi:10.17226/1864
Olsen L (2004) Rättsvetenskapliga perspektiv. Svensk Juristtidning 89(2):105–145
Patel R, Davidson B (2012) Forskningsmetodikens grunder: Att planera, genomföra och rapportera en undersökning. Fjärde upplagan, Studentlitteratur, Lund
Peirce CS (1931–1935) The collected papers of Charles Sanders Peirce, vols I–VI. In: Hartshorne C, Weiss P (eds) Harvard University Press, Cambridge
Piekkari R, Plakoyiannaki E, Welch C (2010) 'Good' case research in industrial marketing: insights from research practice. Ind Mark Manag 39:109–117
Popper K (2005) Logik der Forschung. 11. Auflage. Mohr Siebeck, Tübingen
Posner RA (2002) Legal scholarship today. Harv Law Rev 115(5):1314–1326
Pratt MG (2009) For the lack of a boilerplate: tips on writing up (and rewriting) qualitative research. Acad Manag J 52(5):856–862
Quine WV (1975) The nature of natural knowledge. In: Guttenplan S (ed) Mind and language. Clarendon Press, Oxford, pp 67–81
Ross A (1958) On law and justice. Stevens & Sons, London
Ruddin LP (2006) You can generalize stupid! social scientists, Bent Flyvbjerg and case study methodology. Qual Inq 12(4):797–812. doi:10.1177/1077800406288622
Ryan B, Scapens RW, Theobald M (1992) Research method and methodology in finance and accounting. Academic Press, London
Sandberg J, Alvesson M (2011) Ways of constructing research questions: gap-spotting or problematization? Organization 18:23–44. doi:10.1177/1350508410372151
Sandgren C (2005) Om teoribildning och rättsvetenskap. Juridisk Tidskrift 16(2):297–333
Saurama E, Julkunen I (2012) Approaching practice research in theory and practice. Soc Work Soc Sci Rev 15(2):57–75. doi:10.1921/095352211X636502
Scapens RW (1990) Researching management accounting practice: the role of case study methods. Br Account Rev 22(3):259–281

Strydom H (2014) An evaluation of the purposes of research in social work. Social Work/ Maatskaplike Werk 49(2):149–164. doi:10.15270/49-2-58

Subrt J (2012) History and sociology: what is historical sociology? In: Erasga D (ed) Sociological landscape-theories, realities and trends. Intechopen. Chapter 12, pp 403–416. doi:10.5772/ 38816

Teubner G (1997) Global Bukowina: legal pluralism in the world-society. In: Teubner G (ed) (1997) Global law without a state. Aldershot, Dartmouth, pp 3–28

Torstendahl R (2005) Källkritik, metod och vetenskap. Historisk tidskrift 125(2):209–217

Tracy SJ (2010) Qualitative quality: eight "Big Tent" criteria for excellent qualitative research. Qual Inq 16(1):837–851. doi:10.1177/1077800410383121

von Ranke L (1885) Sämtliche Werke. Bd. 33/34. Duncker & Humblot, Leipzig

Weber M (1904) Die "Objektivität" sozialwissenschaftlicher und sozialpolitischer Erkenntnis. Archiv für Sozialwissenschaft und Sozialpolitik 19(1):22–87

Weber M (1922) Wirtschaft und Gesellschaft – Grundriß der verstehenden Soziologie. J.C.B Mohr (Paul Siebeck), Tübingen

Wesel U (1974) Zur Methode der Rechtsgeschichte. Kritische Justiz 7(4):337–368

Whaples R, Morris AP, Moorhouse JC (1998) What should lawyers know about economics? J Leg Educ 48:120–124

White JB (2002) Legal knowledge. Harv Law Rev 115(5):1396–1431

Wittgenstein L (1922) Tractatus Logico-philosophicus: Logisch-philosophische Abhandlung. Kegan Paul, London

Yates SJ (2004) Doing social science research. SAGE Publications, London

Yin RK (2014) Case study research: design and methods, 5th edn. SAGE Publications, Thousand Oaks

Zweigert K, Kötz H (1996) Einführung in die Rechtsvergleichung auf dem Gebiete des Privatrechts, 3. neubearbeitete Auflage. Mohr Siebeck, Tübingen

Chapter 4
Use of Findings

4.1 General Remarks

The choice of the new point of view of User-Friendly Legal Science can lead to new findings. The user-friendly research approach can contribute to a better understanding of user objectives, the users' legal tools and practices, and the pragmatic syllogisms combining the objectives with the means to reach them.

The findings can be used in many pragmatic ways by the users of legal tools and practices (Chap. 1 and Sect. 4.2). In addition to theory building and system building (Chap. 5), there are pragmatic ways to use the findings even in legal science (Sect. 4.3). Both users and scholars can use the findings of user-friendly studies to deal with legal pluralism (Sect. 4.4). In legal education, User-Friendly Legal Science can contribute to a more practice-ready curriculum (Sect. 4.5).

4.2 Pragmatic and Legal Use

User-Friendly Legal Science is pragmatic and facilitates problem solving. Understanding user objectives and the legal tools and practices to reach them is the difference between the professional and the layman[1] and the conditio sine qua non of rational and reasonable legal work.[2] We can have a look at some of the pragmatic ways to use the findings of user-friendly research.

---

[1]Weber M (1919/2011), p. 13: "Der Dilettant unterscheidet sich vom Fachmann . . . nur dadurch, daß ihm die feste Sicherheit der Arbeitsmethode fehlt, und daß er daher den Einfall meist nicht in seiner Tragweite nachzukontrollieren und abzuschätzen oder durchzuführen in der Lage ist."

[2]Generally, see Weber M (1919/2011), p. 9 on intellectual rationalisation through science; Petersen J (2014), § 2 p. 36.

P. Mäntysaari, *User-friendly Legal Science*, DOI 10.1007/978-3-319-53492-3_4

Guidance. One of the obvious uses is guidance. People can need guidance in many capacities. They use legal tools and practices to reach objectives in their private lives, in the course of business and in other contexts. Providing guidance is a legitimate goal of all 'design sciences' (Sect. 2.5).[3] To produce results that are relevant to many people and society at large is a legitimate goal for legal science as well.

This aspect of legal science has been neglected in the past due to the narrow definition of law and legal science.[4] There is no reason why it should remain so. In the words of Hart: 'Why should not law be equally if not more concerned with the "puzzled man" or "ignorant man" who is willing to do what is required, if only he can be told what it is? Or with the "man who wishes to arrange his affairs" if only he can be told how to do it?'[5]

Legal Advice. One can give guidance to users directly or, through their legal advisors, indirectly. The quality of legal advice can be improved by better information about the context and the pragmatic syllogisms combining objectives and the means to reach them. Legal practitioners need better information to increase the suitability of legal advice to clients. Generally, more suitable and cheaper legal advice can reduce transaction costs and increase overall welfare. This can benefit legal practitioners as well.

Legal practitioners can make a better living if their advice is perceived as relevant and suitable by their clients. A lawyer who does not understand what clients want and how customers can use legal tools and practices to reach their objectives is not well-informed enough to give the kind of advice that customers want to pay for. One tends to quote John Pierpont Morgan, a famous banker, who said: 'Well, I don't know as I want a lawyer to tell me what I cannot do. I hire him to tell how to do what I want to do.' An empirical study in the UK found that specialised but traditional lawyers can see problems too narrowly, if they only understand a narrow field of law. Not only the lack of specialisation but even cognitive narrowness was identified as a source of quality problems.[6]

Better-informed legal practitioners may develop new forms of legal advice. Before developing standardised, automated or online legal services that are

---

[3]van Aken JE (2004), p. 228: "Whereas the typical research product of the explanatory sciences is the causal model, the typical research product of the modern design sciences is the tested and grounded technological rule." For technological rules, see Bunge M (1967), p. 132. However, van Aken finds Bunge's definition as too restrictive and widens its meaning. See also van Aken JE (2004), p. 237 on the utility of technological rules.

[4]See, for example, Dalberg-Larsen J (2005), pp. 48–49 on Alf Ross: "... Ross seems to consider legal action and legal guidance as accessories to any law that is not completely special and aberrant. This conception might indicate that Ross only seldom went out into real life to see what society looked like for ordinary citizens. If he had done so, he would soon have found out that many citizens' lives and welfare are affected by laws, without them even contemplating approaching the courts or lawyers with their problems." See also Mäntysaari P (2013).

[5]Hart HLA (1961/2012), p. 40.

[6]Moorhead R (2010).

cheaper, legal practitioners might benefit from a theory that explains the typical objectives of a certain class of users in a certain context and how these users can reach their objectives by legal tools and practices.

Regulation. Regulating society is a form of practice. Legal norms are expected to have particular societal effects. People and organisations take norms into account by adapting their own behaviour according to their own interests. Better information about the likely effects in the light of such user objectives makes it easier to design more effective norms. Better information about societal mechanisms can thus improve the quality of regulation.[7] Technological change will increase demand for information about societal mechanisms and the implications of the choice of societal objectives.[8]

Moreover, a better understanding of societal mechanisms in the context can reduce the need for state regulation. It might turn out to be possible to replace part of state regulation by party autonomy, education or self-regulation. Sufficiently well-informed private individuals can often adequately protect themselves.

Interpretation. Better information about societal mechanisms can be useful in the context of the interpretation of legal norms, contracts and human behaviour in general.[9] In particular, such information can support arguments about a party's intentions in a context or arguments about the norm content necessary for the attainment of a given purpose (teleological arguments, Sect. 7.3.4).

This can be illustrated with the interpretation of contracts. According to the traditional rule, the court interprets contracts according to the intentions of the parties ('subjectively').[10] However, the interpretation of contracts can only be 'objective' and based on whatever materials are available to the court.[11] It cannot be 'subjective' because judges cannot read anyone's mind and the court lacks verifiable and reliable information about the subjective intentions of the parties.[12] The interpretation of the subjective intentions of the parties becomes a more objective and transparent exercise, if the court receives more objective information about the customary intentions of parties in a certain context and the customary

---

[7]Compare Dalberg-Larsen J (2005), p. 47 on Alf Ross and the sociology of law: "However, Ross' definition of this field of research involves some crucial problems. First, Ross' science only aims at studying whether the law actually has an effect on the citizens' conduct or not. Therefore, it does not really aim at finding out whether the purpose of the law is in fact attained. And often it turns out that even if the citizens do obey the law, it still does not have the desired effect. In other words, the wrong means—regulation of the citizens' conduct—have been used to try to attain the desired end."

[8]Casey AJ, Niblett A (2015).

[9]Weber M (1922), Second Part, Chapter VII, § 6, p. 492: "Die Konsequenzen der rein logischen juristischen Konstruktion verhalten sich vielmehr zu den Erwartungen der Verkehrsinteressenten ungemein häufig gänzlich irrational und geradezu disparat: die vielberedete 'Lebensfremdheit' des rein logischen Rechts hat hier ihren Sitz."

[10]See for example, Article 8(1) of the CISG.

[11]See Articles 8(2) and 8(3) of the CISG.

[12]See Mäntysaari (2010b), section 5.2.

purpose and effect of the legal tools and practices actually used by the parties in that context. The same can be said of the interpretation of any rational human behaviour.

4.3 Pragmatic Uses in Legal Science

The findings of user-friendly studies can be used pragmatically even in legal science (Chap. 1). We can have a look at some of the ways.

First, they can help to build constructions (Sect. 2.5) and theories about user behaviour.[13] Such constructions and theories can be useful when legal norms are made and interpreted.

Second, findings can perhaps be generalised (Sects. 3.4.5 and 3.4.6) or applied in a more specific context. The existence of both general and more specific theories contributes to system building (Chap. 5).[14] System building belongs to the core functions of science.

The existence of alternative perspectives to legal system building could improve the quality of legal science. Law is no exception to the rule that the use of different perspectives and multiple approaches to the study of phenomena in a given field will give a more complete picture.

Since User-Friendly Legal Science primarily does not study law or legal norms, it provides an alternative way to present law as a systematic order. This may sound counter-intuitive. However, law can be presented systematically through the lens of users' objectives in each context. To replace dogmatic and non-scientific areas of law, one can develop new legal disciplines that are functional, theory based and scientific (Sect. 7.2). These new legal disciplines are not limited by national legal traditions and are less path dependent than traditional areas of law.[15]

Third, one can use the findings and theories of User-Friendly Legal Science in the battle for hegemony in the scientific field.

For this purpose, the scientific field can be defined as 'the objective space defined by the play of opposing forces in a struggle for scientific stakes'.[16] The battle for

---

[13]For the traditional and opposite view, see Ross A (1958), p. 34: "What, now, are those social facts which as legal phenomena constitute the counterpart of the legal norms? They must be the human actions regulated by the legal norms ... [T]he legal phenomena as the counterpart of the norms must be the decisions of the courts." See also Dalberg-Larsen J (2005), p. 48 on Alf Ross: "In this field as well as in general, he seems to completely underestimate the importance of developing more general legal-sociological theories to inspire empirical research."

[14]Popper K (2005), number 85.

[15]Ross A (1958), § 44, pp. 202–203: "It would be futile to try to create a systematic classification without roots in tradition. The task of jurisprudence is restricted to revise and refine traditional concepts. The traditions, however, are so different for Continental and Anglo-American law that–with the exception of some few fundamental divisions–it is impossible to discuss problems of systematic arrangements common for both."

[16]Bourdieu P (1975), p. 21. For Bourdieu's sociology of science, see Sismondo S (2011).

hegemony means a battle for the monopoly of scientific authority, that is, a socially recognised capacity to speak and act in an authorised and authoritative way in scientific matters.[17] For example, somebody will give guidance to the legislator and the judge in scientific matters,[18] and scholars apply other researchers' scientific findings in their own work. In order to be relevant, legal science should ensure that it is regarded as a science rather than mere politics or an exercise in rhetorics.[19]

Fourth, the findings of user-friendly research can be used even in other legal disciplines. In doctrinal research, user-friendly theories can support teleological arguments and/or arguments about the relevant objectives (Sects. 4.2 and 7.3.4). In comparative law, they can help to identify social needs (user objectives) and functional equivalents (legal tools and practices) (Sect. 6.4). In law and economics, the findings of user-friendly research can give information about what is relevant and help to question the assumptions and narrow focus of quantitative studies that are based on economic theories.[20]

Fifth, the findings can help to address legal pluralism by giving information about what is relevant in the context.

4.4 Dealing with Legal Pluralism

Both users and scholars may benefit from the findings of user-friendly studies when dealing with legal pluralism.

The notion of legal pluralism means the existence of overlapping legal systems that apply simultaneously.[21] One can distinguish between constitutional pluralism, source pluralism and jurisdictional pluralism. (a) Constitutional pluralism is caused by the fact that different sectors of society have their own constitutional rules and compete against the political legislator. Constitutional pluralism exists both nationally and internationally. There are autonomous legal systems of communities within the nation, and there are communities crossing national boundaries.[22]

---

[17]Bourdieu P (1975), p. 19.

[18]Compare Ross A (1958), § 76, p 331: "[T]here is a place for legal politics, not merely as guidance for the legislator, but also as guidance for the authorities administering the law, in particular the judge."

[19]*Ibid,* § 75, p. 328: "Where then is the place for specific legal politics to be the domain of the lawyers? ... This special body of knowledge can only be sought in the legal-sociological knowledge concerning the causal connection between the normative function of the law and human behaviour, or, we may also say, concerning the possibilities of influencing human action by the apparatus of legal sanctions." See, for example, Graver HP (2008), p. 150.

[20]Hart O (2016). See, for example, Williamson OE (2005) on the notion of contracts in transaction cost economics; Mäntysaari P (2012), section 4.9 on the existence of many legal tools apart from contracts.

[21]Ehrlich E (1912/1967), p. 43. See, for example, Teubner G (1983); Teubner G (1992); Teubner G (1997); de Sousa Santos B (1987); Griffiths J (1986).

[22]Berman HJ (1983), p. 45.

(b) Source pluralism relates to the sources of law. Source pluralism may exist in cross-border situations. The sources of law are increasingly foreign or international because of the cross-border nature of transactions and other dealings in a globalised world and the increasing use of foreign law.[23] However, source pluralism is not limited to cross-border situations. It can exist even in cases that have connections to only one country. Source pluralism may be the consequence of the ideal of coherence. The coherence of the legal system is facilitated by the use of analogy and general principles. Since there is more regulation than ever before, it is more difficult to maintain coherence and there are more sources that could be relevant in a particular case.[24] (c) Moreover, there is jurisdictional pluralism. It may turn out that different competent authorities apply law in different ways.[25]

Legal pluralism has contributed to the fragmentation of law both nationally and internationally[26] and made it more difficult to systematise and interpret law.[27] A rational user will obviously need to pay attention to the relevant legal norms regardless of where they originate, and to the relevant legal sources.

Legal pluralism can increase (a) the user's discretion as the user may choose the suitable legal system (opt-in and opt-out rights), (b) the user's need to manage legal risk as the contents of law may be flexible or unclear and (c) the user's transaction costs as the user may need to invest more in information and risk management and to adapt its own behaviour.[28]

The findings of user-friendly studies could help individual users to address problems caused by legal pluralism because user-friendly studies can choose a well-defined user perspective in the relevant context. In practice, each user will choose the legal system and the legal tools and practices that the user finds useful in each particular context. Where the norms originate is not relevant as such but will be taken into account by the user to the extent that it is relevant for the user. In User-Friendly Legal Science, you can identify and study all relevant legal aspects from the user's perspective.

Users may be able to use the findings of user-friendly studies even collectively. Users can sometimes benefit from cooperation. First, better information about shared objectives and legal tools and practices can help users to create their own legal framework. They can choose industry self-regulation and create non-state law (Sect. 7.5.2).[29] Second, such user-friendly studies can be helpful when interest groups lobby for state law.[30]

---

[23]Teubner G (2012), p. 36; Teubner G (2000).

[24]Dagan H (2011), p. xviii: "For legal realists, the profound and inescapable reason for doctrinal indeterminacy is the availability of multiple and potentially applicable doctrinal sources."

[25]Graver HP (1989).

[26]Sieber U (2010), p. 171.

[27]Mäntysaari P (2013).

[28]See, for example, Mäntysaari P (2010b), sections 2.2 and 4.4.

[29]See, for example, Asano Y (2014), pp. 163 and 165–166.

[30]For firms, see Stigler GJ (1971).

4.5 A More Practice-Ready Curriculum

User-Friendly Legal Science with its theories on how users can reach their objectives by using legal tools and practices could help to make the curriculum more practice ready.

Law is taught at university level in law schools and as a complementary subject in other university departments. Curriculum design depends on what is perceived as 'law', on what is perceived as the needs of practice and on the role of theory.

There is path dependency. The curriculum is influenced by traditions, the researchers' vested interests and efficiency requirements. Existing areas of law and the traditional way of doing things function as platforms that make it easier for people to communicate with each other in legal research and education. Because of time constraints and the scarcity of resources in general, it can be efficient to focus on something in legal education.

Now, traditional legal education focuses on the contents and interpretation of legal norms customarily applied by the court.[31] In doing so, it reflects a rather limited view of legal practice. Most of legal practice is not about litigation or disputes. Moreover, the limited view of what lawyers actually do is combined with the absence of legal theories about societal reality outside the legal system. The limited view also explains the abundance of textbooks that describe legal norms.[32]

From the perspective of clients, the curriculum tends to be less practice ready than it could be. 'Practice-readiness' is obviously related to the users of law, legal tools and legal practices. Many users expect legal practitioners to provide useful advice. A practice-ready curriculum could be based on client needs.

The main reason for the lack of practice readiness seems to be that law schools have looked for the answer in the wrong place.[33] Since the study of law is limited to norms and the way they are interpreted, law schools have failed to focus on client needs and generate theories that reflect their interests.[34]

---

[31]See, for example, Holmes OW (1897) on "the black-letter man".

[32]Ehrlich E (1913), pp. 6–8: "Vom richterlichen Standpunkte aus ist das Recht eine Regel, nach der der Richter die Rechtsstreitigkeiten, die vor ihn gebracht werden, zu entscheiden hat ... An Stelle der wissenschaftlichen Betrachtung ist eben die praktische, auf den richterlichen Beamten zugeschnittene getreten, und der Beamte will doch vor allem die Regel kennen lernen, nach der er selbst vorgehen soll ... Jedes Blatt eines juristischen Werkes, jeder juristische Lehrvortrag bestätigt das, was soeben gesagt worden ist. Aus jedem Worte fast geht es hervor, daß dem Juristen, der von einem Rechtsverhältnisse handelt, immer nur die Frage vorschwebt, wie die Streitigkeiten, die aus diesem Rechtsverhältnisse entstehen, zu entscheiden sind, nicht die davon ganz verschiedene Frage, wie sich die Menschen in diesem Rechtsverhältnisse benehmen und zu benehmen haben."

[33]For the "drunkard's search" generally, see Kaplan A (1964), § 1, pp. 11 and 17.

[34]See even Banakar R (2005), p. 85: "As any practicing lawyer would point out, the practice of law consists of a diverse set of skills, many of which have little if anything at all to do with legal theory."

Law and legal education are not unique in this respect. Other professions face similar challenges. Herbert Simon pointed out that '[a] full solution ... of the organizational problem of the professional schools hinges on the prospect of developing an explicit, abstract, intellectual *theory* of the processes of synthesis and design, a theory that can be analysed and taught in the same way ...'[35]

However, law fares worse than other professional disciplines. Other professional disciplines tend to face a utilisation problem[36] caused by the fact that there is a conflict between the academic reputation system and the professional reputation system.[37] While the academic reputation system rewards rigorous scientific research, the professional reputation system rewards research that is relevant for practitioners. In the absence of scientific theory building and scientific methods in legal science, law professors have an incentive to choose consulting,[38] but consulting experience does not improve scientific theory if scientific rigour and theory building are not regarded as relevant in the first place.

From the perspective of clients, the absence of practice-ready or user-friendly legal theories is likely to reduce the quality of legal advice. It is fair to assume that these quality problems will not go away if one chooses to teach students law courses that make little sense to working lawyers.[39] Neither will the fundamental problems disappear if students are given an education in something else than law. For example, the lack of good 'practice-ready' or 'user-friendly' legal theories cannot be cured by adopting theories from other sciences such as economics or by the increased use of law-and-something courses. Law professors should design their own middle-range theories that are useful for clients.

References

Asano Y (2014) From the theory of private law to legal pluralism: on the reconstruction of private law in the age of globalization. Jpn Yearb Int Law 57:163–178

Banakar R (2005) Anmeldelse af Mauro Zamboni: the policy of law: a legal theoretical framework. Retfærd 28(4):82–87

Berman HJ (1983) Law and revolution: the formation of the Western legal tradition. Harvard University Press, Cambridge

Beyer JM (1982) Introduction to the special issue on the utilization of organizational research. Adm Sci Q 27(4):588–590

Bourdieu P (1975) The specificity of the scientific field and the social conditions of the progress of reason. Soc Sci Inf 14(6):19–47. doi:10.1177/053901847501400602

Bunge M (1967) Scientific research II: the search for truth. Springer, Berlin Heidelberg. doi:10.1007/978-3-642-48138-3

[35] Simon HA (1967), p. 15.

[36] For an introduction, see Beyer JM (1982).

[37] van Aken JE (2004), p. 222.

[38] See Posner RA (2002), p. 1315.

[39] For this discussion generally, see Purcell EA (2014).

Casey AJ, Niblett A (2015) The death of rules and standards. University of Chicago, Public Law Working Paper No. 550; University of Chicago Coase-Sandor Institute for Law & Economics Research Paper No. 738. doi:10.2139/ssrn.2693826

Dagan H (2011) Property: values and institutions. Oxford University Press, Oxford

Dalberg-Larsen J (2005) Alf Ross and the sociology of law. Scand Stud Law 48:39–50

de Sousa SB (1987) Law: a map of misreading. Toward a postmodern conception of law. J Law Soc 14(3):279–302

Ehrlich E (1912/1967) Das lebende Recht der Völker der Bukowina. Reprinted in: Rehbinder M (ed) Eugen Ehrlich, Recht und Leben, Duncker & Humblot, Berlin, pp 43–60

Ehrlich E (1913) Grundlegung der Soziologie des Rechts. Duncker & Humblot, München and Leipzig

Graver HP (1989) Normative systemer – skisse til en oppløsning av rettsbegrepet. In: Basse EM (ed) Regulering og styring. Gad, Copenhagen, pp 53–68

Graver HP (2008) Vanlig juridisk metode? Om rettsdogmatikken som juridisk sjanger. Tidsskrift for Rettsvitenskap 121(2):149–178

Griffiths J (1986) What is legal pluralism? J Leg Pluralism Unofficial Law 18(24):1–55. doi:10.1080/07329113.1986.10756387

Hart HLA (2012) The concept of law, 3rd edn. With an Introduction by Leslie Green. Oxford University Press, Oxford

Hart O (2016) Oliver Hart – Banquet Speech. Nobelprize.org. Nobel Media AB. http://www.nobelprize.org/nobel_prizes/economic-sciences/laureates/2016/hart-speech.html

Holmes OW (1897) The path of the law. Harv Law Rev 10:457–490

Kaplan A (1964) The conduct of inquiry: methodology for behavioral science. Chandler Publishing Company, New York

Moorhead R (2010) Lawyer specialization – Managing the professional paradox. Law Policy 32(2):226–259

Mäntysaari P (2010b) The law of corporate finance: general principles and EU law. Volume II: Contracts in general. Springer, Berlin Heidelberg

Mäntysaari P (2012) Organising the firm: theories of commercial law, corporate governance and corporate law. Springer, Berlin Heidelberg

Mäntysaari P (2013) Was sollte man tun? Ein Plädoyer für anwenderfreundliche Rechtswissenschaft. Rechtstheorie 44(2):189–207. doi:10.3790/rth.44.2.189

Petersen J (2014) Max Webers Rechtssoziologie und die juristische Methodenlehre, 2. Auflage. Mohr Siebeck, Tübingen

Popper K (2005) Logik der Forschung. 11. Auflage. Mohr Siebeck, Tübingen

Posner RA (2002) Legal scholarship today. Harv Law Rev 115(5):1314–1326

Purcell EA Jr (2014) Paradoxes of court-centered legal history: some values of historical understanding for a practical legal education. J Leg Educ 64(2):229–257

Ross A (1958) On law and justice. Stevens & Sons, London

Sieber U (2010) Rechtliche Ordnung in einer globalen Welt. Die Entwicklung zu einem fragmentierten System von nationalen, internationalen und privaten Normen. Rechtstheorie 41(2): 151–198. doi:10.3790/rth.41.2.151

Simon HA (1967) The business school: a problem in organizational design. J Manag Stud 4(1): 1–16. doi:10.1111/j.1467-6486.1967.tb00569.x

Sismondo S (2011) Bourdieu's rationalist science of science: some promises and limitations. Cult Sociol 5(1):83–97. doi:10.1177/1749975510389728

Stigler GJ (1971) The theory of economic regulation. Bell J Econ Manage Sci 2(1):3–21

Teubner G (1983) Substantive and reflexive elements in modern law. Law Soc Rev 17(2):239–285

Teubner G (1992) The two faces of Janus: rethinking legal pluralism. Cardozo Law Rev 13: 1443–1462

Teubner G (1997) Global Bukowina: legal pluralism in the world-society. In: Teubner G (ed) Global law without a state. Aldershot, Dartmouth, pp 3–28

Teubner G (2000) Privatregimes: Neo-Spontanes Recht und duale Sozialverfassungen in der Weltgesellschaft? In: Simon D, Weiss M (eds) Zur Autonomie des Individuums, Liber Amicorum Spiros Simitis. Nomos, Baden-Baden, pp 437–453

Teubner G (2012) Verfassungsfragmente. Gesellschaftlicher Konstitutionalismus in der Globalisierung. Suhrkamp, Berlin

van Aken JE (2004) Management research based on the paradigm of the design sciences: the quest for field-tested and grounded technological rules. J Manag Stud 41(2):219–246

Weber M (1919/2011) Wissenschaft als Beruf. Elfte Auflage. Duncker & Humboldt, Berlin

Weber M (1922) Wirtschaft und Gesellschaft – Grundriß der verstehenden Soziologie. J.C.B Mohr (Paul Siebeck), Tübingen

Williamson OE (2005) Transaction cost economics. In: Menard C, Shirley MM (eds) Handbook of new institutional economics. Springer, Dordrecht, pp 51–65

Chapter 5
System Building

5.1 General Remarks

The presentation of a system is an obvious task for any scientific discipline.[1] Legal science is no exception. You need a systematic order for 'practical reasons' and 'theoretical reasons'.[2] One of the functions of User-Friendly Legal Science must thus be system building.

This new discipline can build its own systems. Since User-Friendly Legal Science primarily studies behaviour rather than law or legal norms, it can produce new systematic orders. They include systems of law (Sect. 5.2), language (Sect. 5.3), contexts (Sect. 5.4) and theories (Sect. 5.5).

Before discussing these new systems, we can have a look at earlier forms of system building in legal science.

Philosophy, Language and Argumentation. System building has long roots in philosophy, science and legal science. The basis of system building is the general system of language and argumentation. Both fall outside the scope of this book. It suffices to say that there are different ways to build such systems. They all require coherence in various forms.

There must be defined concepts and categories.[3] This can be illustrated with the Socratic method. Part of the Socratic method is to define things and distinguish between things. For example, Plato distinguished between four forms of

[1]National Academy of Sciences, National Academy of Engineering, Institute of Medicine (1992), 2 Scientific Principles and Research Practices, p. 38: "In broadest terms, scientists seek a systematic organization of knowledge about the universe and its parts." For finance and accounting, see Ryan B, Scapens RW, Theobald M (1992), pp. 22–23.

[2]Ross A (1958), § 44, p. 202.

[3]See, for example, Augustine of Hippo, De doctrina christiana, Second Book, XXXIX; Friedman M (1953), p. 7; Glaser BG, Strauss AL (1967), pp. 23 and 35–36.

P. Mäntysaari, *User-friendly Legal Science*, DOI 10.1007/978-3-319-53492-3_5

government[4] and Aristotle between four different causal factors.[5] Such definitions can also be based on induction. Cicero proposed to make analytical distinctions and classifications by reducing cases to a smaller number of categories.[6]

There can also be particular practices regarding the form of discourse, that is, forms for the presentation of arguments. This can be illustrated with the dialectical method in early philosophy. (a) The dialectical method was used in Plato's Socratic dialogues. Plato's dialectical method means a discourse between two or more people holding different points of view about a subject but wishing to establish the truth through reasoned arguments in a friendly manner and without the participation of external judges.[7] (b) Thomas Aquinas used the dialectical method in his Summa theologiae. Summa theologiae consists of three parts (partes) reflecting the substance matter of each part. Each part is divided into questions (questiones) and sub-questions (articuli). The questions and sub-questions are supported by arguments (objectiones). The questions and their supporting arguments are followed by counterarguments (sed contra) supporting the author's own view. The author then explains his own view (responsio) starting with a particular opening phrase (respondeo dicendum quod). After that, Thomas Aquinas lists his arguments (ad primam, secundam).

Scientific Disciplines. Modern science has its own concepts and its own rules for the scientific discourse (Sect. 5.5). System building belongs to the core functions of science. It is necessary to build a system for each scientific discipline in order to distinguish between different disciplines (Kant).[8]

Each scientific discipline thus has its own system. A scientific discipline consists of the work of researchers that share their field of study, knowledge interests, research questions, scientific language and methods. The work of many researchers tends to gravitate towards integration.

There are many drivers of system building in scientific disciplines. Some drivers relate to the general nature of argumentation, discourse and scientific theory building. The ideal of coherence contributes to the emergence of a set of general and more specific theories and defined concepts.[9] There are also drivers that relate

---

[4]Timocracy, oligarchy/plutocracy, democracy, and tyranny/despotism.

[5]The material cause/cause materialis, the formal cause/causa formalis, the efficient cause/causa efficiens and the final cause/causa finalis.

[6]Cicero, De oratore, I, § 189; Pound R (1959), Chapter 2 § 3 p. 34. Glaser BG, Strauss AL (1967), p. 23 on grounded theory: "In discovering theory, one generates conceptual categories or their properties from evidence . . .".

[7]Plato, The Republic, 348b.

[8]Kant I (1783), § 1; Kant I (1786), pp. XIII–XIV: "Es ist aber von der größten Wichtigkeit zum Vortheil der Wissenschaften ungleichartige Principien von einander zu scheiden, jede in ein besonderes System zu bringen, damit sie eine Wissenschaft ihrer eigenen Art ausmachen, um dadurch die Ungewißheit zu verhüten, die aus der Vermengung entspringt, da man nicht wohl unterscheiden kann, welcher von beiden theils die Schranken, theils auch die Verirrungen, die sich im Gebrauche derselben zutragen möchten, beyzumessen seyn dürften."

[9]Popper K (2005), number 85.

to researchers rather than research as such. Each researcher tries to ensure the internal coherence of the researcher's own work. Moreover, researchers customarily want the same things as their peers[10] and need to build groups in order to improve their own position in the academic community. They have strong personal incentives to belong to the winning side in the battle for hegemony.

Triadic System. In practice, a university department tends to adopt just one system for each scientific discipline rather than many competing systems. However, the progress of science is a process of triadic system building. Johann Fichte, a German philosopher, described the triad of a thesis, an antithesis and a synthesis.[11] An intellectual proposition (thesis) may be countered by its negation (antithesis). The conflict may be solved by forming a new intellectual proposition (synthesis).

Inspired by Ludwik Fleck,[12] Thomas S. Kuhn offered a more detailed description of the development of scientific system building based on the triad. First, there is a 'preconsensus', 'immature' or 'pre-paradigm' phase in the field with competing intellectual schools addressing the same issues. Second, there is some integration. Third, the consensus school focuses on the dominant 'paradigm' or 'disciplinary matrix'. Fourth, once the field of research has matured to 'normal science', researchers apply the dominant principles in their own work. Fifth, researchers find 'anomalies' that are irreconcilable with the dominant paradigm (Chap. 7). Anomalies accumulate. Sixth, there is again competition between different schools of thought. The existing consensus may prevail, or a 'paradigm shift' may occur as a result of a 'scientific revolution' that establishes a new consensus.[13]

Plurality Rather than Unity of Science. Immanuel Kant argued for the separation of scientific disciplines but assumed that it would lead to the completeness of sciences (Vollständigkeit der Wissenschaften).[14] However, there is no unity of science.

The unity of science (unified science, scientific monism) belonged to the goals of the Vienna Circle and the unified science (Einheitswissenschaft) movement that regarded metaphysics as its main opponent. Metaphysics was perceived as the main opponent due to its lack of empiricism (Chap. 6).

The Vienna Circle cofounder Otto Neurath was a pioneer of the unified science movement.[15] The characteristic aspects of Neurath's unified science were the use of the inductive method, the existence of a network of theories at different levels of abstraction, the use of quantitative methods, interaction between members of the community of researchers to verify results, the use of

---

[10]Girard R (1961) discussed the mimetic character of desire as a psychological law.

[11]Fichte JG (1794).

[12]Fleck L (1935/1979).

[13]Kuhn T (1996); Cheffins BR (2004).

[14]Kant I (1786), pp. XIV–XV. See also Suppes P (1993), p. 52.

[15]See, for example, Carnap P (1934), p. 248; Haller R (1985). See also Carnap R, Hahn H, Neurath O (1929), p. 314 on "der Geist wissenschaftlicher Weltauffassung" and socialism.

a standardised language and the use of a common encyclopaedia (Enzyklopedie) as a platform for communication.[16]

The opposite of the unity of science is the pluralist view. One of the representatives of the pluralist view is Patrick Suppes. According to Suppes, unity of science does not reflect the reality of science. There is no unity of method. The languages of scientific disciplines cannot be reduced to just one language. The building of grand theories is 'out of fashion', and the 'application of working scientific theories to particular areas of experience is almost always schematic and highly approximate in character'. Therefore, 'there is, at least in the current scientific temperament, total support for the thesis of incompleteness'.[17]

In other words, there is plurality in the sciences.[18] This reflects even the fact that different systems reflect different interests. Because of the existence of different points of view, there are bound to be different theories about one and the same phenomenon.[19]

There are nevertheless drivers of the convergence of sciences. One might ask whether the unified science movement has taken a big step forward now that English has become the lingua franca of researchers and research is digitalised. This is perhaps not straightforward.

On one hand, digitalisation has reduced the cost of global communication. The low cost of Internet-based communication has facilitated the emergence of scientific databases and cross-border communication, easier and faster publication, easier access to publications and the chance to verify and use findings worldwide. Easier access to a large number of scientific publications may act as a driver of convergence even across the boundaries of different scientific disciplines. For example, economics has a global reach. Economics has influenced the language and thinking of researchers in law and social sciences in general.

On the other hand, digitalisation is likely to increase the segmentation of science. The vast amount of publications can be a driver for increased specialisation. There are incentives to publish more in the academic community regardless of whether

---

[16]Compare Kellert SH, Longino HE, Waters CK (2006), p. x: "We take scientific monism to be the view that 1. the ultimate aim of a science is to establish a single, complete, and comprehensive account of the natural world (or the part of the world investigated by the science) based on a single set of fundamental principles; 2. the nature of the world is such that it can, at least in principle, be completely described or explained by such an account; 3. there exist, at least in principle, methods of inquiry that if correctly pursued will yield such an account; 4. methods of inquiry are to be accepted on the basis of whether they can yield such an account; and 5. individual theories and models in science are to be evaluated in large part on the basis of whether they provide (or come close to providing) a comprehensive and complete account based on fundamental principles."

[17]Suppes P (1993), p. 53.

[18]Kellert SH, Longino HE, Waters CK (2006), pp. ix–x: "It is useful to distinguish between plurality in the sciences and pluralism about the sciences. The former is a feature of the present state of inquiry in a number of areas of scientific research . . . These are characterized by multiple approaches, each revealing different faces of a phenomenon . . . Pluralism is a view about this state of affairs . . .".

[19]See *ibid*, p xii.

the findings can be verified on not.[20] The convergence of sciences is hampered by the existence of too much noise.

Traditional Legal Science. The presentation of a system is an obvious task for traditional legal science.[21] However, traditional system building faces new challenges due to the existence of drivers of convergence.

Traditional systems of legal science have not only functions shared by the systems of scientific disciplines in general but even other functions due to the normative nature of law and the fact that normal legal science focuses on legal norms.

Legal norms necessarily come in systems depending on their substance matter. For example, there are fundamental divisions such as the distinction between national and international law, Swedish law and Finnish law, public and private law or substantive and procedural law.[22] Such systems are limited by national legal traditions.[23]

Jurisprudence has produced even systems, models and tools for system building unrelated to the substance matter of legal norms. They can be illustrated with the following examples:

- There are systems of normative language such as systems based on deontic logic. Deontic logic was developed as a branch of symbolic logic in twentieth century philosophy.[24]
- According to Kelsen's pure theory of law (Reine Rechtslehre), the validity of a legal norm is derived from a higher legal norm.[25] Ultimately, there is a basic norm (Grundnorm). There is a fundamental difference between the system of natural science and the system of law according to Kelsen. While specific theories can be derived from general theories in natural science, the contents of a legal norm cannot be derived deductively from a higher legal norm. A legal norm can only be made.[26]

---

[20]Smaldino PE, McElreath R (2016).

[21]Weber M (1922), p. 395: "… widerspruchloses, und vor allem prinzipiell lückenloses System von Regeln …" Ross A (1958), § 44, p. 202: "A systematic order is valuable first for practical reasons … Systematic arrangement is valuable also for theoretical reasons … A rational scheme of arrangement is therefore an obvious task for jurisprudence."

[22]*Ibid*, § 44, p. 203.

[23]*Ibid*, § 44, pp. 202–203: "It would be futile to try to create a systematic classification without roots in tradition. The task of jurisprudence is restricted to revise and refine traditional concepts. The traditions, however, are so different for Continental and Anglo-American law that–with the exception of some few fundamental divisions–it is impossible to discuss problems of systematic arrangements common for both."

[24]von Wright GH (1951).

[25]Kelsen H (1934), number 27, p. 62.

[26]*Ibid*, number 28, p. 64.

- There are also systems of argumentation and interpretation. Due to the vagueness of legal terms, these systems have a close connection to rhetoric (Sect. 7.3).[27]

The functions of a system of traditional legal science include the following[28]: increasing pedagogical efficiency, increasing continuity in time (increasing both predictability and path dependency), extending the scope of law through implied characteristics of the legal norms that belong to a particular area of law (general principles), directing the interpretation of law through the combination of general rules or principles and more specific norms that build on the general rules or principles and contributing as part of jurisprudence to a system of decision norms for the judge.[29]

However, legal pluralism (Sect. 4.3) and the drivers of convergence make traditional legal system building increasingly more difficult and reduce its relevance. This can again be illustrated with Kelsen's pure theory of law, and even by the emergence of law-and-something research with its external point of view. (a) According to Kelsen, every two norms that derive their validity from the same basic norm belong to the same legal system. The basic norm is thus used to explain the systematic nature of legal norms. But if law is fragmented both internationally and nationally and there is legal pluralism,[30] the basic norm cannot be identified and the relevant legal norms cannot be presented as a hierarchical system. (b) The need to comply with the traditional requirements of scientific research and the absence of legal theories explaining societal reality have increased the popularity of law-and-something research (Sect. 6.3). Legal phenomena can be regarded as a field of study in other social sciences. While the characteristics of law and legal norms can be analysed and classified through the lens of the theories and methods of the relevant scientific discipline, traditional legal system building basically lacks relevance in the process.

User-Friendly Legal Science. After this rather lengthy introduction, we can conclude by saying that there is room for new legal system building that is aligned with the customary scientific requirements. We can have a look at the new systems of User-Friendly Legal Science.

[27]For legal rhetoric, see, for example, Mäntysaari P (2016a).

[28]Ehrlich E (1913), pp. 268–273.

[29]See, for example, Ehrlich E (1913), pp. 14 and 234.

[30]Sieber U (2010), p. 171.

5.2 Systems of Law

User-Friendly Legal Science can provide a new way to present law as a systematic order. Legal tools and the norms that facilitate them can be presented systematically through the lens of users' objectives in each context. The new areas of law are thus 'functional' rather than 'dogmatic' (see also Sect. 6.4).

Unlike the systems built in traditional jurisprudence, these systems are not limited by national legal traditions, and a system does not need to be limited to one jurisdiction only.[31] In principle, a system can nevertheless be limited to the law of a certain jurisdiction where the context is defined so narrowly that there are no cross-border connections or connections to foreign legal norms. In the long run, however, user-friendly system building could facilitate the emergence of similar systems in the legal science of different countries and improve the comparability of law across jurisdictions.

Since user-friendly systems of law are functional, they do not need to be aligned with the traditional dogmatic areas of law. Neither are they limited to external regulation. There are parallels to Eugen Ehrlich's 'living law'.[32]

For example, one could choose the firm as the user and define 'corporate governance' as its context. The firm probably has particular objectives and will use particular kinds of legal tools and practices to reach them in this context. When doing so, the firm will need to pay attention to various kinds of legal norms by adapting to them or avoiding them. The relevant legal norms may be found in one or more jurisdictions and in various areas of law such as corporate law, capital markets law, contract law, tax law, insolvency law, inheritance law and so forth. In contrast, the study of 'corporate law' in one or more jurisdictions is not a study of functional equivalents.[33] 'Corporate law' does not mean the same thing in all countries. While doctrinal corporate law is a bunch of legal norms defined more or less arbitrarily by national traditions such as pedagogical conventions, the functional area of corporate governance must be defined in a more structured way. It cannot be defined without some prior research (Sect. 2.5). Of course, one can redefine even corporate law functionally as an area of User-Friendly Legal Science.[34]

[31] Compare Ross A (1958), § 44, pp. 202–203.

[32] Ehrlich E (1913), pp. 405–406.

[33] For example, Kraakman R et al. (2004) was not really a functional study.

[34] Mäntysaari P (2012); Mäntysaari P (2016b).

5.3 System of Language

User-Friendly Legal Science describes the behaviour of users and, to some extent, market behaviour and other societal mechanisms. It is also defined as part of legal science. This must influence its language. The language of this new discipline consists of many components.

Everyday Language. The semantic basis of law is everyday language.[35] Obviously, everyday language is the starting point when you describe legal norms, interpret contracts and study normative relationships in general. You can find examples of this in case law[36] and literature.[37]

Everyday language is the starting point even in User-Friendly Legal Science. You need everyday language to describe the field, the users, the users' objectives and other circumstances.

Legal Concepts. In addition, User-Friendly Legal Science purports to describe behaviour by using legal concepts and the specific language of law and jurisprudence. There are three fundamental reasons for this.

First, the use of a common language platform is characteristic of all scientific disciplines. This new discipline should therefore primarily use the language of legal science rather than the language of sociology, economics or other social sciences.

Second, legal concepts can (and should) be used to describe societal reality. Legal concepts describe different actors, relationships between the different actors and the legal tools or practices that they customarily use in their dealings with other actors.

Third, the usefulness of legal concepts is increased by the fact that they tend to be connected to legal norms and sanctions enforceable by the state. Legal concepts are particularly useful when describing legal phenomena and the use of legal tools and practices, that is, things that are based on or influenced by legal norms (for epistemology, see Sect. 5.5.4).

Rational users tend to adapt their behaviour to legal norms for various reasons. Rational users may take into account the costs and benefits of compliance or non-compliance. Legal norms can also be binding as social norms. However, the concepts of other social sciences are not to the same extent linked to normative rules of behaviour and the threat of legal sanctions for non-compliance.

Moreover, because of the normative nature of law, legal concepts tend to be based on a more holistic approach. Legal norms must be applied to real people—homo sapiens—in the complex circumstances of real life. They are not applied to

[35]Ross A (1958), § 24.

[36]Lord Hoffmann in Mannai Investment Co Ltd. v Eagle Star Assurance [1997] UKHL 19; [1997] AC 749; [1997] 3 All ER 352; [1997] 2 WLR 945 (House of Lords).

[37]See, for example, Kramer A (2003); Mäntysaari P (2010b), section 5.2.4 on the "real method of interpretation".

fictive people—such as homo economicus—in circumstances reduced to a few variables.

Legal Concepts v Economics. The concepts of other social sciences are not necessarily aligned with legal reality. If they do not take into account legal reality as it is, they do not describe societal reality as well as they could.

This can be illustrated with the theory of the firm and corporate law. We can first have a look at economic theory and the language of economics. (a) The neoclassical theory of the firm started with the publication of two articles: Alchian and Demsetz (1972) and Jensen and Meckling (1976). Jensen and Meckling (1976) suggest that the behaviour of the firm is like the behaviour of the market. They assume that the firm is 'a legal fiction'.[38] The firm and the legal entity are used interchangeably in that article.[39] Moreover, Jensen and Meckling assume that there is an owner-manager.[40] (b) Fama (1980) argues that a corporation does not have owners in any meaningful sense and that a modern corporation does not have an entrepreneur. However, Fama also assumes that each factor in the firm is owned by somebody. The firm is just 'the set of contracts covering the way inputs are joined to create outputs and the way receipts from outputs are shared among inputs'.[41] (c) Both Jensen and Meckling (1976) and Fama (1980) choose the principal-agent approach.[42] The agent should act in the interests of the principal. Since Jensen and Meckling (1976) assume that the firm has an owner-manager,[43] they also assume that managers should act in the interests of the owner-manager. Fama treats shareholders as residual claimants, risk bearers and principals.[44] (d) These theories have been very influential worldwide. It is customary to talk about shareholders as owners of the firm and assume that it is the function of board members and managers to act in the best interests of shareholders. For example, it is assumed that they should return funds to shareholders when this is the best way to increase share price.

However, the language of economics does not describe legal relationships in real life. Neither does it describe market reality as market participants need to take into account existing laws.[45] (a) Because of separate corporate personality, a corporation has no owners. Shareholders and bondholders are owners of securities that

[38]Jensen MC, Meckling WH (1976), p. 311: "The firm is not an individual. It is a legal fiction . . .".

[39]*Ibid,* p. 310: "It is important to recognize that most organizations are simply legal fictions which serve as a nexus for a set of contracting relationships among individuals. This includes firms . . ." The authors define legal fiction in footnote 12: "By legal fiction we mean the artificial construct under the law which allows certain organizations to be treated as individuals."

[40]*Ibid*, p. 312. For a critical view, see Fama EF (1980), pp. 290–291.

[41]Fama EF (1980), p. 290.

[42]Wilson R (1968); Arrow KJ (1971); Jensen MC, Meckling WH (1976). For an overview, see Eisenhardt KM (1989).

[43]Jensen MC, Meckling WH (1976), p. 312. See also Fama EF (1980), pp. 290–291.

[44]Fama EF (1980), p. 291.

[45]See Mäntysaari P (2012); Mäntysaari P (2010a).

provide certain limited rights to the holder. (b) Because of separate corporate personality, the assets of the corporation belong to the corporation. They belong neither to shareholders nor to anyone else. (c) The legal entity is the 'hub' of all contracts. There are neither implied nor statutory contracts between the different resource providers. For example, there are no contracts between managers and shareholders, but there are contracts between managers and the corporation. (d) Shareholders may or may not have acted as suppliers of funding to the corporation. Most shareholders in listed companies have not provided any funding to the corporation. It is thus misleading to say that excess funds should be 'returned' to shareholders to whom the assets 'belong'. Shareholders may not have provided any funds to the corporation in the first place, and the assets of the corporation belong to the corporation. (e) The legal entity is not the same thing as the firm. The business of the firm can be organised by using various kinds of legal entities as tools. In German law, it is customary to distinguish between the firm (das Unternehmen) and the legal entity as the carrier of the firm (Unternehmensträger). There is a related distinction in French law (Sect. 7.5.3).[46] (f) Corporate law tends to protect the firm against all stakeholders, including shareholders.[47]

We can see that the language of economics and the language of legal science can paint very different pictures of societal reality.

Neutral Concepts. The use of legal concepts is not without problems. Normative legal concepts are embedded in a legal framework that is context specific. The context customarily is the national law of a certain country, an international convention between many states or a non-state legal framework. Different rule-makers may use different legal languages and different legal concepts. If legal concepts tend to be context specific[48] rather than universal, one may ask what legal concepts one should use in User-Friendly Legal Science.

The choice of legal concepts depends on the context even in this new discipline. If the context is purely national and limited to just one country, it is easier to use the normative legal concepts of the law of that country. If the context is international or global, this would not be meaningful and more neutral concepts would become necessary. The question of neutral concepts has been discussed in comparative law in greater detail.[49]

There are even other fundamental reasons to develop new concepts that are less dependent on the legal framework and more universal.

First, the point of view of User-Friendly Legal Science requires the use of many concepts that do not have a normative meaning. You may need non-normative concepts to define the user, the context and the user's objectives in the context. You may need non-normative concepts even to define many legal tools and practices

[46]The opposite view is that the firm is the same thing as the legal entity. See Jensen MC, Meckling WH (1976); Orts EW (2015), pp. 28 and 53.

[47]See, for example, Mäntysaari P (2005).

[48]See also Augustine of Hippo, De doctrina christiana, Third Book, XXV.

[49]See, for example, Hansen N (2008), section II.5.

such as 'compliance programmes' and 'the principle of four eyes'. Everyday language may not be sufficient to describe these things in an unambiguous and efficient manner.

Second, you need ideal types. The use of ideal types allows for a rational, structured description of social reality.[50] Ideal types neither are nor have to be perfectly aligned with the doctrinal concepts of the jurisdictions to which the study has connections. By definition, ideal types are more neutral.

Third, neutral concepts facilitate the choice of a broader context or a higher level of generality and a higher level of explanatory power (Sect. 2.5). Neutral concepts can be universal and used globally.

5.4 System of Contexts

Users use legal tools and practices to achieve their objectives in various contexts. Each researcher chooses and defines the relevant context for the particular study. The number of potential contexts is unlimited. As each context depends on the choice of the user, the number of contexts is increased by the existence of different user perspectives. There can thus be a patchwork of contexts in user-friendly legal studies.

Contexts obviously are not coordinated in society. To some extent, they can be overlapping (coupled) and interrelated. Theories describing these contexts can form systems. The contexts of theories can be coupled in various ways. In the long run, the findings can be consolidated (see Sect. 5.1 for drivers of convergence).

Users. Generally, the context depends on the user. In one transaction between two parties, one can identify two at least partly overlapping user contexts. For example, there is a buyer and a seller in a sales transaction. Since buyers and sellers can be different, the buyer context can include elements that are not characteristic of the seller context, and the seller context can include elements that are not characteristic of the buyer context. The buyer and the seller have objectives that are partly similar, partly different.

Levels of Generality. The context depends on the level of generality (abstraction). There are general contexts and specific contexts. For example, firms use legal tools and practices generally to reach their objectives, but firms also use legal tools and practices in specific contexts such as the particular context of corporate governance. The specific contexts are part of the general context.

Actions. From a user perspective, a context is not static. Contexts are things that the user may be able to address. The user may be able to manage contexts through opt-in and opt-out. In other words, it can accept contexts and adapt to them, exit contexts or avoid contexts.

[50]For comparative law, see *ibid*, section II.5.

For example, a firm that is in the business of aviation manufacturing can choose whether to build light consumer aircraft or commercial passenger aeroplanes and whether to sell the products in the US or in Europe. Product liability is an obvious risk that the manufacturer will be exposed to, and it will address it one way or another. The firm might accept the European product liability regime and adapt to it and avoid the US product liability regime by staying out of the market and outside the reach of US product liability laws. Moreover, the firm might prefer to avoid the risks inherent in the sale of light consumer aircraft and choose to manufacture commercial passenger aeroplanes only.

Alternatives. From the user perspective, specific contexts can be alternatives. One may then need to ask whether they really belong to the same context. This depends on the level of generality and the question whether the contexts are functional equivalents.

For example, many firms choose whether to remain private or go public when they analyse their funding options. Private share ownership and public share ownership are alternatives from the perspective of the firm. However, both contexts are united in the more general context of corporate finance.

Specific contexts can even be functional equivalents from the user perspective. One may be able to achieve more or less the same result in alternative ways. For example, one can achieve the same commercial result in commodities markets by physical contracts (supply contracts) or financial contracts (derivatives).

Therefore, alternatives belong to the same context when they can be regarded as functional equivalents. Whether they can be regarded as functional equivalents depends on the level of generality.

Complements. When potential contexts are complements from the chosen user perspective, they belong to the same context.

For this purpose, the notion of complementarity applies to a situation where the attainment of objectives in one context customarily influences the attainment of objectives in another context. For example, there can be a trade-off between two objectives, or there can be increased positive effects when one tries to reach objectives in the two contexts at the same time.

This can be illustrated with the contexts of corporate governance and innovation. Reasonable and socially acceptable objectives in the context of corporate governance will not be met in the long term if the firm is unable to adapt to changes in the marketplace and is wiped out by market forces. The organisation of a firm's corporate governance influences its cabability to innovate. Therefore, corporate governance and innovation should belong to the same context.[51]

Consolidation. The study of partly overlapping contexts increases understanding and can be followed by the consolidation of theories.[52]

---

[51]Mäntysaari P (2012), pp. 113 and 129.

[52]See also Glaser BG, Strauss AL (1967), p. 79: "[S]ubstantive theory is a strategic link in the formulation and generation of grounded formal theory."

Studying the phenomena under investigation from one perspective can improve the understanding of the phenomena from other perspectives as well. For example, one can study the legal aspects of logistics from many user perspectives such as the perspective of the freight forwarder, the manufacturer of industrial goods, the retailer or the consumer. For each user category, the context is a bit different. The different user categories have partly conflicting interests (most parties would prefer to pay less and charge more, each party prefers to allocate risk to somebody else unless it gets paid for bearing risk), partly interests that are aligned (duties and costs should be allocated in the most efficient way to keep overall costs down, the goods must not be damaged) and perhaps even other interests. Although some interests may be unique to a particular user category and may not be characteristic of other user categories, many of the questions that the parties manage are the same or related and the way the parties manage them depends on the interests and behaviour of other parties in this field.

Findings can be consolidated at a higher level of generality. In other words, the study of interrelated contexts can contribute to the building of more general theories. For example, one may be able to define logistics at a higher level of abstraction as an ideal type with characteristic actors, characteristic interests and characteristic legal tools and practices. At a more concrete level, one can define more specific contexts each with its own particular characteristics.

5.5 System of Theories

5.5.1 General Remarks

A theory is a system of terms that describe a particular part of reality, in scientific research according to the knowledge interests of the discipline.[53] One can talk about a system of theories when two or more theories are interrelated.

There is a system of theories in User-Friendly Legal Science. Since the number of potential contexts is virtually unlimited (Sect. 5.4) and there are different kinds of actors in each context, one can build very many user-friendly theories to describe how users use legal tools and practices to reach their objectives in different contexts. These theories can be interrelated and consolidated into coherent systems.

One can distinguish between different theories according to their function (main theories and method theories, Sect. 5.5.2), level of generality (general theories and specific theories, Sect. 5.5.2), substance matter (how they form groups, Sect. 5.5.3) and scientific level (how they are at different stages of scientific discourse, Sect. 5.5.4).

[53] See, for example, Patel R, Davidson B (2012), p. 21.

It is useful to organise theories into systems. Theories differ in their explanatory power and empirical content (Sect. 2.5) but benefit from integration.[54] A new theory can be aligned with existing theories, and a general theory can unify subordinate theories.[55] The integration of theories is facilitated by the processes of deduction, induction, abduction and grounded theory. These processes foster the convergence of science and help to mitigate plurality in the sciences (Sect. 5.1).

Deduction. Theories for narrow contexts (that is, at a more concrete level) can thus be applications of theories for broader contexts (that is, at a higher level of generality). For example, this theory of User-Friendly Legal Science is an application of broader theories of scientific research in social sciences. Such theories include, for example, the theory of abduction (Peirce),[56] the theory of falsification (Popper),[57] the theory of interpretive understanding (Weber),[58] grounded theory (Strauss and Corbin)[59] and the middle-range theory (Merton).[60]

Induction. On the other hand, theories for broader contexts can also be the result of the unification and consolidation of theories for narrower contexts or the application of a previous narrow theory at a higher level of generality. For example, a theory of corporate finance law[61] gave rise to a theory of management-based commercial law at a higher level of generality,[62] and the latter theory contributed to the theory of User-Friendly Legal Science at an even higher level of generality.[63]

Abduction and Grounded Theory. Abduction and grounded theory help to find existing theories that are relevant, define their place in the system, build new theories and define even their place in the system. This can be illustrated with this book. The book was rewritten several times. The text of the book was intended to be clear, complete and internally coherent. When surprising things (such as gaps or internal conflicts) emerged, it was necessary to modify the text to ensure coherence or to find theories to explain the surprising things and ensure coherence

---

54 Popper K (2005), numbers 35–36.

55 Aroney N (2013), p. 10: "Fourth, the explanatory power of a theory is augmented by its consilience with other theories (which themselves have their own explanatory power). This consilience can occur either through integration with coordinate or superordinate theories or a theory's capacity to unify the explanations provided by subordinate theories."

56 Peirce CS (1931–1935), 5.145.

57 Popper K (1935).

58 Weber M (1922).

59 Strauss AL, Corbin JM (1990).

60 Merton RK (1968); Boudon R (1991). For an application in finance, see Merton RC, Bodie Z (2005).

61 Mäntysaari P (2010a, b, c).

62 Mäntysaari P (2012).

63 Mäntysaari P (2013).

in a new way. Where theories could not be found, they had to be built. In order to be integrated in a rational and coherent manner, the theories had to be organised.

Integration. Theories can be integrated in various ways. Potentially conflicting theories can be modified and aligned. Theories can be unified to a higher-level theory with a wider range. There is an incentive to integrate theories because a theory has more explanatory power if it is compatible with other theories.[64]

5.5.2 Main Theories and Method Theories, General Theories and Specific Theories

One can distinguish between (a) domain theories (main theories) and method theories (complementary theories), and (b) theories that describe a wider range of phenomena (general theories) and theories with a narrower scope (specific theories).

Domain Theories, Main Theories. A domain theory defines a scientific discipline, as well as its fundamental concepts. A scientific research project is therefore based on at least one domain theory as its main theory. In this new discipline, the main theory could thus be the theory of User-Friendly Legal Science.

General Theories and Specific Theories. Different theories can describe the same context at different levels of generality. General theories explain a wide range of things but are less specific. It is more difficult for a theory to explain phenomena over a relatively wide range. Specific theories explain things with a higher level of detail and precision.[65]

Method Theories, Complementary Theories. The main theory and the specific theories can be complemented by method theories from other scientific disciplines. Method theories are not the same thing as the method. Method theories explain relevant phenomena by using the language of another scientific discipline and provide useful concepts.

Method theories are particularly useful in User-Friendly Legal Science with its dualistic fields. For example, method theories can be a valuable source of information about user objectives in the context. Where the user is the firm, the theory of User-Friendly Legal Science and the context-specific user-friendly theories could be complemented by one or more theories from economic sciences as method theories. Method theories can also provide a framework for value-based decisions and a framework for assessing different alternatives from the user perspective. For example, in the context of an 'ethical firm's' human resources management (HRM), one may be able to define the 'ethical firm's' objectives with the help of stakeholder

[64]Aroney N (2013), p. 10; Mæhle SS (2015), p. 152.

[65]Popper K (2005), number 35; Aroney N (2013), p. 10; Mæhle SS (2015), p. 151.

theories, theories about corporate social responsibility and the particular HRM theories of business science.

Method theories are context specific. The choice of complementing method theories depends on the research question, the context and the researcher's knowledge interests. There can be alternative method theories. They should therefore not be chosen uncritically.[66]

Legal Dogmatics. The theoretical framework of legal dogmatics can be regarded as a method theory that complements the main theory or theories. This is because one cannot describe any legal tools and practices in a reliable manner without taking into account their legal regulation and how the legal framework might be interpreted. User-Friendly Legal Science requires, to some extent, even the interpretation and systematisation of law.

5.5.3 Approaches to the Substance Matter

In addition to the distinction (a) between main theories and method theories and (b) between general theories and specific theories), one can distinguish (c) between various approaches to the substance matter.

Same Object or Persistent Themes. In principle, the theories of User-Friendly Legal Science can build systems in two ways on the basis of their subject matter. They can refer to one and the same object, or there can be persistent themes.

This is in the light of Foucault. Foucault made an attempt to define a science as a group of statements. He first identified four hypotheses. Statements could form a group because (1) they refer to one and the same object,[67] (2) there are relations between statements due to their form and type of connection,[68] (3) one has determined a system of permanent and coherent groups[69] or (4) the interconnections of statements are described and the statements are presented under unitary forms with persistent themes.[70] Foucault ended up rejecting these hypotheses, but

[66]See Olsen L (2004), pp. 130–131 on the problems caused by the use of theories imported from social sciences in legal dogmatics.

[67]Foucault M (1972), Part II, Chapter 2: "First hypothesis . . . : statements different in form, and dispersed in time, form a group if they refer to one and the same object."

[68]*Ibid,* Part II, Chapter 2: "Second hypothesis to define a group of relations between statements: their form and type of connexion."

[69]*Ibid,* Part II, Chapter 2: "Another direction of research, another hypothesis: might it not be possible to establish groups of statements, by determining the system of permanent and coherent groups involved?".

[70]*Ibid,* Part II, Chapter 2: "Lastly, a fourth hypothesis to regroup the statements, describe their interconnexion and account for the unitary forms under which they are presented: the identity and persistence of themes."

they help to identify two early ways to make the subject matter of theories count in system building.

In User-Friendly Legal Science, theories can share the same object or the same theme, for example where they share the same context (context-based systems) or the same users (user-based systems).

User-Based Systems. Theories can share the same users (user-based systems). For example, the firm uses legal tools and practices in very many contexts. At a high level of generality, all firms may nevertheless have the same fundamental objectives and may even choose from the same set of basic legal tools and practices. For this reason, there can be a general legal theory describing the behaviour of firms (Sect. 7.5) and more specific user-based theories for different contexts. The specific theories are interrelated because of the same fundamental objectives and the same set of basic legal tools and practices in each context.

Context-Based Systems. Context-based systems can relate to the same field from the perspective of different users. For example, one can build theories on the legal aspects of logistics from the different perspectives of the relevant actors (the supplier perspective, the seller perspective, the buyer perspective, the consumer perspective, the freight forwarder perspective, the carrier perspective and so forth). These different theories are interrelated as the interests of one user category and the use of legal tools and practices in their interests influence the behaviour of other user categories.

Context-based systems can be at different levels of generality. For example, statements concerning things that are characteristic of the most relevant actors in the context of logistics could help to build a general theory of logistics that belongs to legal science in general and User-Friendly Legal Science in particular.

However, a context-based system tends to be at a higher level of generality compared with a user-based system. This is because the increased complexity of the larger context requires the use of more general ideal types. Without more general ideal types, it would be difficult to describe the context in a more general way and to facilitate understanding.

5.5.4 Scientific Level

There is no science without systematic cumulation of knowledge.[71] However, the nature of cumulation may change in the course of time. There are thresholds that must be crossed on the way to scientificity. These thresholds can be relevant in system building as there can be a different system for each stage. One can study the path to scientificity deductively (in this case, with the help of the notion of

[71]Bourdieu P (1975), p. 39.

discursive formations) and inductively (by studying the scientificity discourse of another discipline).

Discursive Formations. Foucault's notion of a discursive formation provides one of the ways to understand these thresholds and the path to scientificity. There is a discursive formation when one can define a regularity between objects, types of statements, concepts or thematic choices.[72] Regularity means that these elements are subjected to rules of formation[73] and that there are particular strategies to manage them.[74] For discursive formations, Foucault defined the following thresholds: positivity, epistemologisation, scientificity and formalisation.[75]

Formalisation is the highest stage. Formalisation could also take the form of a 'primary model' that is based on certain crucial assumptions.[76]

At the time of writing, it would be too much to analyse the discourse of User-Friendly Legal Science because the number of participants is so small. However, the thresholds suggested by Foucault can set an agenda for its theory building and system building.

The purpose of this book is both to contribute to the individualisation of User-Friendly Legal Science as a discursive formation,[77] and to help it cross the threshold of positivity and reach the stage of formalisation.

Empiricism. An alternative way to obtain information about the path to scientificity could be to study the explicit theory-building discourse of a different area of social sciences. In the light of the theory-building discourse of management accounting, one can identify the following stages:

- There is increasing awareness of the needs of users and a shift towards research that is useful.[78]

[72]Foucault M (1972), Part II, Chapter 2: "[W]henever, between objects, types of statement, concepts, or thematic choices, one can define a regularity ... we will say ... that we are dealing with a discursive formation ...".

[73]*Ibid,* Part II, Chapter 2: "The conditions to which the elements of this division (objects, mode of statement, concepts, thematic choices) are subjected we shall call the rules of formation."

[74]*Ibid,* Part II, Chapter 6: "Such discourses as economics, medicine, grammar, the science of living beings give rise to certain organizations of concepts, certain regroupings of objects, certain types of enunciation, which form, according to their degree of coherence, rigour, and stability, themes or theories ... Whatever their formal level may be, I shall call these themes and theories 'strategies'."

[75]*Ibid,* Part IV, Chapter 6, section (d).

[76]Ryan B, Scapens RW, Theobald M (1992), pp. 22–23 (on finance and accounting).

[77]Foucault M (1972), Part II, Chapter 6: "A discursive formation will be individualized if one can define the system of formation of the different strategies that are deployed in it; in other words, if one can show how they all derive ... from the same set of relations."

[78]Ryan B, Scapens RW, Theobald M (1992), pp. 42–43.

- The discipline is criticised for lacking a proper theoretical basis.[79] The counterargument is that the criticism is misleading as the discipline uses theories from other social sciences.[80]
- The absence of a proper theoretical basis is proposed to be cured by using the paradigm of another discipline.[81] However, there can be competing disciplines and paradigms in social sciences,[82] and the adoption of just one paradigm may lead to a view that is regarded as too narrow.[83]
- It is proposed that the discipline should start building its own theories. This requires defining the core concepts.[84] For example, one must define the field and the relevant actors or practitioners in the field.[85] One may be able to define the discipline by studying practices in the field.[86]
- The question arises whether the discipline should only be regarded as a field that is studied empirically by applying the theories of other social sciences or as a field of science with its own theories.[87]
- After this, one distinguishes between the discipline's own domain theories (field theories, main theories) and complementing theories from other disciplines (method theories).[88]

User-Friendly Legal Science follows a similar path. The fundamental problem of normal legal science is its lack of a proper scientific basis. To cure the problem, there have been many attempts to make law an empirical science either in its own right or by applying the theories and empirical methods of other social sciences in the field of law (Chap. 6). This new discipline is an attempt to get around the fundamental problems of legal science by increasing the scope of legal science, focusing on behaviour rather than norms and building new legal theories that are scientific.

---

[79]Zimmerman JL (2001); Ittner CD, Larcker DF (2002). See also Ittner CD, Larcker DF (2001).

[80]Hopwood A (2002).

[81]Zimmerman JL (2001), p. 423.

[82]Ittner CD, Larcker DF (2001), p. 357.

[83]Lukka K, Mouritsen J (2002).

[84]Ahrens T, Chapman CS (2006). For a different model, see Silverman D (1993), pp. 1–2.

[85]Malmi T, Granlund M (2009a); Quattrone P (2009); Malmi T, Granlund M (2009b); Al-Htaybat K, von Alberti-Alhtaybat L (2013).

[86]For example, Al-Htaybat K, von Alberti-Alhtaybat L (2013), p. 13.

[87]Lukka K, Vinnari E (2014).

[88]Lukka K (2005). In addition to Bruno Latour, the most well-known representatives of the actor-network theory include Michel Callon and John Law. See Latour B (2005). For the use of the actor-network theory in management accounting research, see, for example, Ahrens T, Chapman CS (2007).

References

Ahrens T, Chapman CS (2006) Doing qualitative field research in management accounting: positioning data to contribute to theory. Account Organ Soc 31(8):819–841
Ahrens T, Chapman CS (2007) Management accounting as practice. Account Organ Soc 32 (1/2):1–27
Alchian AA, Demsetz H (1972) Production, information costs, and economic organization. Am Econ Rev 62(5):777–795
Al-Htaybat K, von Alberti-Alhtaybat L (2013) Management accounting theory revisited: seeking to increase research relevance. Int J Bus Manage 8(18):12–24
Aroney N (2013) Explanatory power, theory formation and constitutional interpretation: some preliminaries. Aust J Leg Philos 38:1–31
Arrow KJ (1971) Essays in the theory of risk bearing. Markham Publishing Co., Chicago
Augustine of Hippo (426-427) De doctrina christiana
Boudon R (1991) What middle-range theories are. Contemp Sociol (Am Sociol Assoc) 20 (4):519–522
Bourdieu P (1975) The specificity of the scientific field and the social conditions of the progress of reason. Soc Sci Inf 14(6):19–47. doi:10.1177/053901847501400602
Carnap P (1934) Logische Syntax der Sprache. Springer, Wien. doi:10.1007/978-3-662-25375-5
Carnap R, Hahn H, Neurath O (1929) Wissenschaftliche Weltauffassung. Der Wiener Kreis. Veröffentlichungen des Vereins Ernst Mach. Artur Wolf Verlag, Wien
Cheffins BR (2004) The trajectory of (corporate law) scholarship. Camb Law J 63(2):456–506. doi:10.1017/S0008197304006658
Cicero, De oratore
Ehrlich E (1913) Grundlegung der Soziologie des Rechts. Duncker & Humblot, München and Leipzig
Eisenhardt KM (1989) Agency theory: an assessment and review. Acad Manag Rev 14(1):57–74
Fama EF (1980) Agency problems and the theory of the firm. J Polit Econ 88(2):288–307
Fichte JG (1794) Grundlage der gesammten Wissenschaftslehre: als Handschrift für seine Zuhörer. Bei Christian Ernst Gabler, Leipzig
Fleck L (1979) Genesis and development of a scientific fact. The University of Chicago Press, Chicago. Originally published in German as Fleck L (1935) Entstehung und Entwicklung einer wissenschaftlichen Tatsache. Einführung in die Lehre vom Denkstil und Denkkollektiv. Schwabe, Basel
Foucault M (1972) The archaeology of knowledge. Tavistock Publications Limited, London. Originally published as Foucault M (1969) L'Archéologie du savoir. Editions Gallimard, Paris
Friedman M (1953) The methodology of positive economics. In: Friedman M (ed) Essays in positive economics. University of Chicago Press, Chicago, pp 3–43
Girard R (1961) Mensonge romantique et vérité romanesque. Editions Bernard Grasset, Paris
Glaser BG, Strauss AL (1967) The discovery of grounded theory: strategies for qualitative research. Aldine de Gruyter, New York
Haller R (1985) Das Neurath-Prinzip: Grundlagen und Folgerungen. In: Dahms HJ (ed) Philosophie, Wissenschaft, Aufklärung: Beiträge zur Geschichte und Wirkung des Wiener Kreises. De Gruyter, Berlin, pp 204–220
Hansen N (2008) Comparative law and comparative knowledge. In: Reimann M, Zimmermann R (eds) The Oxford handbook of comparative law. Oxford handbooks in law. Oxford University Press, Oxford, Chapter 9, pp 305–338
Hopwood A (2002) "If only there were simple solutions, but there aren't": some reflections on Zimmerman's critique of empirical management accounting research. Eur Account Rev 11:777–785
Ittner CD, Larcker DF (2001) Assessing empirical research in managerial accounting: a value-based management perspective. J Account Econ 32:49–410

Ittner CD, Larcker DF (2002) Empirical managerial accounting research: are we just describing management consulting practice. Eur Account Rev 11:787–794

Jensen MC, Meckling WH (1976) Theory of the firm: managerial behavior, agency costs and ownership structure. J Financ Econ 3(4):305–360

Kant I (1783) Prolegomena zu einer jeden künftigen Metaphysik die als Wissenschaft wird auftreten können. Johann Friedrich Hartknoch, Riga

Kant I (1786) Metaphysische Anfangsgründe der Naturwissenschaft. Johann Friedrich Hartknoch, Riga

Kellert SH, Longino HE, Waters CK (2006) Introduction: the pluralist stance. In: Kellert SH, Longino HE, Waters CK (eds) Scientific pluralism. Minnesota studies in the philosophy of science, vol 19. University of Minnesota Press, Minneapolis, pp vii–xxix

Kelsen H (1934) Reine Rechtslehre: Einleitung in die rechtswissenschaftliche Problematik, 1. Aufl. Deuticke, Leipzig Wien. / Jestaedt M (ed) (2008) Studienausgabe. Mohr Siebeck, Tübingen

Kraakman R, Davies P, Hansmann H, Hertig G, Hopt KJ, Kanda H, Rock EB (2004) The anatomy of corporate law: a comparative and functional approach. Oxford University Press, Oxford

Kramer A (2003) Common sense principles of contract interpretation (and how we've been using them all along). Oxf J Leg Stud 23(2):173–196

Kuhn TS (1996) The structure of scientific revolutions, 3rd edn. University of Chicago Press, Chicago

Latour B (2005) Reassembling the social: an introduction to actor-network theory. Oxford University Press, Oxford

Lukka K (2005) Approaches to case research in management accounting: the nature of empirical intervention and theory linkage. In: Jönsson S, Mouritsen J (eds) Accounting in Scandinavia: the northern lights. Liber & Copenhagen Business School Press, Kristianstad, pp 375–399

Lukka K, Mouritsen J (2002) Homogeneity or heterogeneity of research in management accounting? Eur Account Rev 11:805–811

Lukka K, Vinnari E (2014) Domain theory and method theory in management accounting research. Account Audit Account J 27(8):1308–1338

Mæhle SS (2015) Rettsvitenskapelig forskningsmetodikk – i lys av grunnleggende forskningsverdier. Tidsskrift for Rettsvitenskap 128(2):125–157

Malmi T, Granlund M (2009a) In search of management accounting theory. Eur Account Rev 18 (3):597–620

Malmi T, Granlund M (2009b) Agreeing on problems, where are the solutions? A reply to Quattrone. Eur Account Rev 18(3):631–639

Mäntysaari P (2005) Comparative corporate governance: shareholders as a rule-maker. Springer, Berlin Heidelberg

Mäntysaari P (2010a) The law of corporate finance: general principles and EU law. Volume I: cash flow, risk, agency, information. Springer, Berlin Heidelberg

Mäntysaari P (2010b) The law of corporate finance: general principles and EU law. Volume II: contracts in general. Springer, Berlin Heidelberg

Mäntysaari P (2010c) The law of corporate finance: general principles and EU law. Volume III: funding, exit, takeovers. Springer, Berlin Heidelberg

Mäntysaari P (2012) Organising the firm: theories of commercial law, corporate governance and corporate law. Springer, Berlin Heidelberg

Mäntysaari P (2013) Was sollte man tun? Ein Plädoyer für anwenderfreundliche Rechtswissenschaft. Rechtstheorie 44(2):189–207. doi:10.3790/rth.44.2.189

Mäntysaari P (2016a) Auditorier och retorik. Tidsskrift for Rettsvitenskap 129(1):1–42. doi:10.18261/issn.1504-3096-2016-01-01

Mäntysaari P (2016b) Oikeudenaloista tieteenaloihin. Lakimies 114(2):297–304

Merton RK (1968) Social theory and social structure. Free Press, New York

Merton RC, Bodie Z (2005) Design of financial systems: towards a synthesis of function and structure. J Invest Manage 3(1):1–23

National Academy of Sciences, National Academy of Engineering, Institute of Medicine (1992) Responsible science: ensuring the integrity of the research process. Volume I. The National Academies Press, Washington. doi:10.17226/1864
Olsen L (2004) Rättsvetenskapliga perspektiv. Svensk Juristtidning 89(2):105–145
Orts EW (2015) Business persons: a legal theory of the firm. Oxford University Press, Oxford
Patel R, Davidson B (2012) Forskningsmetodikens grunder: Att planera, genomföra och rapportera en undersökning. Fjärde upplagan. Studentlitteratur, Lund
Peirce CS (1931–1935) The collected papers of Charles Sanders Peirce, vols I–VI. In: Hartshorne C, Weiss P (eds) Harvard University Press, Cambridge
Plato, The Republic
Popper K (1935) Logik der Forschung. Verlag von Julius Springer, Wien
Popper K (2005) Logik der Forschung. 11. Auflage. Mohr Siebeck, Tübingen
Pound R (1959) Jurisprudence, vol 1. West Publishing Co., St. Paul, Minn
Quattrone P (2009) We have never been post-modern. Eur Account Rev 18(3):621–630
Ross A (1958) On law and justice. Stevens & Sons Limited, London
Ryan B, Scapens RW, Theobald M (1992) Research method and methodology in finance and accounting. Academic Press, London
Sieber U (2010) Rechtliche Ordnung in einer globalen Welt. Die Entwicklung zu einem fragmentierten System von nationalen, internationalen und privaten Normen. Rechtstheorie 41(2):151–198. doi:10.3790/rth.41.2.151
Silverman D (1993) Interpreting qualitative data. Sage, London
Smaldino PE, McElreath R (2016) The natural selection of bad science. R Soc Open Sci 3:160384. doi:10.1098/rsos.160384
Strauss AL, Corbin JM (1990) Basics of qualitative research: grounded theory procedures and techniques. Sage, London
Suppes P (1993) Models and methods in the philosophy of science: selected essays. Springer, Dordrecht. doi 10.1007/978-94-017-2300-8
von Wright GH (1951) Deontic logic. Mind 60:1–15
Weber M (1922) Wirtschaft und Gesellschaft – Grundriß der verstehenden Soziologie. J.C.B Mohr (Paul Siebeck), Tübingen
Wilson R (1968) On the theory of syndicates. Econometrica 36(1):119–132
Zimmerman JL (2001) Conjectures regarding empirical managerial accounting research. J Account Econ 32:411–427

Chapter 6
Previous Attempts to Increase the Scientificity of Legal Science

6.1 General Remarks

User-Friendly Legal Science differs in fundamental ways from earlier attempts to turn the study of law into an empirical science. We can have a brief look at the most important earlier approaches in order to learn more about what User-Friendly Legal Science is not. At the same time, we can learn more about its nature and what it is.

There have been several attempts to bring more empiricism into legal science[1]:

- Some of them are based on the 'internal point of view' of traditional legal science (Sect. 6.2).
- The internal point of view can also be combined with an interdisciplinary approach.
- The interdisciplinary approach is combined with the 'external point of view' in law-and-something disciplines (Sect. 6.3). The law-and-something approach means the study of law through the lens of the theories and methods of non-legal scientific disciplines. Well-known examples of this approach include the sociology of law, the history of law and law and economics.
- Comparative law has its own characteristics. It is an empirical science with its own theory building and methods (Sect. 6.4). It is also a legal discipline that chooses the 'external point of view'.

Legal disciplines have thus chosen the internal point of view or the external point of view. The choice either is or is not combined with an interdisciplinary approach. The interdisciplinary approach has become so popular that it is sometimes difficult to distinguish between the internal and external approaches.[2]

[1]See, for example, Leiter B (2001a); Leiter B (2007); Leiter B (2009); Mæhle SS (2015), p. 143.

[2]Epstein RA (2002), p. 1289: "The most tempting generalization to make about the evolution of legal analysis over the past thirty or forty years is that the rickety wall that once separated the internal from the external analysis of law has crumbled."

P. Mäntysaari, *User-friendly Legal Science*, DOI 10.1007/978-3-319-53492-3_6

6.2 Traditional Legal Science

6.2.1 General Remarks

Traditional legal science (legal scholarship) consists of legal dogmatics (doctrinal research) and legal theory (jurisprudence). It studies law and legal rules applied by the court and is normative in character.[3] Traditional legal science has problems with scientificity (Sect. 6.2.2). There have been many attempts to cure them in the past. The interdisciplinary approach has become very influential in modern legal research. However, it has its own problems (Sect. 6.2.3). This leaves room for other approaches (Sect. 6.2.4) and User-Friendly Legal Science (Sect. 6.2.5).

6.2.2 Problems with Scientificity

One may ask whether doctrinal research is scientific and whether legal dogmatics is a science.[4] Legal dogmatics does have its own theory that defines its field (the legal system and legal norms), its point of view (interpretation and systematisation), and to some extent its own methods (legal sources and legal rhetoric).[5] When the purpose of legal research is to simulate the normative use of law, it is customarily embedded[6] in the interpretation rules of the chosen jurisdiction.

However, the core of the legal method consists of rhetoric. Rhetoric cannot be regarded as a scientific method (Sect. 7.3).[7] It nevertheless plays a central role in legal research because law is closely connected to subjective value preferences and politics.[8] Legal norms provide a way to address the problem of conflicting interests in society.[9]

---

[3]Holmes OW (1897); Kelsen H (1934); Hart HLA (1961/2012); von Wright GH (1963).

[4]See Vaquero AN (2013) on the notions of legal science.

[5]Olsen L (2004), pp. 113, 121–122 and 126.

[6]Rakoff TD (2002), p. 1279 distinguishing between "embedded" and "non-embedded" legal scholarship; Fleischer H (2007b), pp. 52–53 commenting on the distinction made by Rakoff; Fleischer H (2007a), pp. 501–502.

[7]Mäntysaari P (2016a).

[8]See, for example, Holmes OW (1897), pp. 457–478; Ross A (1958), p. 331. See also Larenz K (1966), p. 12 on the function of legal science: "Die Aufgabe der Rechtswissenschaft ... ist eine dreifache. Sie legt die Gesetze aus, sie bildet das Recht gemäß den der Rechtsordnung immanenten Wertmaßstäben und den in ihr liegenden gedanklichen Möglichkeiten fort und sie sucht immer aufs neue die Fülle des Rechtsstoffes unter einheitlichen Gesichtspunkten zu erfassen." This can be illustrated by the use of the values of the Catholic Church in Thüsing G (2015).

[9]Heck P (1914).

The point of view and method of traditional legal science are unable to produce propositions about the legal system that are true or false.[10] The art of rhetoric can be used for any purpose.[11]

Legal rules can be systematised and interpreted in different ways depending on the interests that one wants to further. A wide range of rhetorical tools[12] can be employed to win an argument, further particular interests in the interpretation of legal norms[13] or otherwise. Propositions of legal doctrine are designed to influence judicial decision-making and can therefore be described as 'political acts'.[14]

Moreover, traditional legal science is unable to produce useful scientific theories about society outside the legal system. The lack of scientific theories is caused by the limited scope of traditional legal science (the internal point of view) and its failure to observe the basics of scientific research (such as the formulation of falsifiable theories, the choice of interpretive understanding as the goal of research and the use of scientific research methods).[15]

The political nature of law and legal science, their close connection to moral and value preferences, the subjective nature of the interpretation of legal norms, the absence of scientific theories about societal reality and the absence of scientific methods mean that traditional legal science is not scientific.[16]

Because of the lack of scientificity, traditional legal science has become increasingly marginal. Laws should preferably be drafted on the basis of useful information about societal reality, that is, on the basis of theories about how society works. Scientific theories can influence the interpretation of laws. If legal science does not produce useful theories about societal reality, lawmakers and researchers have reason to turn to other social sciences such as economics for guidance. Legal science is ill equipped to face competition from other social sciences. 'It takes a theory to beat a theory,'[17] but traditional legal science does not produce the necessary theories as it focuses on existing norms rather than societal reality.

The absence of sufficient theory building makes it more difficult for traditional legal science to cope even in its core area. Focusing on legal norms has contributed

---

[10]See also Dellavalle S (2016): "Following Koskenniemi's interpretation, the law has no truth content because no universal rationality can be presumed."

[11]See already Augustine of Hippo, De doctrina christiana, Fourth Book, II; Schopenhauer A (1830).

[12]For example, Perelman C, Olbrechts-Tyteca L (1971); Gast W (2015); Mäntysaari P (2016a).

[13]For example, Stigler GJ (1971).

[14]Ross A (1953), p. 61; Ross A (1958), p. 49; Zahle H (2003), p. 809.

[15]See, for example, van Gestel R, Micklitz HW, Maduro MP (2012), p. 8: "It is probably no coincidence that so many colleagues nowadays perceive doctrinal research(ers) to be intellectually rigid and inward-looking. Unfortunately one reason for this is that doctrinalists all too often have: shown a preoccupation with technicalities and topics with little or no theoretical relevance, and have often limited themselves to repeating existing knowledge ('facing future problems backwards') and, more in general, have failed to connect law to life."

[16]Larenz K (1966), p. 11; von Jhering R (1868); von Kirchmann J (1848); Ulen TS (2002).

[17]Kuhn TS (1970).

to over-regulation[18] and the fragmentation of law, and increased legal pluralism (Sect. 4.3). Fragmentation and legal pluralism have made it more difficult to interpret and systematise law[19] and left more room for the use of rhetorical techniques (Sect. 7.3).

6.2.3 Early Attempts to Define Doctrinal Research as a Science

There have been various attempts to address the problems of traditional legal science. One is to try to define doctrinal research as a science. Such attempts range from the German historical school to new legal realism and from Kelsen's pure legal science to the interdisciplinary approach.

Historical Sources. In the first half of the nineteenth century, Friedrich Carl von Savigny and the German historical school of law that he represented treated law as an expression of the convictions of the people and required lawyers to ascertain the will of the people on the basis of historical sources (Sect. 6.3.3). It was not enough just to apply the letter of the law.[20] The core assumption of the German historical school is perhaps summarised in the following words of von Savigny:

> In the earliest of times to which authentic history extends, the law will be found to have already attained a fixed character, peculiar to the people, like their language, manners and constitution.[21]

The Case Method. In the second half of the nineteenth century and after the US civil war, Christopher Columbus Langdell defined law as a 'science' consisting of 'certain principles or doctrines'. He advocated the case method. The case method had a connection to legal history. Langdell sought a connection between a manageable number of current principles and doctrines on one hand and the cases that contributed to such theory on the other. His primary sources were cases. He defined his case method as follows[22]:

> Law, considered as a science, consists of certain principles or doctrines . . . Each of these doctrines has arrived at its present state by slow degrees; in other words, it is a growth, extending in many cases through centuries. This growth is to be traced in the main through a series of cases; and much the shortest and best, if not the only way of mastering the doctrine effectually is by studying the cases in which it is embodied. But the cases which are useful and necessary for this purpose at the present day bear an exceedingly small proportion to all

[18]Maslow AH (1966), p. 15: "I suppose it is tempting, if the only tool you have is a hammer, to treat everything as if it were a nail."

[19]Sieber U (2010), p. 171; Mäntysaari P (2013).

[20]von Savigny FC (1814), pp. 5–6. Posner RA (2002b), p. 1314: "[T]he earliest recognizably protomodern academic legal scholarship was that of Friedrich Carl von Savigny . . ."

[21]von Savigny FC (1814), p. 8, translated in von Savigny FC (1831), p. 24.

[22]Langdell CC (1871), Preface, pp. vi–vii. See also Walker A (2014), pp. 149–150.

> that have been reported. The vast majority are useless and worse than useless for any purpose of systematic study. Moreover, the number of fundamental legal doctrines is much less than is commonly supposed; the many different guises in which the same doctrine is constantly making its appearance, and the great extent to which legal treatises are a repetition of each other, being the cause of much misapprehension. If these doctrines could be so classified and arranged that each should be found in its proper place, and nowhere else, they would cease to be formidable from their number. It seemed to me, therefore, to be possible to take such a branch of the law as Contracts, for example, and, without exceeding comparatively moderate limits, to select, classify, and arrange all the cases which had contributed in any important degree to the growth, development, or establishment of any of its essential doctrines; and that such a work could not fail to be of material service to all who desire to study that branch of law systematically and in its original sources.

Societal Effects. Doctrinal research was influenced by the sociology of law. In the 1910s, Eugen Ehrlich developed a sociological approach to the study of law (Sect. 6.3.2). He distinguished between positive law and 'lebendes Recht' ('living law").[23] His 'living law' consists of the rules of conduct that dominate social life. Because of compliance with the norms of 'living law', people seldom end up in court.

Roscoe Pound was influenced by Ehrlich.[24] Pound distinguished between the analytical, the historical, the philosophical and the sociological methods as the four methods of jurisprudence.[25] Moreover, Pound regarded sociology of law as a theoretical science and sociological jurisprudence as an applied science.[26]

In an article published slightly earlier than Ehrlich's book, Pound distinguished between law in the books and law in action.[27] There can be a difference between how law actually is applied and how it should be applied according to law in the books. However, Pound (a representative of sociological jurisprudence) did not go as far as Ehrlich (a representantive of legal sociology). Pound's law in action seems

---

[23]Ehrlich E (1913), pp. 31 and 405–406: "Die Erforschung des lebenden Rechts ist es also, womit die Soziologie des Rechts beginnen muß ... Aber die wissenschaftliche Bedeutung des lebenden Rechts beginnt nicht erst da, wo es für die Entscheidungsnormen der Gerichte oder für den Inhalt der Gesetze bestimmend wird. Es hat seinen eigenen Erkenntniswert, und dieser liegt darin, daß es die Grundlage der rechtlichen Ordnung der menschlichen Gesellschaft ist." English translation Ehrlich E (1936). For living law in legal history, see Berman HJ (1983), pp. 4–5. For Max Weber and law, see Petersen J (2014).

[24]Pound R (1959), Chapter 1, p. 20. See Nobleman E (1961), pp. 187, 189 and 197; Likhovski A (2003), pp. 632–633, 646 and 637, citing Hull NEH (1997), pp. 108–109.

[25]Pound R (1959), Chapter 1, pp. 14–20.

[26]*Ibid*, Chapter 6, § 27, p. 344. See also pp. 337–338: "Mr. Justice Holmes was at least the forerunner of sociological jurisprudence in the United States ... Experience upon the bench and wide reading of and deep reflection upon the juristic writing of the time, led him at the end of the century to the sociological position ... In American sociological jurisprudence the outstanding work is that of Mr. Justice Cardozo."

[27]Pound R (1910).

to be limited to law as applied by state agencies. Pound left the meaning of law in action unclear.

In the 1930s, Karl Llewellyn and other legal realists argued that law is not a deductive science. Llewellyn wrote that what judges, lawyers and law enforcement officers 'do about disputes is ... the law itself'.[28] Law was thus defined as dispute settlement and dispute avoidance.

Like Langdell, Llewellyn favoured the case method. However, Llewellyn argued that the function of law can only be ascertained from the perspective of ordinary people: 'the meaning of law in life and in the practice of lawyers is its meaning not to courts, but to laymen'.[29] The functions of lawyers were therefore '(a) the handling of specific suits caused by disputes (getting the judge to do what you would like to have him to do) and (b) counselling laymen how to shape their conduct in anticipation of what courts are likely to do if a dispute arises; and, as a part of that job inventing "device to make it easier for people to accomplish what they want in their relations with other people."'[30]

Pure Law. In Europe, Hans Kelsen chose a very different approach. His starting point reflected the positivist phase of the development of sciences that was popular at the time. Kelsen distinguished between positivist and normative sciences[31] and assumed that sociology and historical disciplines were positivist (which they currently are not; see Sect. 2.1).[32] Kelsen wanted to preserve the purity of the study of law by limiting the work of the legal scholar to linguistic and logical analysis.[33]

Prognosis Theory. Kelsen's approach was rejected by Alf Ross, who described the idea of a purely logical interpretation, free of all pragmatism, as 'an illusion'.[34] However, Ross still preferred to adhere to logical positivism.[35] This reflected the popular thinking of the time.[36]

---

[28]Llewellyn KN (1930), p. 3. Similarily Bobbitt P (1991), p. 24: "Law is something we do, not something we have as a consequence of something we do."

[29]Llewellyn KN (1930), p. 24.

[30]Frank J (1931).

[31]Kelsen H (1911/2000): "The contrast between 'is' and 'ought' is decisive for the fundamental distinction between all scholarly disciplines."

[32]Kelsen H (1911/2000): "The natural sciences, in particular, belong to the explanatory or causal disciplines, as do the historical disciplines; among the normative disciplines are found ethics, logic, and grammar." "If I now call sociology—a natural science of human society that strives to find the natural laws of social life, to explain what happens in society just as it actually happens in reality—if I call this sociology an explanatory, causal science, I believe I will encounter little opposition."

[33]Kelsen H (1934).

[34]Ross A (1958), p. 338. For Kelsen's reply, see Kelsen H (2013).

[35]See Zahle H (2003).

[36]Pound R (1959), Chapter 6, § 23, p. 299: "[T]here was a tendency to take a mathematical-physical view of everything. Men sought to find the mathematical of mechanical laws according to which all things came into exitence and by which they were governed in the course of their existence. As this was the type of thought of the first positive philosophers, it came to be that of the first positive philosophies of law, and so of the first stage of sociological jurisprudence."

Like Kelsen, Ross distinguished between legal dogmatics (or jurisprudence, the study of legal norms) and the sociology of law (the study of law in action). According to Ross, legal-sociological knowledge concerned 'the causal connection between the normative function of the law and human behaviour'.[37] Although Ross was clearly inspired by sociology,[38] he did not want to apply its scientific methods.[39] For Ross, the behaviour of judges belonged to the domain of legal dogmatics rather than the sociology of law.[40] He regarded the sociology of law as the basis of 'legal politics' and legal politics as applied legal sociology.[41]

Ross found a new way to define legal doctrine as an empirical science. Ross started with 'the working hypothesis that it must be possible to define and explain the concept "valid law" in principle in the same fashion as the concept "valid norms of chess"'. He argued for what became known as the prognosis theory: 'The working hypothesis implies that the legal norms, like the norms of chess, serve as a scheme of interpretation for a corresponding set of social acts, the law in action, in such a way that it becomes possible to comprehend those actions as a coherent whole of meaning and motivation and to predict them within certain limits. This capacity within the system is based on the fact that the norms are effectively complied with because they are felt to be socially binding.'[42]

According to the prognosis theory of Alf Ross, statements of valid law refer to the future and a statement that a certain rule is part of valid law can be true or false. If the rule is applied in a future judgment, the statement is true. If it is not applied in the future, the statement is false.[43] In other words, the validity of statements

[37]*Ibid*, p. 328. See also Dalberg-Larsen J (2005), p. 47.

[38]Ross A (1958), p. 34: "What, now, are those social facts which as legal phenomena constitute the counterpart of the legal norms? They must be the human actions regulated by the legal norms ... [T]he legal phenomena as the counterpart of the norms must be the decisions of the courts." Ross A (1958), p. 35: "[T]he law provides the norms for the behaviour of the courts, and not for private individuals."

[39]See, for example, von Holderstein Holtermann J, Christensen MJ, Madsen MR (2013); Dalberg-Larsen J (2005), p. 48: "In this field as well as in general, he seems to completely underestimate the importance of developing more general legal-sociological theories to inspire empirical research."

[40]See, for example, Dalberg-Larsen J (2005), p. 40. It is of course possible to study judicial behaviour even in the sociology of law. See, for example, Posner RA (2010).

[41]Ross A (1958), p. 331: "[T]here is a place for legal politics, not merely as guidance for the legislator, but also as guidance for the authorities administering the law, in particular the judge." Ross A (1958), p. 328: "Where then is the place for specific legal politics to be the domain of the lawyers? ... This special body of knowledge can only be sought in the legal-sociological knowledge concerning the causal connection between the normative function of the law and human behaviour, or, we may also say, concerning the possibilities of influencing human action by the apparatus of legal sanctions." See also Dalberg-Larsen J (2005), p. 47.

[42]Ross A (1958), p. 29.

[43]Ross A (1953), pp. 53–54 and 64; Ross A (1958), pp. 41 and 50–51; Zahle H (2003), pp. 806–807.

depends on the power of legal rhetoric and actual positions of power in a future case.[44]

Scandinavian Legal Realism. Alf Ross represented Scandinavian legal realism. Like other doctrinal approaches, it studied law and legal norms. It was characteristic of Scandinavian legal realism that it tried to define normative terms as empirical predictions about the behaviour of authorities. However, because of its focus on law and legal norms, Scandinavian legal realism did not really take into account the subjective goals of any actors in the field.[45] Ross was not interested in the user perspective.[46]

Interpretive Understanding. The work of Kelsen and Ross was influenced by a limited view on science in the positivist phase (Sect. 2.1). They missed the rise of qualitative and narrative research and the fact that interpretive understanding can be a legitimate goal of science. This new way of scientific thinking could be taken into account in later research, which can be illustrated by H.L.A. Hart. Unlike Kelsen, Hart could describe law as a social construction.[47] Moreover, Hart showed that one cannot understand the social phenomenon of law without taking into account the perspective of the relevant actors, and that Scandinavian legal realism had failed to do so.[48]

American Legal Realism and the Interdisciplinary Approach. Many of the early attempts to upgrade traditional legal science into a science were originally based on the 'internal point of view'.[49] However, one could find more theories about societal reality outside legal dogmatics. The 'internal point of view' could be influenced by an interdisciplinary approach, or legal research could be embedded in the theoretical framework of other social sciences and take the 'external point of view'.

Langdell's case method was not enough for American legal realists such as Karl Llewellyn, Oliver Wendell Holmes, Louis D. Brandeis and Benjamin Cardozo. They believed that extra-legal considerations such as societal effects should be taken into account in dispute resolution.[50] Llewellyn, who had discovered the limitations of the case method, lobbied for the merger of case study with contextual

---

[44]Mäntysaari P (2016a).

[45]See, for example, Bjarup J (2005); Dalberg-Larsen J (2005). See also Leiter B (2009).

[46]Compare Dalberg-Larsen J (2005), pp. 48–49 on Alf Ross: "... Ross seems to consider legal action and legal guidance as accessories to any law that is not completely special and aberrant. This conception might indicate that Ross only seldom went out into real life to see what society looked like for ordinary citizens. If he had done so, he would soon have found out that many citizens' lives and welfare are affected by laws, without them even contemplating approaching the courts or lawyers with their problems."

[47]Hart HLA (1961/ 2012).

[48]See Leiter B (2009).

[49]Hart HLA (1961/ 2012), pp. 88–90; Shapiro SJ (2006), p. 1158.

[50]See van Gestel R, Micklitz HW, Maduro MP (2012), p. 11.

material. He argued that students need to understand the context of legal rules in order to effectively counsel clients.[51]

This required a more interdisciplinary approach to the study of law. In the 1930s, the interdisciplinary approach became the standard way to bridge the gap between law and other social sciences in the US.[52] The interdisciplinary approach has since enabled some empirical research in legal science even in the absence of scientific theories in this discipline.[53]

Combined with the internal point of view, the interdisciplinary approach has influenced legal scholarship not only in the US but also worldwide. Its current state can perhaps be illustrated with the papers presented at the symposium titled 'Law, Knowledge, and the Academy' hosted by Harvard Law School (2001)[54]; papers presented at the conference 'Beyond the State – Rethinking Private Law' organised by the American Journal of Comparative Law and Rabels Zeitschrift (2007)[55]; concerns about the absence of scientificity in legal dogmatics raised in the edited book 'Das Proprium der Rechtswissenschaft' (2007)[56]; and the proposals presented in the edited books 'Privatrechtstheorie' (2015)[57] and 'Rethinking Legal Scholarship' (2016).[58] The underlying theme seems to be that doctrinal research should be reformed by the increased use of a broad range of theories from other social sciences.

Around 1970, many law professors in the US went further by choosing the external point of view.[59] Movements such as law and economics, new legal realism and empirical legal studies contributed to an empirical turn in US legal science. In law and economics, the theories and methods of economics are applied in the field of law. New legal realism is 'an effort to understand the sources of judicial decisions on the basis of testable hypotheses and large data sets'.[60] In empirical legal studies, researchers apply quantitative methods to the study of law.

---

[51]Llewellyn KN (1935), p. 669.

[52]See Directors of the Columbia Law Review Association, Inc. (1964), p. 724.

[53]Ulen TS (2002), p. 900: "The puzzling absence of a core theory in law has not, somewhat curiously, led to the total absence of empirical work in law. Indeed . . . even the doctrinalists had an interest in empirical work, and, indeed, they did some empirical work. The reason for this interest in empiricism in the absence of theory lies . . . in the pattern of the development of American jurisprudence in the twentieth century. When legal formalism gave way to legal realism in the 1930s and 1940s, the desire for empirical work was born."

[54]Harvard Law Review 115(5):1277–1431.

[55]For a conference report, see Flohr M (2008). For the articles, see American Journal of Comparative Law 56(3):527–844.

[56]Engel C, Schön W (eds) (2007).

[57]Grundmann S, Micklitz HW, Renner M (eds) (2015).

[58]van Gestel R, Micklitz HW, Rubin EL (eds) (2016).

[59]Posner RA (2002b), p. 1316.

[60]Miles TJ, Sunstein CR (2008), p. 831.

Results. The results of the previous attempts to increase the scientificity of doctrinal research have been rather poor. The early attempts failed to upgrade traditional legal research into a science. Langdell's case method turned out to have practical rather than scientific purposes. The prognosis theory of Ross has hardly been applied in the study of law.[61] New legal realism and empirical legal studies have failed to produce a relevant theoretical base for their respective fields of study. The lack of theories can be explained by the fact that new legal realism and empirical legal studies focus on methods rather than theory building and by their very broad scopes.

The interdisciplinary approach has its own problems. The core problem of the interdisciplinary approach is that non-legal disciplines do not necessarily reflect the nature of law and the values that laws are based on.

First, law is normative. The perspective of law must be holistic because legal norms must be applied to a wide range of people and organisations that exist in real life. It must take into account the complexities of society. In contrast, social sciences are not normative. Whether they reflect or do not reflect real-life complexity depends on the chosen point of view. It is not necessary for non-normative social sciences to choose the holistic approach. Each scientific discipline defines its own narrow perspective. For example, the use of quantitative methods would not be possible without reducing the phenomena under investigation into a small number of variables that are given a numeric value. Some scientific disciplines such as mainstream economics are based on very narrow assumptions (see also Sect. 5.3).[62]

Second, law and non-normative social sciences can be based on different values. Since legal norms are applied to real people in real life, law is a way to balance various conflicting interests according to the prevailing societal values. In contrast, each scientific discipline has its own limited perspective and can be based on its own set of values. The reception of theories from other social sciences such as economics would thus go hand in hand with the reception of the values that the theories are based on.

Third, theories in social sciences can be self-fulfilling. When people base their actions on theories, they might create the social mechanisms that the theories

[61]Zahle H (2003), p. 814: "... Ross' project achieved ... broad support and even until this very day has its supporters. Paradoxically this acceptance has been strengthened by the fact that no author of legal doctrine has seriously studied and written in accordance with the line of thinking presented by Ross."

[62]Weber M (1949), pp. 43–44: "Economic theory is an axiomatic discipline in a way which is logically very different from that of the systematic science of law. Its relationship to economic reality is very different from the relationship of jurisprudence to the phenomena treated by the history and sociology of law. The concepts of jurisprudence may and should be used as ideal-types in empirical legal studies. Pure economic theory, in its analysis of past and present society, utilizes ideal-type concepts exclusively. Economic theory makes certain assumptions which scarcely ever correspond completely with reality but which approximate it in various degrees and asks: how would men act under these assumed conditions, if their actions were entirely rational? It assumes the dominance of pure economic interests and precludes the operation of political or other non-economic considerations."

describe and contribute to the outcome that the theories predict.[63] Law is not an exception. Consequently, the lack of theories about societal reality in legal science and the use of theories from other social sciences as transplants is a threat to the values that laws are based on.

Fourth, theory transplants[64] and rules based on theories from other social sciences can become theory irritants or legal irritants.[65] It is widely known that legal transplants do not necessarily work properly in the host legal system, although they might work adequately in the home legal system (the legal system in which the transplants originate). Theory transplants from other social sciences cannot be expected to work better than legal transplants. They can be expected to be worse. This is because of fundamental differences between law and theories from other social sciences. Generally, 'round data' should not be forced into 'square categories'.[66]

Fifth, the interdisciplinary approach does not help to cure the problems of the doctrinal study of law. This can be illustrated with the edited book 'Privatrechtstheorie' (2015)[67] in which a group of German scholars chooses hermeneutics as the way to integrate theories from scientific disciplines in legal dogmatics. This approach is not likely to cure the problems of doctrinal research for the following reasons:

- The approach proposed in the book seems to be based on the assumption that a broad range of theories can lead to a unified view. But the dream of the unity of science has already been replaced by the pluralist view in the theory of science (Sect. 5.1).
- The use of a larger number of theories from social sciences is not likely to reduce problems caused by legal pluralism (Sect. 4.3). On the contrary, it is designed to increase the number of arguments perceived as legitimate, increase the creative use of rhetorical techniques and make the problem worse.
- Since the point of view is still that of legal dogmatics, the choice of particular theories as the basis of the hermeneutical approach reflects the subjective preferences of the researcher. For example, the theories that the group highlighted were largely from economics and sociology rather than the humanities.[68] The choice and use of theories from other scientific disciplines is a form of rhetoric (Sect. 7.3.4).
- Moreover, the group does not distinguish between the different functions of the theories. (It is proposed in this book that one can distinguish between domain/ main theories and method/complementary theories, Sects. 3.3 and 5.5.2.)

---

[63]For a case showing how economic theories can influence legislation, see Ferraro F, Pfeffer J, Sutton RI (2005); Kieser A (2004); André T Jr. (1998).

[64]Watson A (1974).

[65]For legal irritants, see Teubner G (1998).

[66]Glaser BG, Strauss AL (1967), p. 37.

[67]Grundmann S, Micklitz HW, Renner M (eds) (2015).

[68]For the humanistic study of law, see Sarat A, Anderson M, Frank CO (2010).

6.2.4 New Points of View

There are even other approaches to bring legal dogmatics closer to a science. It may require new points of view apart from the mere interpretation and systematisation of legal norms.

Pound distinguished between the dogmatic and critical modes of treatment when the methods of jurisprudence are applied to the study of the legal system. He defined the critical mode of treatment as 'consideration of ... what ought to be in the light of [dogmatic] analysis, or history, or social ends to be served, or all of these'. He added that '[a]nalytical jurists hold that such criticism ... is no part of jurisprudence'.[69]

In the past, such new points of view have related to impact, internal coherence, comparison or policy. Consequently, Graver distinguishes between impact analyses, systematic analyses, synthetic analyses, comparative analyses and policy analyses. In these cases, doctrinal research may exhibit some of the characteristics of other areas of legal science such as legal sociology, legal policy or legal theory[70]:

- In an impact analysis, the point of view is whether the stated objectives of regulation or a legal norm have been met.[71]
- A systematic analysis has a connection to system building and the internal coherence of the legal system. It can focus on distinctions between different existing or new legal areas, as well as the use of existing or new legal concepts.[72] A systematic analysis can also study legal norms in the context of foreign law or international law.[73]
- A synthetic analysis deals with two levels of generality. It can define general principles on the basis of legal norms or more concrete model cases on the basis of general clauses or standards.[74]
- A policy analysis studies whether regulation is adequate. It can also propose a reform.[75]

Such ideas are not totally new. They bring us one back to Friedrich Carl von Savigny, who distinguished between the linguistic, systematic, historic and teleologic elements of the interpretation of legal norms.[76]

---

[69]Pound R (1959), Chapter 1, p. 23.

[70]See Graver HP (2008), pp. 172–173.

[71]*Ibid*, p. 173.

[72]*Ibid*, p. 173.

[73]*Ibid*, p. 173.

[74]*Ibid*, p. 174.

[75]*Ibid*, p. 174.

[76]von Savigny FC (1840), Chapter 4, § 33: "Das grammatische Element ... Das logische Element ... Das historische Element ... Das systematische Element ..."

6.2.5 Traditional Legal Science and User-Friendly Legal Science

There are fundamental differences between traditional legal science and User-Friendly Legal Science. While doctrinal research focuses on legal norms applied by the court, User-Friendly Legal Science primarily focuses on behaviour rather than legal norms, and the behaviour that it focuses on is user behaviour rather than the behaviour of the court. Unlike traditional legal science, this new discipline puts more emphasis on theory building and empirical evidence.

However, User-Friendly Legal Science needs doctrinal legal scholarship because it focuses on the use of legal tools and practices rather than social practices in general. The legal tools and practices that users apply for the purpose of reaching their objectives are based on or influenced by legal norms. The theories of doctrinal research should therefore be applied as method theories (Sects. 3.3 and 5.5.2).

One may ask how it can be possible to combine the interpretation of legal norms, which largely is an unscientific exercise, with research that claims to be scientific.[77] The answer is that one should just focus on the point of view of User-Friendly Legal Science and the fundamental knowledge interests of the particular study.

The relevant point of view is how users can use legal tools and practices to reach their objectives in different contexts. The main objective is not to interpret legal norms. It is more important for users to identify ways of legal action. However, the interpretation of legal norms is relevant because the substance of legal norms cannot be defined otherwise. The substance of legal norms, perhaps in most cases, can be defined as a doctrinal exercise with sufficient accuracy for the purposes of the user-friendly study regardless of the inherent absence of scientificity. The doctrinal exercise can, in other words, lead to a very strong prognosis (Llewellyn, Ross). The inherent flexibility of interpretation means that the user can be exposed to legal risk depending on the context. It may turn out in the course of the user-friendly study that the management of this risk belongs to user objectives in the context. The management of the interpretation risk can be studied by applying the theories and methods of User-Friendly Legal Science.[78]

One may note that the relationship between User-Friendly Legal Science and doctrinal research does not have to be one-way traffic. Doctrinal research can benefit from the new discipline (Chap. 4).

[77]See also Rhode DL (2002); van Gestel R, Micklitz HW, Maduro MP (2012), p. 8.

[78]See, for example, Mäntysaari P (2010b), Chapter 5.

6.3 Law and Something

6.3.1 General Remarks

The approach of law-and-something disciplines can bring benefits. The study of legal phenomena through the lens of the theories and methods of other social sciences includes the use of scientific methods – which replace the laissez-faire method culture of traditional legal scholarship and the use of legal rhetoric as the main method – and a more international orientation.[79] The external point of view of this approach has been more successful than the internal point of view in bringing legal science closer to the threshold of scientificity (Sect. 5.5.4).[80]

However, law is regarded as a mere field in law-and-something disciplines.[81] This can undermine the position of legal science as an independent discipline. Moreover, the respective points of view of non-legal disciplines are not necessarily aligned with the fundamental nature of law (Sect. 2.3) and its values (Sect. 6.2.4).

Three influential law-and-something disciplines stand out: the sociology of law (Sect. 6.3.2), the history of law (Sect. 6.3.3) and law and economics (Sect. 6.3.4). A study of these three disciplines can help to understand the nature of User-Friendly Legal Science as a distinct area of science with its own particular characteristics (Sect. 6.3.5).

Part of law-and-something research is positivist. One of the characteristics of such research is the predominance of causally functional and empirical accounts of law: 'The theory is that law is a purposive or functional activity; people create law, or make use of law in a particular way for a reason, and the result of these activities, whether intended or not, is that law becomes what it becomes and society becomes what it becomes.'[82] This way of thinking still persists in much of law and economics.

In the late 1970s, critical theory turned against such causally functional and empirical accounts of law: 'Theories of causal regularities in law/society relations were elusive and unstable; they tended to break down under critique into indeterminacy marked by complexity and contingency.'[83]

[79]van Gestel R, Micklitz HW (2014); van Gestel R, Micklitz HW, Maduro MP (2012), p. 12: "So what are the new and more pressing questions with respect to the role of methodology in law? The answer has to do with the fact that law is a 'discipline in transition' moving, among others, from: a predominantly monodisciplinary (doctrinal) tradition towards more and more attention for multidisciplinary and empirical legal research, from a national to a more international and global orientation and from a research culture of 'laissez faire' towards more monitoring, managerial control, and research programming on the basis of output indicators. What needs to be done is to meet the needs of those who study law by describing the demands these transitions pose for legal scholarship."

[80]See, for example, Ulen TS (2002); Fisk C, Gordon RW (2011), p. 521.

[81]See, for example, Tomlins C, Comaroff J (2011), p. 1040: "'Law and' relies on empirical context to situate law as a domain of activity."

[82]Fisk C, Gordon RW (2011), p. 521.

[83]*Ibid*, p. 522. See also Ryan B, Scapens RW, Theobald M (1992), pp. 4–5 on finance and accounting.

There are thus different kinds of law-and-something disciplines. User-Friendly Legal Science shares some of its characteristics with the sociology of law and legal history. In contrast, User-Friendly Legal Science is the opposite of law and economics in many respects. We will now have a look at the most important law-and-something disciplines before discussing the similarities and differences (Sect. 6.3.5).

6.3.2 The Sociology of Law

Sociology was developed at the turn of the twentieth century. Emilé Durkheim defined sociology as the study of social facts. A social fact is identifiable through the power of external coercion that it exerts or is capable of exerting on people.[84] Durkheim represented positivism. According to Durkheim, social facts must be considered as 'things' for research purposes.[85] In contrast, Max Weber assumed that the most appropriate way to gain knowledge about the social world is through interpretive understanding (Verstehen).[86]

The sociology of law builds on the theories and methods of sociology. Eugen Ehrlich is regarded as one of the founders of the sociology of law. The founders regarded legal sociology as the scientific study of law.[87] This became the accepted view in legal science.[88] The terms sociology of law and socio-legal studies are nowadays used interchangeably, which has not always been the case.[89]

While doctrinal research focuses on legal norms, legal sociology is a science that studies human behaviour relating to legal norms.[90]

---

[84]Durkheim É (1894), Chapter I.

[85]*Ibid*, Chapter II.

[86]Weber M (1922).

[87]Ehrlich E (1913), p. 19: "Da das Recht eine gesellschaftliche Erscheinung ist, so gehört jede Art der Jurisprudenz den Gesellschaftswissenschaften an, aber die eigentliche Rechtswissenschaft ist ein Teil der theoretischen Gesellschaftswissenschaft, der Soziologie. Die Soziologie des Rechts ist die wissenschaftliche Lehre vom Rechte."

[88]See Ross A (1958), § 4; Pound R (1959) Chapter 6 § 27, p. 344.

[89]According to Campbell CM, Wiles P (1976), the "sociology of law" seeks to understand the nature of social order by using theory in the study of law, and "socio-legal studies" is characterised by the employment of social scientific approaches as a tool for data collection. The distinction between "socio-legal studies" and "legal sociology" is nowadays regarded as unnecessary. Banakar R, Travers M (2005a), p. xii; Banakar R (2006), p. 78.

[90]See already Ehrlich E (1912/1967), p. 43: "Es leben im Herzogtum Bukowina gegenwärtig, zum Teile sogar noch immer ganz friedlich nebeneinander, neun Volksstämme ... Ein Jurist der hergebrachten Richtung würde zweifellos behaupten, alle diese Völker hätten nur ein einziges, und zwar genau dasselbe, das in ganz Österreich geltende österreichische Recht. Und doch könnte ihn schon ein flüchtiger Blick davon überzeugen, dass jeder dieser Stämme in allen Rechtsverhältnissen des täglichen Lebens ganz andre Rechtsregeln beobachtet."

According to Nicholas S. Timasheff, the sociology of law focuses on the following questions: How does law determine behaviour? What forces determine the making, change or repeal of legal norms? What relationships exist between legal phenomena and other social phenomena?[91]

Models of Legal Sociology. Modern sociology of law focuses on the relationship between legal norms or decisions and other societal structures.[92] There are different models of legal sociology.

Thomas Mathiesen calls the dominant models of legal sociology the norm model, the coercion model and the experience model[93]: The 'norm model' has its roots in Durkheim's positivist school. Legal rules and other norms are regarded as forces that influence the behaviour of people.[94] The coercion model has its roots in Marxist theory. It is based on the assumption that behaviour is the product of the power that humans exercise against each other.[95] The coercion model can thus be deduced from the forces of the economic system.[96] The experience model is rooted primarily in phenomenological philosophy. It is based on the assumption that behaviour is a product of people's special understanding of each other.[97] Therefore, the experience model is part of the socio-cultural system and can be analysed in terms of norms and patterns of behaviour.[98]

The existence of three dominant models each with its own notions of norms and law, and each with its own point of view, can explain why it can be difficult for legal sociologists to define legal sociology and to compare law and legal sociology as disciplines. According to Roger Cotterrell, the comparison of (what he defines as) law and sociology as intellectual disciplines is 'all but impossible' on grounds that both 'are to be understood primarily as social phenomena'.[99]

Characteristics of Modern Legal Sociology. Legal sociology was originally designed as a scientific discipline. It shares its methods with other social sciences.[100] However, its particular characteristics look unclear.[101]

---

[91]Timasheff NS (1937); Schiff D (1981), p. 403.

[92]Mathiesen T (1973), p. 10; Svensson M (2008), pp. 33–34: "Det övergripande rättssociologiska kunskapsintresset är inriktat mot frågor som rör samspelet mellan rättsliga regler och beslut å ena sidan och övriga samhälls- strukturer å den andra ..."

[93]Mathiesen T (1973), pp. 9–14; Svensson M (2008), pp. 33–34.

[94]Hydén H (2011), p. 120.

[95]*Ibid*, pp. 120–121.

[96]*Ibid*, p. 123.

[97]*Ibid*, pp. 120–121.

[98]*Ibid*, p. 123.

[99]Cotterrell R (1995), pp. 42–43.

[100]Banakar R, Travers M (2005a), p. ix: "Many socio-legal researchers would argue that their undertaking requires no special methods besides those already used in the social sciences."

[101]Hydén H (2011), p. 127 on the present "identity crisis" of the discipline; Banakar R (2006).

Legal sociology has a very broad field that does not seem to be limited to the relationship between the legal system and society. Although the field of legal sociology is linked to 'law' and 'norms',[102] these notions are very broad in this discipline.

The notion of norms can be based on all three dominant models: the norm model, the coercion model and the experience model.[103] Basically, norms underscore what 'ought' to be done.[104] Håkan Hydén writes that one can 'get from "is" to "ought"'.[105] According to him, norms seem to be limited to two aspects in sociology. One is expectations emanating from individuals. The other is expectations arising out of the underlying rationality of a system.[106] While societal systems are not explicitly normative, there is a built-in rationality that 'decides what is right and what is wrong'. This is the way to get from 'is' to 'ought'. One can illustrate this with economics. Economics is not explicitly a normative science. Economics is nevertheless designed to 'offer dependable normative advice about how one should act in various situations'. Therefore, economics produces norms for the purposes of legal sociology.[107]

The very broad notion of norms is complemented by a broad notion of law for the purposes of legal sociology.[108] Cotterrell defines law 'in its broadest sociological sense' as 'a field of experience shaped and structured by problems of government, social control, and social order'.[109] The definition of law is thus not limited to the legal system or positive law but includes even Ehrlich's living law[110] and more.

Not only does legal sociology have a very broad field; it has even a very broad point of view. Legal sociology is not limited to the study of Durkheim's social facts since it covers even the coercion model and the experience model. For example, Cotterrell includes the latter models in the definition of the point of view of legal sociology: 'Sometimes it is an experience of power available for the citizen's use; an experience of having the ability to coerce, influence, make things happen, and get things done; of being able to invoke the aid of the state or, at least, to make use of certain procedures, practices, or circumstances of state agencies to further or protect one's interests.'[111]

---

[102]Hydén H (2013), p. 207.

[103]Hydén H (2011), p. 120.

[104]See, for example, Banakar R (2015), p. 216.

[105]The opposite, the traditional severing of "is" from "ought", is called Hume's guillotine. Hume D (1739), book III, part I, section I. See also Kelsen H (1911/2000): "The contrast between 'is' and 'ought' is decisive for the fundamental distinction between all scholarly disciplines." "The methodological contrast between sociology and jurisprudence taken as a starting point for the following discussion is one between 'is' and 'ought'."

[106]Hydén H (2011), p. 121.

[107]*Ibid*, p. 122.

[108]See Banakar R (2015), pp. 42–43.

[109]Cotterrell R (1995), pp. 3–4.

[110]Ehrlich E (1913), pp. 405–406. English translation Ehrlich E (1936).

[111]Cotterrell R (1995), p. 4.

Legal sociology seems to be defined in relation to legal dogmatics. According to Balakar, '[t]he interdisciplinary character of socio-legal studies enables it to highlight aspects of law, legal institutions and legal practice which neither law nor sociology can articulate by itself.'[112] Cotterrell distinguishes between 'normative legal theory' and 'empirical legal theory'. The latter means the scientific study of law 'from the outside'.[113] Cotterrell points out that the '[s]ociological analysis of law has as its sole unifying objective the attempt to remedy the assumed inadequacy of lawyers' doctrinal analyses of law'. If this is true, it can be difficult to define the point of view of legal sociology because legal sociology would then cover a very broad range of phenomena indeed.

Although legal sociology seems to be defined in relation to legal dogmatics, it is not focused on legal norms.[114] Hydén points out that law is 'treated as a black box' in most studies: 'Law is looked upon as a single uniform entity. The legal design is regarded as being without any impact.'[115] While 'the legal scientist and practitioner is interested in the interpretation and proper application of law in concrete cases, the social scientist raises other questions about the legal system'.[116]

6.3.3 Legal History

Historical evidence is important both in the science of history and in legal science. Legal sources are used as evidence of historical facts in the study of history, and historical facts are used as evidence of law in legal science. The doctrinal study of law is always based on historical sources. Legal history is also a particular area of legal science. Information about the characteristics of legal history as a legal discipline is helpful when defining User-Friendly Legal Science as a legal discipline.

Legal Sources as Evidence in the Science of History. The science of history shares many of its theories and methods with other social sciences, in particular sociology.

Modern source-based history was founded by Leopold von Ranke.[117] He introduced the ideas of reliance on primary sources (empiricism) and an emphasis on narrative history. According to von Ranke, historical research should tell you how

[112] Banakar R (2006), p. 78.

[113] Cotterrell R (1995), pp. 24–25. For the internal and external point of views, see Hart HLA (1961/ 2012), pp. 88–90.

[114] Campbell CM, Wiles P (1976), p. 553; Banakar R, Travers M (2005a), p. xi; Banakar R, Travers M (2005b), pp. 11 and 22.

[115] Hydén H (2011), p. 127.

[116] *Ibid*, p. 126.

[117] Iggers GG (1962), p. 17: "Indeed, almost every major debate in German or American historical thought on the nature and methods of historical research has centered around, or at least involved, the question of the acceptance or rejection of Ranke's methodology and philosophy of history."

things actually were.[118] Such source-based history used to be based on induction in the positivist tradition rather than on deduction.[119]

However, it turned out that over-reliance on the positivist methods of natural sciences can reduce the usefulness of information about historical facts. The Annales[120] school of thought provided an alternative. According to this school, one should try to understand the bigger picture of history.[121] For the Annales school, understanding (comprendre) was not limited to knowledge (savoir) of social phenomena but included even an attempt to explain them. Although causal explanations were still regarded as necessary, the Annales schools brought the science of history closer to hermeneutics.[122]

The hermeneutical circle[123] is now regarded as a suitable model for the understanding of historical facts. In hermeneutics, it is assumed that there is a connection between information about a thing and its parts. The hermeneutical perspective is to take into account the relevant context of the people under investigation, draw general conclusions on the basis of information about historical details and draw conclusions about details on the basis of more general information about historical facts. The researcher's own context is equally important. The process is called a circle because the researcher's own prior information (Vorverständnis) and understanding (Verstehen) improve during the course of the research and the researcher can obtain better information the better he starts to understand the things under investigation.[124] For example, the researcher may define and redefine ideal types during the course of the research.

Historians have regularly made use of legal sources in order to understand historical facts. In the words of Frederic W. Maitland: 'Think for a moment what lies concealed within the hard rind of legal history. Legal documents, documents of the most technical kind, are the best, often the only evidence that we have for social and economic history, for the history of morality, for the history of practical religion.'[125] The oldest written sources tend to be legal documents. One can gain information about, say, Mesopotamian society by studying legal sources.[126]

---

[118]von Ranke L (1885), p. VII: "Man hat der Historie das Amt, die Vergangenheit zu richten, die Mitwelt zum Nutzen zukünftiger Jahre zu belehren, beigemessen: so hoher Ämter unterbindet sich gegenwärtiger Versuch nicht: er will blos zeigen, wie es eigentlich gewesen."

[119]Lamprecht K (1896), p. 3: "Die Geschichtswissenschaft ist im Rahmen der für die Induktion geltenden erkenntnistheoretischen Kautelen und Ergänzungen eine induktive Wissenschaft; also kann nur der jeweilige Charakter des induktiven Beweisverfahrens und dessen verschiedenartige Auffassung wahrhaft wissenschaftliche Gegensätze und Strömungen in ihr begründen."

[120]The journal Annales d'histoire économique et sociale was founded by Lucien Febvre and Marc Bloch in Strasbourg in 1929.

[121]Berglund L, Ney A (2015), p. 154.

[122]Iggers GG (1984), p. 45.

[123]Ast DF (1808), pp. 179–180; Heidegger M (1926), § 63.

[124]Firat AF (1987); Berglund L, Ney A (2015), pp. 121–126.

[125]Maitland FW (1911), pp. 485–486.

[126]See, for example, Van de Mieroop M (2005), pp. 17–18; Berglund L, Ney A (2015), pp. 130–131.

History and Sociology. History is closely related to sociology, which has provided useful concepts and methods. Sociology has also influenced the choice of the research perspective in the science of history by showing how to study societal structures.[127] There are nevertheless fundamental differences between these two disciplines.

The most important difference is not the time perspective. For example, August Comte studied the stages of societal evolution in the light of history, and Max Weber showed how the long lines of history influence present society.[128] Societal facts are anchored in the past, and the present becomes history.

The most important differences seem to relate to primary sources, the discipline's point of view and the researcher's knowledge interests.

In the science of history, primary sources consist of original materials from the time under investigation (von Ranke). Secondary sources such as prior research help to choose relevant research questions and contribute to a better understanding of the context and the primary sources. The researcher must choose a research question that can reasonably be answered on the basis of the study of primary sources.

Now, it can be difficult and time consuming to search for information about historical facts on the basis of primary sources. In practice, it can require specialisation that only a proper education can provide. For these reasons, you cannot ask sociologists to comply with similar requirements. In sociological studies, information about historical facts tends to be based on secondary sources, that is, prior studies. This makes it possible to study broader questions such as questions about the evolution of the societal structure.

The nature of the primary sources influences the point of view of the discipline and the knowledge interests of the researcher.

Varieties of Legal History. Legal history is the study of how law has evolved and why it has changed. The legal historian tries to understand and describe how earlier legal systems 'work'.[129] The primary interest of legal historians tends to be in law or in history.

There are varieties of legal history.[130] The first was the German historical school of law (Sect. 6.2.3). Friedrich Karl von Savigny, its founder, recommended the study of the people and their history for the doctrinal study of law.[131] Legal scholars

[127]See, for example, Berglund L, Ney A (2015), pp. 45 and 87–88.

[128]Weber M (1904–1905).

[129]Stolleis M (2008), p. 47: "Wie Recht 'funktioniert' … ist Stoff der Rechtsgeschichte." Stolleis M (2008), p. 43: "Sieht man das generelle Interesse des Rechtshistorikers darin, daß er verstehen und beschreiben will, wie vergangene Rechtsordnungen 'funktionieren', dann hat er bestimmte grundlegende Aufgaben vor sich. Helmut Coing hat sie in seiner ihm systematischen und nüchternen Art beschrieben." Citing Coing H (1976).

[130]See, for example, Stolleis M (2008), pp. 11–19; Lobban M (2012).

[131]von Savigny FC (1814), p. 8.

were thus expected to be historians.[132] The German historical school of law was significant as it inspired legal scholars to look for scientific methods for the study of law and legal phenomena.[133] The German historical school was the start of the interdisciplinary approach in legal science. Doctrinal legal history was later attacked by legal realists.[134]

The second variety of legal history tried to cement the position of legal history by seeking a closer connection to existing law. It tried to find two things in earlier law, one the roots of the current legal doctrine[135] and the other evidence of big ideas or particular values.[136]

The third variety of legal history focused less on current legal doctrine. Instead, it looked at how law developed in society.[137] This enabled a broader notion of 'law'[138] and the alignment of legal history with the wider context of social and economic history.[139]

These variations – and many other – still exist.[140] Doctrinal legal history has been reinvigorated as one of the many variations.[141] Legal historians may seek a connection to theory.[142] There are even statistical and economic approaches to legal history.[143]

The Approach and Methods of Legal History. Legal history customarily takes a holistic approach because of the nature of law and society. Law constitutes society and society constitutes law. For example, various schools of legal theory have been used in the past to change society and law.[144]

---

132 Wesel U (1974), p. 337.

133 Ehrlich E (1913), p. 2: "Die Bedeutung der Rechtsgeschichte für die Rechtswissenschaft beruht aber nicht so sehr darauf, daß sie eine Geschichte, als darauf, daß sie eine reine Wissenschaft ist, fast die einzige Wissenschaft vom Rechte, die es heute gibt."

134 Holmes OW (1897), p. 469: "It is revolting to have no better reason for a rule of law than that so it was laid down in the time of Henry IV. It is still more revolting if the grounds upon which it was laid down have vanished long since, and the rule simply persists from blind imitation of the past."

135 Stolleis M (2008), p. 12.

136 *Ibid*, p. 13.

137 See Lobban M (2012), paragraph 4 on the method of Sir Henry Maine.

138 *Ibid*, paragraph 19 (on Hurst).

139 Stolleis M (2008), p. 17.

140 Lobban M (2012), paragraphs 24–25: "The generations which followed Hurst in America took legal history in two different directions. One direction was to return to doctrine. The 1970s and 1980s saw a flowering of critical legal histories, which sought to show how the doctrine which developed had been the product of contestation between rival interests . . . Another direction was to take up Hurst's call for focused and local studies, but to turn attention away from the economic development which Hurst concentrated on, towards social relations."

141 *Ibid*, paragraph 17 (on Milsom).

142 Berman HJ (1983), p. 44: "The second task of social theory of law today is to adopt a historiography that is appropriate to legal history . . ."

143 Klerman DM (2002).

144 Berman HJ (1983), p. 13.

The methods of legal history vary widely.[145] It is characteristic of legal history to use multiple perspectives and diverse sources.[146]

Oversimplified concepts of causation in the context of law are out.[147] Legal historians are expected not to use unidirectional theories of causation: 'Legal history is not trying to be an empirical social science aiming to identify a series of variables and use the past as an experiment to prove that one or two variables produced particular effects.' Moreover, 'one would have to be arrogant, deluded, or ignorant of a quarter century's critical theory to believe that any historical event worth writing about was indisputably the product of only one or two prior events or phenomena'.[148]

Narrative matters in legal history[149]: 'the contingency and complexity have to be pushed aside enough to tell a story that a reasonably literate reader can follow'.[150]

Legal historians are expected to use historical primary sources and 'attempt to think like a lawyer of the age' they study.[151] The conventional sources of legal history include 'judicial opinions, statutes, treatises, lawyer's pleadings and other writings, and court records of trials and testimony'.[152] In other words, they can include both primary and secondary sources of law of the relevant age, as well as other historical sources relating to law.[153] There can even be other sources such as the conventional sources of intellectual and social history.[154]

Legal positivism is rejected. A study in legal history is preceded by several choices that reflect the subjective values of the researcher.[155]

---

[145]Fisk C, Gordon RW (2011), p. 525.

[146]Vec M (2001); Fisk C, Gordon RW (2011), p. 526.

[147]Berman HJ (1983), p. 44. Compare nevertheless Capra F, Mattei U (2015), pp. 11–12: "Humans were able to employ science and law to transform common holdings into a commodity and then into capital; we also have the ability to reverse this path, transforming some of our now overabundant capital into renewed commons."

[148]Fisk C, Gordon RW (2011), p. 525.

[149]See, for example, Berman HJ (1983), p. 1: "This book tells the following story . . ." See also Berman HJ (1983), p. 12: "If analytical jurisprudence, or, as it is now more often called, legal positivism, is an inadequate theoretical basis for grasping the narrative of the development of Western legal institutions, what theory or theories would provide a better basis?"

[150]Fisk C, Gordon RW (2011), p. 525.

[151]Lobban M (2012), paragraph 14.

[152]Fisk C, Gordon RW (2011), p. 526.

[153]See, for example, Cohen ML (2007).

[154]Fisk C, Gordon RW (2011), p. 526.

[155]Wesel U (1974), p. 353: "Der juristische Positivismus lebte von der Illusion, der Jurist könne Entscheidungen treffen ohne eigene Wertungen im Wege rein logischer Deduktion aus dem System der Rechtsnormen. Diese Illusion haben wir inzwischen überwunden, ohne allerdings bis jetzt zu wissen, woher der Jurist denn nun die Kriterien für die notwendigen eigenen Entscheidungen nehmen soll. Ähnlich ist es in der allgemeinen Geschichte. Langsam wird sich auch dort das Bewußtsein durchsetzen, daß man ohne eigene philosophische Vorentscheidungen nicht feststellen kann, wie es nun eigentlich gewesen ist."

6.3.4 Law and Economics

The economic analysis of law has been the most influential of the interdisciplinary approaches so far. Oliver Wendell Holmes regarded economics as the future: 'For the rational study of the law . . . the man of the future is the man of statistics and the master of economics.' According to Wendell Holmes, the use of economics is necessary due to the theory deficit of legal science: 'We have too little theory in the law rather than too much.'[156] Today, law professors in the top twenty-six US law schools are most likely to have a PhD in economics, if they have a PhD. Few have a PhD in law: 'By hiring Ph.D.s, the law schools are, in large part, hiring statisticians.'[157] There is a canon of law and economics articles and other works customarily referred to in legal education.[158] Interestingly, law and economics seems to be the opposite of User-Friendly Legal Science in many respects.

Law and economics means the study of the efficiency of legal norms and the legal system. It can be intended as a means to replace the vagueness inherent in the design and interpretation of legal norms. There is some vagueness because laws tend to based on what is regarded as a reasonable way to balance various kinds of conflicting societal interests. In law and economics, this inherent vagueness is replaced by a single goal and models reduced to a few variables.

However, law and economics is no exception to the rule that both the choice of societal outcomes and the interpretation of legal norms are based on subjective preferences and values.[159] Law and economics is based on the core assumption that socially optimal results are the results produced by the pursuit of self-interest in market-mediated exchanges.[160] This assumption can be regarded as a political agenda with an intended societal impact. It is designed to increase the wealth of economic elites that are in a position to pursue their self-interest in market-mediated exchanges at the cost of most people who do not share the same

---

[156]Holmes OW (1897).

[157]LoPucki LM (2016), p. 538.

[158]See Whaples R, Morris AP, Moorhouse JC (1998); Fleischer H (2001).

[159]For the use of economic concepts in legal reasoning, see Malloy RP (2004). See also Posner RA (1995), p. 132: "Efficiency . . . is an important social value and hence internalised by most judges, and it may be the only social value that judges can promote effectively, given their limited remedial powers and the value pluralism of our society. So it should be influential in judicial decision making . . ." Capra F, Mattei U (2015), p. 127: "The triumph of economics among the social sciences, combined with a variety of neo-Darwinian evolutionary ideas, made jurists believe that the legal system naturally evolves toward economic efficiency . . . The mechanistic and abstract vision of the law has helped to progressively expropriate resources from the 99 percent in favor of the 1 percent." Goode RM (1998), p. 29: "[T]he law cannot be concerned solely with economic efficiency as the yardstick by which to measure the success of social goals." Eidenmüller H (2005), pp. 169–170, 487 and 490: "Die Gerichte können keine Promotoren des Effizienzdenkens sein." Mestmäcker EJ (2007), p. 13: "Wealth maximization is no substitute for the purpose of law in general." Critically even Grundmann S, Micklitz HW, Renner M (eds) (2015), p. 16.

[160]Ferraro F, Pfeffer J, Sutton R (2005), p. 12.

opportunities in the absence of the necessary financial and social resources. The assumption can also become a self-fulfilling prophecy.[161] There is a bias for Americanisation.[162]

You cannot sell a political agenda without rhetoric (Sect. 7.3). Law and economics has its own canons of rhetoric.[163] They include, in particular, the primacy of mathematical methods, the characterisation of law and the legal system in the language of incentives and costs, the concept of efficiency and the rational choice theory.[164]

However, the use of mathematical methods would not have been possible without reducing phenomena into a few variables[165]; all forms of rationality are not regarded as relevant in economics, neither are all incentives and costs; there are different views about efficiency; and there are different forms of rationality.

The reduction of society to a number of variables is likely to contribute to views that do not reflect its complexity and can be seen as simplistic and radical. The choice of variables depends on the subjective preferences of the researcher.

The rationality of law and economics is limited to what is regarded as rational in the technical or mathematical sense (Zweckrationalität). Other forms of rationality such as rationality as what is reasonable (Wertrationalität) or affectual are excluded.[166] Interestingly, many of the core ideas of law and economics originally were not stated in mathematical terms.[167]

Focusing on what is rational in the technical or mathematical sense contributes to a limited view on incentives and costs.[168] This is connected to the underlying

---

[161] *Ibid.*

[162] For Americanisation generally, see Juusola K, Kettunen K, Alajoutsijärvi K (2015). For examples, see La Porta R, Lopez-de-Silanes F, Shleifer A, Vishny RW (1998); André TJ Jr. (1998); Mäntysaari P (2005), pp. 245–246.

[163] McCloskey DN (1988); Murray MD (2012).

[164] Murray MD (2012).

[165] See also Krugman P (2009).

[166] For different forms of rationality, see Weber M (1922), Erster Teil, Kapitel I, § 2: "Wie jedes Handeln kann auch das soziale Handeln bestimmt sein 1. zweckrational ... 2. wertrational ... 3. affektuell ... 4. traditional ..." See also Simon HA (1991), p. 30 on motivation. For applications of rationality and bounded rationality, see Williamson OE (1985), p. 44; Kahneman D (2003). For the contingency theory, see Woodward J (1958); Schoonhoven CB (1981).

[167] Zimmerman JL (2001), p. 419: "Consider Fama's (1965, 1970) statement of the efficient markets hypothesis, Williamson's (1975, 1985) transaction cost economics, and the Jensen and Meckling (1976) agency theory ... Other examples of non-mathematical theories abound: Coase's (1937) theory of firms versus markets, Stigler's (1971) theory of regulation, the Watts and Zimmerman (1978, 1986) positive theory of accounting choice, the Scholes and Wolfson (1992) tax framework, and the Smith and Watts (1992) predictions regarding incentives and firms' investment opportunity sets."

[168] Hart O (2016): "After 47 years working in the area, I have learned that economics is both more and less powerful than people think. It is more powerful because it provides an indispensable set of tools for understanding human behavior ... This is the good news about economics ... The bad news is that it is not the whole story. For understanding many questions other things matter too:

political agenda. First, the prevailing rhetoric of economics is designed to allocate capital and income to wealthy economic elites that are not constrained by other incentives or costs in their pursuit of economic benefits. Second, the overemphasis on financial incentives, especially in the context of rewarding executives and other members of economic elites, is likely to contribute to too high compensation levels in the light of the fact that there are even other incentives.[169] Third, it is also designed to allocate costs that are difficult to determine or whose existence depends on personal preferences to somebody else. For example, there are things that do not have a market price but are very important for the functioning of Western society such as its Christian heritage,[170] equality, a working representative democracy and the rule of law. However, it would be difficult to define the price of such institutions, and even more difficult to define the societal effect and price of changes that make them weaker bit by bit (the sorites paradox).

One can also note that law and economics does not just reduce societal complexity to a small number of variables in its quest for efficiency. There are also different notions of 'efficiency'.[171] While the choice of efficiency as a benchmark depends on subjective values, even the choice of a particular notion of efficiency depends on them. Efficiency is thus not an 'objective' benchmark.

At the end of the day, efficiency is a bad benchmark for legislation. First, 'the law cannot be concerned solely with economic efficiency as the yardstick by which to measure the success of social goals'.[172] Second, '[w]ealth maximization is no substitute for the purpose of law in general'.[173]

Law and economics works much like any other political platform that has just one agenda. If one accepts that legal norms and the legal system only need to serve a single goal, one must accept that there can be competing platforms with just as legitimate goals. The choice of economic 'efficiency', whatever it means, as the guiding light for the design and interpretation of legal norms[174] is not less political than using other platforms such as 'the ecology of law'[175] or 'socialism' for the same purpose.

---

psychology, history, sociology, politics. This is the sense in which economics is less powerful than people think. It provides only part of the answer."

[169]For a broader view on managers' incentives, see Simon HA (1991), p. 30. See also Bebchuk LA, Fried JM (2003).

[170]Spencer N (2016).

[171]Malloy RP (2004), p. 20: "Efficiency and wealth maximization are both ambiguous and highly contested ideas."

[172]Goode RM (1998), p. 29. For commercial law, see also Mäntysaari P (2012), sections 3.6 and 3.7.

[173]Mestmäcker EJ (2007), p. 13.

[174]For a critique, see, for example, Posner EA (2002a); Mäntysaari P (2012), section 3.6.

[175]Capra F, Mattei U (2015), p. 128: "In order to solve our systemic problems, we need a total critique that leads out of the mechanistic trap. This is provided by an ecological understanding of law."

Early sociology had a connection to economics.[176] However, sociology and economics grew apart and became very different. Max Weber did not regard economics as a reality science: 'Economic theory makes certain assumptions which scarcely ever correspond completely with reality but which approximate it in various degrees and asks: how would men act under these assumed conditions, if their actions were entirely rational? It assumes the dominance of pure economic interests and precludes the operation of political or other non-economic considerations.'[177]

Economics thus has its own characteristic problems. Since law and economics means the application of economics in the field of law, it is plagued by the same problems as economics in general. They are caused by the fact that it is based on fictions, its narrow view, the vagueness of its core assumptions such as 'efficiency' and its focus on the welfare of economic elites. Moreover, the use of economics in legal science is coupled with problems caused by 'theory irritants'[178] (Sects. 2.3 and 6.2.3).

6.3.5 Law and Something and User-Friendly Legal Science

Experiences from the sociology of law, the science of history and law and economics may help to place User-Friendly Legal Science on the map of legal science and to understand its approach.

There is a fundamental difference between User-Friendly Legal Science and law and economics. Law and economics is positivist, while User-Friendly Legal Science is not. User-Friendly Legal Science has more common ground with legal sociology and legal history (as well as comparative law, Sect. 6.4).

The distinction between User-Friendly Legal Science and legal sociology is particularly important for the status of the former as an independent discipline.

Legal sociology and the new discipline are clearly united in their scientific ambitions and fields that consist of law in the broad sense and society. Whether the new discipline belongs to legal sociology obviously depends on how legal sociology is defined. One does find similarities between User-Friendly Legal Science and Eugen Ehrlich's theory of the sociology of law. Their primary sources seem to overlap.[179]

---

[176] Weber M (1949), pp. 64–65.

[177] Weber M (1949), pp. 43–44.

[178] For legal transplants and legal irritants, see Watson A (1974); Teubner G (1998).

[179] Ehrlich E (1913), pp. 405–406: "Die Erforschung des lebenden Rechts ist es also, womit die Soziologie des Rechts beginnen muß ... Es hat seinen eigenen Erkenntniswert, und dieser liegt darin, daß es die Grundlage der rechtlichen Ordnung der menschlichen Gesellschaft ist. Um diese kennen zu lernen, müssen wir die Übungen, Herrschafts- und Rechtsverhältnisse, Verträge, Satzungen, letztwilligen Erklärungen feststellen, ganz unabhängig davon, ob sie in einer Entscheidung oder in einem Gesetze bereits Ausdruck gefunden haben oder je darin Eingang finden würden." For living law in legal history, see Berman HJ (1983), pp. 4–5.

However, the new discipline does not belong to the sociology of law. These two disciplines describe societal reality in different ways. They do not share the same point of view. Moreover, one can assume that the reason why law and sociology remain separate after 100 years of efforts to integrate them[180] reflects the fact that the point of view of legal sociology is not aligned with the needs of legal practice. In contrast, User-Friendly Legal Science is designed as a practice-ready discipline.

Holistic Approach. User-Friendly Legal Science has as its goal interpretive understanding, takes a holistic approach and tries to describe societal reality from different perspectives. In this it resembles legal sociology and legal history.

The holistic research approach should play a role in research design when one chooses complementing theories for the research project (method theories, Sect. 3.3). Some theories are designed to share the holistic approach and to reflect existing societal reality. Other theories do not share the holistic research approach.

Economics is based on methodological individualism and a narrow view on societal reality.[181] One should therefore understand to what extent economic theories can be used in User-Friendly Legal Science. Economic concepts – and the concepts of law and economics – do not necessarily reflect existing laws and acceptable societal outcomes. This can be illustrated with company law (Sect. 5.3). Shareholders do not really own a limited liability company (they own shares issued by the company), and there are no legally enforceable contracts between providers of different resources to the firm (the hub of all contracts is the legal entity, that is, the limited liability company). States need good firms, but aligning the interests of managers with the interests of shareholders is not likely to make firms better (it is likely to make firms worse because the firm is not the same thing as its shareholders).[182] It is designed to increase the wealth of executives and short-term shareholders.

Field. The law-and-something disciplines and User-Friendly Legal Science partly share the same field. They share the field only partly because their respective fields (or coupled systems, Sect. 2.2) are discipline specific. In law-and-something disciplines, both the legal field and the other field are determined by the disciplinary requirements of the non-legal discipline (the 'something').[183] The fields (or coupled systems) of User-Friendly Legal Science are not limited by any other discipline.

---

[180]Banakar R (2015), pp. 21–22.

[181]See also Bourdieu P (1992), Part II, Chapter 1.

[182]In 2014, the share of manufacturing as value added of GDP was 23% in Germany, 12% in the US, and 10% in the UK. In Germany, board members have a legal duty to act in the interests of the firm. This may have contributed to the existence of better manufacturing firms in Germany. http://data.worldbank.org/indicator/NV.IND.MANF.ZS.

[183]For example, see Bourdieu P (1987), p. 817 for the juridical field: "The juridical field is the site of a competition for monopoly of the right to determine the law. Within this field there occurs a confrontation among actors possessing a technical competence which is inevitably social and which consists essentially in the socially recognized capacity to interpret a corpus of texts sanctifying a correct or legitimized vision of the social world." Bourdieu P (1987), p. 831: "The juridical field is a social space organized around the conversion of direct conflict between directly

Point of View. The law-and-something disciplines have different points of view. The point of view of law and economics is that of economics (the study of economic efficiency) applied in the legal field.[184] The point of view of legal sociology is that of sociology applied in the legal field. Since legal sociology is not limited to the study of Durkheim's social facts but covers even the coercion model and the experience model, it can be difficult to define its point of view.[185]

User-Friendly Legal Science is again different. Its point of view is how users can reach their objectives by legal tools and practices in different contexts. The point of view of User-Friendly Legal Science is that of a 'design science' or a science that produces 'constructions' (Sect. 2.5).

For example, while the study of Durkheim's social facts means the study of some external things that make people behave in certain ways,[186] User-Friendly Legal Science focuses on what people can do with legal tools in order to make external things happen.

Moreover, while both law and norms are defined in a very broad sense in legal sociology according to Ehrlich[187] and the different models of legal sociology, the legal tools of User-Friendly Legal Science are connected to their direct or indirect legal effect, that is, enforceability by external entities, rather than mere perceived normativity.

Primary Sources. Primary sources help to distinguish between User-Friendly Legal Science and the law-and-something disciplines. In order to be regarded as a legal science, the primary sources of the new discipline should consist of legal materials.

The primary sources are discipline specific. Each law-and-something discipline has its own primary sources. This can contribute to different knowledge interests. For example, both history and sociology belong to social sciences and are sometimes regarded as the same thing,[188] but the fact that they have different primary sources has influenced their knowledge interests.

---

concerned parties into juridically regulated debate between professionals acting by proxy. It is also the space in which such debate functions."

[184]Posner RA (1975).

[185]See already Ross A (1958), p. 20: "Sociology of law as a branch of science is as yet so new and undeveloped that it is difficult to state with which problems it is concerned."

[186]Durkheim É (1894).

[187]Ehrlich E (1913), p. 19: "Da das Recht eine gesellschaftliche Erscheinung ist, so gehört jede Art der Jurisprudenz den Gesellschaftswissenschaften an, aber die eigentliche Rechtswissenschaft ist ein Teil der theoretischen Gesellschaftswissenschaft, der Soziologie. Die Soziologie des Rechts ist die wissenschaftliche Lehre vom Rechte." Bourdieu P (1987), p. 814: "A rigorous science of the law is distinguished from what is normally called jurisprudence in that the former takes the latter as its object of study." Ross A (1958), § 5: "Jurisprudential analysis may direct its attention to both branches of the study of law–to the doctrinal study of law and to sociology of law."

[188]Giddens A (1984).

The primary sources and the point of view are thus interrelated. If the whole point of User-Friendly Legal Science is to study how different kinds of users use legal tools and practices to reach their objectives in different contexts, the primary sources cannot be limited to legislative materials, case law and law in the books. It is important to identify the legal tools and practices and to study as primary sources the legal texts in which they are documented. For example, the documents that provide information about the use of legal tools and practices can include legislative materials, contracts, wills, company documents, stock exchange rules, disclosures of financial information and other legal materials. In this respect, User-Friendly Legal Science seems to resemble legal history.

The Role of Legal Dogmatics. While legal sociology is more interested in law in general rather than its substance, the substance of law plays an important role in User-Friendly Legal Science because of its point of view and its role as the 'middle term' between law and practice (Chap. 1). The theoretical framework of legal dogmatics will thus need to be applied as a method theory in User-Friendly Legal Science (Sect. 3.3.3).

6.4 Comparative Law

6.4.1 General Remarks

There are similarities between User-Friendly Legal Science and comparative law.[189] Both use a functional approach and ideal types.[190] Both use a broad range of primary sources. Both can have a global reach.

Comparative law has long roots.[191] It was influenced by the scientific ideals of the twentieth century.[192] It is nowadays a research area that can use scientific methods.

One can distinguish between comparative law in the narrow and broad sense. In the broad sense, the contents of foreign law can be taken into account without

[189]See, for example, Mäntysaari P (2013), pp. 197–199; Zweigert K, Kötz H (1996), § 3 II; Glaser BG, Strauss AL (1967), pp. 25–26 (on one-case studies).

[190]For comparative law, see Hansen N (2008), section II.5: "This, the use of ideal types, 'prototypes', or constructed types both allows for a rational, structured description of social reality and replaces misleading taxonomic classifications with complex typologies. Such concepts offer a means of comparing complex matters of fact: similarities and differences may be formulated as deviations from the idealized concept."

[191]See Hug W (1932); Basedow J (2014); Basedow J (2016).

[192]Rabel E (1924): "Fassen wir ihre Aufgaben so streng, als das wissenschaftliche Ideal es verlangt." Zweigert K, Kötz H (1996), § 2 I: "Die primäre Funktion der Rechtsvergleichung ist – wie die aller wissenschaftlichen Methoden – Erkenntnis."

applying the comparative legal method as such.[193] Roscoe Pound argued that comparative aspects must be included in any methods of jurisprudence.[194] Foreign law is often taken into account in the context of legal dogmatics or national rule-making.[195]

In the narrow sense, comparative law is a research area with its own methods. This is a relatively late phenomenon. It started to flourish in continental Europe in the 1920s.[196] European integration, Community law and the approximation of Member States' laws have brought comparative aspects to mainstream legal science in Europe.[197]

A comparative study can be a legal requirement under certain circumstances. The legal requirements can be illustrated with the following examples (Jürgen Basedow):

- The 'general principles of law recognized by civilized nations' are regarded as a source of international law.[198] Identifying these general principles of law is an inductive exercise that requires a comparative legal study: 'Comparative law research plays an important role in uncovering these principles and determining them as precisely as possible.'[199]
- The general principles of law common to many countries may need to be taken into account when interpreting international conventions designed to harmonise the provisions of the participating states' laws.[200]
- International private law and the law of the international jurisdiction of courts have a close connection to comparative law.
- Comparative studies can play an important role in EU law. For example, there are references to the general principles common to the laws of the Member States,[201] the prohibition of restrictions that are not in compliance with the four

[193]An early example of this approach in international law was Grotius H (1625).

[194]Pound R (1959), Chapter 1, p. 21: "The analytical, historical, and analytical methods, as methods of jurisprudence must be comparative."

[195]Kadner TM (2007), pp. 248–249.

[196]In 1920, Lambert founded the Institut de droit comparé in Lyon. L'Académie internationale de droit comparé (the International Academy of Comparative law) was founded in 1924. In 1926, Rabel founded the Kaiser-Wilhelm-Institut für ausländisches und internationales Privatrecht in Berlin, now the Max Planck Institute for Comparative and International Private Law in Hamburg. In the same year, L'Institut international pour l'unification du droit privé (Unidroit, the International Institute for the Unification of Private Law) was set up in Rome as an auxiliary organ of the League of Nations. In 1931, Lévy-Ullmann and Capitant founded the Institut de droit comparé of the University of Paris.

[197]Kadner TM (2007), p. 249: "Bei allen auf Europäisierung des Privatrechts gerichteten Initiativen kommt der rechtsvergleichenden Methode eine Schlüsselrolle zu."

[198]Article 38 of the International Court of Justice Statute. See Basedow J (2016).

[199]Mosler H (1995), p. 517. See also Rabel E (1927), p. 11; Basedow J (2016).

[200]See Article 7 of the CISG; Basedow J (2016).

[201]See, for example, Article 340(2) TFEU.

freedoms are complemented by the prohibition of measures that produce an equivalent effect[202] and comparative law obviously plays an important role even in the approximation of Member States' laws.
- Moreover, the minimum scope of human rights may depend on a comparative analysis of the protection granted by the laws of many countries.[203]

We will focus on comparative law in the narrow sense (Sect. 6.4.2) and have a look at the similarities and differences between comparative law and User-Friendly Legal Science (Sect. 6.4.3).

6.4.2 The Comparative Method

Comparative law and the comparative method are chosen for a reason.[204] The choice depends on the ultimate goal of the study and can be a question of subjective, political or other preferences rather than a purely scientific exercise or a question of compliance with legal requirements. The choice may depend on the expected results of the study. For example, comparative legal arguments based on a study of certain jurisdictions can support a particular interpretation of existing national law or a particular legislative or regulatory alternative or give reason to solve societal problems either this way or that way such as through regulation or unregulation. The choice of other jurisdictions might provide counterarguments.

Just like in other disciplines, research design largely depends on subjective values.[205] However, this does not render the whole research process arbitrary and unscientific. There is room for the application of scientific methods based on the chosen research design.

The findings can be used in various ways depending on the ultimate goal of the study and the knowledge interests of the user. This may require evaluation.[206] For Ernst Rabel, evaluation was not part of comparison.[207] In any case, evaluation depends on the chosen framework: you cannot say what outcome is 'the best' or

[202]Case 120/78 Rewe-Zentral AG v Bundesmonopolverwaltung für Branntwein (Cassis de Dijon), paragraph 8. See nevertheless Case C-384/93 Alpine Investments BV v Minister van Financiën, paragraph 51. Basedow J (2016).

[203]See Basedow J (2016).

[204]See, for example, *ibid*: "Grund und Zweck der Rechtsvergleichung sind also zwar nicht identisch, sie greifen aber ineinander. Dies hat zur Folge, dass der erwartete Nutzen oft genug zurückwirkt auf die Initiierung und die Ausgestaltung rechtsvergleichender Forschung."

[205]Basedow J (2014): "The difficulties start as soon as we tackle any specific subject and try to design comparative research."

[206]Zweigert K, Kötz H (1996), § 2 I: "Die Rechtsvergleichung ... bietet dem kritischen Betrachter die Chance, die für die jeweilige Zeit und den jeweiligen Raum »bessere Lösung« zu erkennen."

[207]Rabel E (1924).

desirable unless there is a framework for the assessment of the quality of different outcomes in the chosen context.[208]

Purpose. Generally, a comparative study can serve different purposes, and there is a 'broad array of scholarly interests in comparative enquiries'. One can compare 'for the sole sake of understanding' or in order to 'pursue a given purpose' such as for the purposes of legislation, interpretation, education and harmonisation.[209] The comparative study can be a legal requirement[210] or not required by laws. Moreover, the purpose of a comparative study can be (1) epistemological (understanding legal rules and institutions), (2) comparative (achieving comparability), (3) presumptive (emphasising similarity), (4) formalising (system building), (5) evaluative (determining the better law), (6) universalising (preparing legal unification) or (7) critical (providing tools for the critique of law).[211]

Methods. The choice of the method depends on the nature of the study. One can distinguish between traditional comparative law and comparative empirical study of law and between micro-comparison and macro-comparison.

Traditional Comparative Law, the Functional Method. In the field of traditional comparative law, one can distinguish between micro-comparison and macro-comparison. The functional method is the mainstream legal method in micro-comparison.[212] The purpose of the functional method is simply to facilitate the comparison of comparable things. It means the comparison of sets of all legal norms that share the same chosen function. The function and common denominator (tertium comparationis) that permits comparison is the attainment of a particular social purpose. The functional method is not suitable for macro-comparison.

At the core of the functional method lies functionalism. There are several notions of functionalism across disciplines.[213] However, the existence of different

---

[208]For example, history provided such a framework in von Jhering R (1868), pp. 75–76: "Denn die Geschichte selber ist, wie Hegel gesagt hat, das Weltgericht; die Sünden der Väter strafen sich an den Kindern, und wer in der Geschichte suchen will, was gut und böse, der wird es erkennen können an dem Segen, der auch hier auf der guten, und dem Fluch, der auf der bösen Tat ruht."

[209]Basedow J (2014); Zweigert K, Kötz H (1996), § 2 I.

[210]See Basedow J (2016).

[211]Michaels R (2008), Chapter 10, Section III.

[212]Zweigert K, Kötz H (1996) is a standard work on comparative law and the functional method. For the functional method, see also Husa J (2003); Brand O (2007); Michaels R (2008); De Coninck J (2010).

[213]Michaels R (2008), Chapter 10, Section II: "In fact, one can distinguish at least seven different concepts of functionalism across disciplines: (1) finalism, a neo-Aristotelian functionalism based on inherent teleogy, (2) adaptionism, an evalutionary functionalism in a Darwinian tradition, (3) classical (Durkheimian) functionalism, explaining institutions through their usefulness for society, (4) instrumentalism, a normative theory of usign law for social engineering, (5) refined functionalism, a functionalist method that replaces certain postulates of classical functionalism with empirically testable hypotheses, (6) epistemological functionalism, an epistemology that focuses on functional relations rather than on the ontology of things, and (7) equivalence functionalism, building on these concepts but emphasizing the non-teleological, non-causal aspect of functional relations."

notions of functionalism has not been regarded as relevant in functionalist comparative law.[214]

Since comparative law is an area of legal science rather than sociology, the functional method primarily focuses on sets of legal things that share the same function rather than sets of social things that share the same function.[215] This partly answers the question of primary sources and the question how deep the researcher is expected to go.

The functional method can be applied provided that the research question is defined so narrowly that it only covers a limited number of phenomena. Unless the research question is defined narrowly, the researcher cannot take into account all relevant sets of legal things.[216]

The researcher is also expected to identify similarities and differences between the ways the issue has been addressed by legal means in the chosen jurisdictions and to explain their existence. In order to describe the reason for the existence of similarities and differences, the researcher may need to dig deeper into legal practice and legal culture and to study economic, social and cultural factors. For example, it may turn out that differences in laws are connected with general societal differences: the function (say, ensuring gender equality in employment) enables the comparison of laws as tertium comparationis, but the comparative study can reveal differences in the relevance of the function attributable to cultural or religious reasons (say, between Sweden and Saudi Arabia).[217] On the other hand, different legal systems can give very different solutions to the same problems (say, corporate governance) even where the societies are relatively similar (say, the US and Germany).[218]

One must therefore distinguish between the choice of comparable things for the comparative study, the comparison of the comparable things and describing the reason for the existence of similarities and differences.

Before answering the research question in the light of the ultimate goal of the study, the researcher may need a theoretical platform that acts as a frame of reference (and method theory). For example, functionality often serves as an evaluative criterion when functionalist comparative law is reduced to a better-law comparison: 'the better of several laws is that which fulfils its function better than

[214]Michaels R (2008), Chapter 10, Section II.8: "Which of these concepts underlies the functional method of comparative law? The answer is: all of the above. Comparative lawyers pick and choose different concepts, regardless of their incompatibility."

[215]For the connection between comparative law and sociology, see Cotterrell R (2006), Chapters 8–9.

[216]See, for example, Mäntysaari P (2005), section 2.3.5; Likhovski A (2003), pp. 630–631.

[217]Differences in the relevance of the function were perhaps not fully recognised by Zweigert K, Kötz H (1996), § II–III. They assumed that the legal problems of all countries are similar.

[218]Zweigert K, Kötz H (1996), § 3 III assumed that different developed legal systems give the same or very similar solution to the same problems of life. However, they also pointed out that legal norms may not be necessary where social norms serve the same purpose. See *ibid*, § 3 II.

the others'.[219] In principle, there should be a theory providing a framework for the assessment of when the function is 'fulfilled better'. Some comparatists have turned to economic theory: 'The proximity between functionalist comparative law and economics has been recognized before: economic efficiency can serve as a benchmark against which legal systems are measured.'[220] Consequently, law and economics scholars have questioned the relevance of comparative law.[221]

Comparative Empirical Study of Law. Traditional comparative law is complemented by the comparative empirical study of law. Unlike the functional method of traditional comparative law that tries to include all legal factors that share the same function, the empirical study of law means that legal phenomena are reduced to a small number of variables that can be given a numeric value.[222] It can also take the form of qualitative comparative analysis (QCA).[223]

Related concepts include law and economics, law and finance, and legal origins.[224] (a) Law and economics and the comparative empirical study of law share the use of quantitative research methods. The difference is that law and economics focuses on overall social welfare and does not need to compare different jurisdictions. (b) There is a bigger difference between the comparative empirical study of law and law and finance. While the former means the use of particular numerical and statistical methods, law and finance is a research area. The best-known study in the area of law and finance is La Porta, Lopez-de-Silanes, Shleifer and Vishny (1998).[225] (c) The legal origins approach is in the intersection point of comparative empirical study of law and law and finance.[226] There is a stream of research in law and finance explaining differences between the financial markets

[219]Michaels R (2008), Chapter 10, Section I.

[220]Michaels R (2009), p. 777.

[221]Basedow J (2014): "In more recent years, I attended a conference on the international sale of goods organized by the New York University School of Law at Fiesole/Italy. Most of the American speakers turned out to adhere to the economic analysis of law; their papers did not refer to any specific national sales law, but discussed the economic pros and cons of hypothetical solutions for hypothetical cases. Quite to the contrary, the European attendees struggled with various national rules of sales law and the conflicts they may bring about in cross-border cases. In the discussion following my own presentation, one of the American professors asked: 'What can we learn from comparative law that we do not already know from economic theory?'"

[222]Lieder J (2010), p. 228.

[223]Herala N (2004), p. 17: "Qualitative comparative analysis, or QCA, combines two ways of simplifying complexity. It both examines similarities and differences between a limited number of cases, and it inspects relations between variables (Ragin 1987:XIII). QCA could be described as a variable-oriented qualitative comparative method." See also Ragin CC (1987).

[224]Lieder J (2010), pp. 228–230; Eidenmüller H (2007), pp. 486–495.

[225]La Porta R, Lopez-de-Silanes F, Shleifer A, Vishny RW (1998). See also Djankov S, La Porta R, Lopez-de-Silanes F, Shleifer A (2008); Djankov S, Glaeser E, La Porta R, Lopez-de-Silanes F, Shleifer A (2003).

[226]Gleaser EL, Shleifer A (2002); Lieder J (2010), pp. 229–230; Michaels R (2009).

of different countries by the presumed quality of each country's legal system. In other words, 'legal origins matter'. The results have been controversial.[227]

6.4.3 Comparative Law and User-Friendly Legal Science

User-Friendly Legal Science shares many things with comparative law. Both are creations of legal science rather than applications of other disciplines in the legal field. Moreover, both share the functional research perspective.

In epistemological respects, there can be similarities between the method of User-Friendly Legal Science and the functional method of comparative law applied in micro-comparison. The similarities can be explained by three things.

First, when the researcher chooses and defines the research question in User-Friendly Legal Science, the researcher's approach is 'functional'. A comparative study that is based on the use of the functional method and focuses on the interests of a particular class of users can reveal at least some of the users' objectives[228] and some of their legal tools and practices. This works the other way round as well. There could be two-way traffic. A user-friendly study can provide useful information about the parties' objectives, tools and practices.

Second, the nature of the functional method[229] is scientific. What is not scientific in comparative law is, for example, the choice of the ultimate goal of the study and the use of its results as argumentum ad rem in legal rhetoric.

Third, User-Friendly Legal Science and comparative law define their respective scopes in relation to sociology in related ways. Comparative law studies legal norms rather than social facts in general, and its primary sources are normative. Some older functionalists have even turned to fictions of societal reality in order to exclude the need to study social facts. They assume that different legal systems address similar needs and end up addressing them in similar ways.[230] User-Friendly Legal Science studies the use of legal tools and practices rather than social facts, and its primary sources should include legally relevant materials.

However, because of its point of view, User-Friendly Legal Science does not study exactly the same phenomena as comparative law.

User-Friendly Legal Science is not comparative as such. The context nevertheless has a geographical scope that can influence the number of jurisdictions relevant for the study (Sect. 2.2).

---

[227]See Klerman DM, Mahoney PG (2007).

[228]You can find an example about comparative corporate governance and corporate governance in Mäntysaari P (2005), section 2.3; Mäntysaari P (2010a), section 8.2 and Mäntysaari P (2012), Chapters 7–9.

[229]Zweigert K, Kötz H (1996), § 2 I and § 3 I.

[230]Zweigert K, Kötz H (1996), § 3 III. For a critique, see Brand O (2007), pp. 409–410.

Moreover, comparative legal studies must focus on a narrower range of legal instruments. In a comparative and functional study, you study how a certain social need has been addressed in two or more jurisdictions by legal norms. Legal norms are the product of external rule-making.[231] They are customarily adopted by the state. In contrast, User-Friendly Legal Science is not limited to the study of external legal norms in this or that jurisdiction. It can study all relevant legal tools and practices subject to the geographical scope of the context.

References

André T Jr (1998) Cultural hegemony: the exportation of Anglo-Saxon corporate governance ideologies to Germany. Tulane Law Rev 73:69–171

Ast DF (1808) Grundlinien der Grammatik, Hermeneutik und Kritik. Bei Jos. Thomann, Buchdrucker und Buchhändler, Landshut

Augustine of Hippo (426–427) De doctrina christiana

Banakar R (2006) How can sociology and jurisprudence learn from each other? A reply to Mauro Zamboni. Retfærd 29(2):75–84

Banakar R (2015) Normativity in legal sociology: methodological reflections on law and regulation in late modernity. Springer International Publishing, Switzerland. doi:10.1007/978-3-319-09650-6

Banakar R, Travers M (2005a) Introduction. In: Banakar R, Travers M (eds) Theory and method in socio-legal research. Hart Publishing, Oxford and Portland Oregon, pp ix–xvi

Banakar R, Travers M (2005b) Law, sociology and method. In: Banakar R, Travers M (eds) Theory and method in socio-legal research. Hart Publishing, Oxford and Portland Oregon, pp 1–25

Basedow J (2014) Comparative law and its clients. Am J Comp Law 62(4):821–857

Basedow J (2016) Hundert Jahre Rechtsvergleichung – von wissenschaftlicher Erkenntnisquelle zur obligatorischen Methode der Rechtsanwendung. JuristenZeitung 71(6):269–280

Bebchuk LA, Fried JM (2003) Executive compensation as an agency problem. J Econ Perspect 17 (3):71–92

Berglund L, Ney A (2015) Historikerns hantverk: om historieskrivning, teori och metod. Studentlitteratur, Lund

Berman HJ (1983) Law and revolution: the formation of the Western legal tradition. Harvard University Press, Cambridge

Bjarup J (2005) The philosophy of Scandinavian legal realism. Ratio Juris 18:1–15. doi:10.1111/j.1467-9337.2005.00282.x

Bobbitt P (1991) Constitutional interpretation. Blackwells, Oxford and Cambridge, Mass

Bourdieu P (1987) The force of law: toward a sociology of the juridical field. Hastings Law J 38:814–853

Bourdieu P (1992) Les règles de l'art: genèse et structure du champ littéraire. Seuil, Paris

Brand O (2007) Conceptual comparisons: towards a coherent methodology of comparative legal studies. Brooklyn J Int Law 32(2):405–466

[231] Zweigert K, Kötz H (1996), § 3 II: "Bei allen diesen Beispielen ist es freilich immer noch so, daß es *rechtliche* Regeln (wenn auch unterschiedlicher systematischer Verkleidung) sind, die wir miteinander in Bezug setzen müssen. Oft genug muß der Rechtsvergleicher aber darüber hinausgreifen . . ."

Campbell CM, Wiles P (1976) The study of law in society in Britain. Law Soc Rev 10(4):547–578. doi:10.2307/3053297
Capra F, Mattei U (2015) The ecology of law: toward a legal system in tune with nature and community. Berrett-Koehler Publishers, Inc., Oakland
Cohen ML (2007) Researching legal history in the digital age. Law Libr J 99(2):377–393
Coing H (1976) Aufgaben des Rechtshistorikers. Sitzungsberichte der wissenschaftlichen Gesellschaft an der Johann-Wolfgang-Goethe-Universität Frankfurt am Main, Bd. XIII, Nr. 5. Frank Steiner, Wiesbaden, pp 146–184
Cotterrell R (1995) Law's community: legal theory in sociological perspective. Clarendon Press, Oxford
Cotterrell R (2006) Law, culture and society: legal ideas in the mirror of social theory. Ashgate, Aldershot
Dalberg-Larsen J (2005) Alf Ross and the sociology of law. Scand Stud Law 48:39–50
De Coninck J (2010) The functional method of comparative law: quo Vadis? Rabels Zeitschrift für ausländisches und internationales Privatrecht 74:318–350
Dellavalle S (2016) Law as a linguistic instrument without truth content? On the epistemology of Koskenniemi's understanding of law. Max Planck Institute for Comparative Public Law & International Law (MPIL) Research Paper No. 2016–08
Directors of the Columbia Law Review Association, Inc. (1964) Notes. Modern trends in legal education. Columbia Law Rev 64(4):710–734
Djankov S, Glaeser E, La Porta R, Lopez-de-Silanes F, Shleifer A (2003) The new comparative economics. J Comp Econ 31:595–619
Djankov S, La Porta R, Lopez-de-Silanes F, Shleifer A (2008) The law and economics of self-dealing. J Financ Econ 88:430–465
Durkheim É (1894) Les régles de la méthode sociologique. Revue philosophique
Ehrlich E (1912) Das lebende Recht der Völker der Bukowina. Reprinted in: Rehbinder M (ed) (1967) Eugen Ehrlich, Recht und Leben, Duncker & Humblot, Berlin, pp 43–60
Ehrlich E (1913) Grundlegung der Soziologie des Rechts. Duncker & Humblot, München and Leipzig
Ehrlich E (1936) Fundamental principles of the sociology of law. Harvard University Press, Cambridge
Eidenmüller H (2005) Effizienz als Rechtsprinzip. Die Einheit der Gesellschaftswissenschaften 90. Mohr Siebeck, Tübingen
Eidenmüller H (2007) Forschungsperspektiven im Unternehmensrecht. Zeitschrift für Unternehmens- und Gesellschaftsrecht 36(4):484–499
Engel C, Schön W (eds) (2007) Das Proprium der Rechtswissenschaft. Recht – Wissenschaft – Theorie. Mohr Siebeck, Tübingen
Epstein RA (2002) Let "the fundamental things apply": necessary and contingent truths in legal scholarship. Harv Law Rev 115(5):1288–1313
Ferraro F, Pfeffer J, Sutton RI (2005) Economics language and assumptions: how theories can become self-fulfilling. Acad Manag Rev 30(1):8–24. doi:10.5465/AMR.2005.15281412
Firat AF (1987) Historiography, scientific method, and exceptional historical events. In: Wallendorf M, Anderson P (eds) Advances in consumer research, vol 14. Association for Consumer Research, Provo, Utah, pp 435–438
Fisk C, Gordon RW (2011) Foreword: "law as ...": theory and method in legal history. UC Irvine Law Rev 1(3):519–541
Fleischer H (2001) Grundfragen der ökonomischen Theorie im Gesellschafts- und Kapitalmarktrecht. Zeitschrift für Unternehmens- und Gesellschaftsrecht 30(1):1–32
Fleischer H (2007a) Zur Zukunft der gesellschafts- und kapitalmarktrechtlichen Forschung. Zeitschrift für Unternehmens- und Gesellschaftsrecht 36(4):500–510
Fleischer H (2007b) Gesellschafts- und Kapitalmarktrecht als wissenschaftliche Disziplin – Das Proprium der Rechtswissenschaft. In: Engel C, Schön W (eds) Das Proprium der Rechtswissenschaft. Recht - Wissenschaft - Theorie 1. Mohr Siebeck, Tübingen, pp 50–76

Flohr M (2008) Beyond the state – Rethinking private law symposium in Hamburg am 12. Und 13. Juli 2007. Rabels Zeitschrift für ausländisches und internationales Privatrecht 72(2):391–396. doi:10.1628/003372508784080645
Frank J (1931) The Bramble Bush: some lectures on law and its study by K. N. Llewellyn. Yale Law J 40(7):1120–1125
Gast W (2015) Juristische Rhetorik. 5., überarbeitete und erweiterte Auflage. C.F. Müller Verlag, Heidelberg
Giddens A (1984) The constitution of society: outline of the theory of structuration. Polity Press, Oxford, and University of California Press, Berkeley and Los Angeles
Glaser BG, Strauss AL (1967) The discovery of grounded theory: strategies for qualitative research. Aldine de Gruyter, New York
Gleaser EL, Shleifer A (2002) Legal origins. Q J Econ 117:1193–1229
Goode RM (1998) Commercial law in the next millenium. The Hamlyn Lectures. Forty-ninth Series. Sweet & Maxwell, London
Graver HP (2008) Vanlig juridisk metode? Om rettsdogmatikken som juridisk sjanger. Tidsskrift for Rettsvitenskap 121(2):149–178
Grotius H (1625) De jure belli ac pacis libri tres. Apud Nicalaum Buon, Pariisis
Grundmann S, Micklitz HW, Renner M (eds) (2015) Privatrechtstheorie. Mohr Siebeck, Tübingen
Hansen N (2008) Comparative law and comparative knowledge. In: Reimann M, Zimmermann R (eds) The Oxford handbook of comparative law. Oxford handbooks in law. Oxford University Press, Oxford, Chapter 9, pp 305–338
Hart HLA (2012) The concept of law, 3rd edn. With an introduction by Leslie Green. Oxford University Press, Oxford
Hart O (2016) Oliver Hart - Banquet Speech. Nobelprize.org. Nobel Media AB. http://www.nobelprize.org/nobel_prizes/economic-sciences/laureates/2016/hart-speech.html
Heck P (1914) Gesetzesauslegung und Interessenjurisprudenz. Archiv für die civilistische Pracis 112:1–318
Heidegger M (1926) Sein und Zeit. Max Niemeyer Verlag, Tübingen
Herala N (2004) Use of Qualitative Comparative Analysis (QCA) in comparative law. Acta Wasaensia 124, Universitas Wasaensis, Vaasa
Holmes OW (1897) The path of the law. Harv Law Rev 10:457–490
Hug W (1932) The history of comparative law. Harv Law Rev 45:1027–1070
Hull NEH (1997) Roscoe Pound and Karl Llewellyn: searching for an American jurisprudence. University of Chicago Press, Chicago
Hume D (1739) A treatise of human nature. John Noon, London
Husa J (2003) Farewell to functionalism or methodological tolerance? Rabels Zeitschrift für ausländisches und internationales Privatrecht 67:419–447
Hydén H (2011) Looking at the world through the lenses of norms. Nine reasons for norms: a plea for norm science. In: Papendorf K, Machura S, Andenaes K (eds) Understanding law in society. Developments in socio-legal studies. LIT Verlag, Berlin, pp 120–159
Hydén H (2013) Rättssociologi: om att undersöka relationen mellan rätt och samhälle. In: Korling F, Zamboni M (eds) Juridisk metodlära. Studentlitteratur, Lund, pp 207–237
Iggers GG (1962) The image of Ranke in American and German historical thought. Hist Theory 2 (1):17–40. doi:10.2307/2504333
Iggers GG (1984) New directions in European historiography. Wesleyan University Press, Middletown, Connecticut
Juusola K, Kettunen K, Alajoutsijärvi K (2015) Accelerating the Americanization of management education: five responses from business schools. J Manage Inq 24:347–369. doi:10.1177/1056492615569352
Kadner TM (2007) Die Europäisierung der juristischen Perspektive und der vergleichenden Methode – Fallstudien. Zeitschrift für vergleichende Rechtswissenschaft 106(3):248–271
Kahneman D (2003) Maps of bounded rationality: psychology for behavioral economics. Am Econ Rev 93(5):1449–1475

Kelsen H (1911) Über Grenzen zwischen juristischer und soziologischer Methode, Vortrag gehalten in der Soziologischen Gesellschaft zu Wien. J.C.B. Mohr (P. Siebeck), Tübingen. / Partly translated into English by Cooper B in Kelsen H (2000) On the borders between legal and sociological method. In: Jacobson AJ, Schlink B (eds) Weimar: a jurisprudence of crisis. University of California Press, Berkeley, Los Angeles and London, pp 57–63

Kelsen H (1934) Reine Rechtslehre: Einleitung in die rechtswissenschaftliche Problematik, 1. Aufl. Deuticke, Leipzig Wien. / Jestaedt M (ed) (2008) Studienausgabe. Mohr Siebeck, Tübingen

Kelsen H (2013) A "realistic" theory of law and the pure theory of law: remarks on Alf Ross's on law and justice. In: d'Almeida LD, Gardner J, Green L (eds) Kelsen revisited: new essays on the pure theory of law. Hart Publishing, Oxford and Portland, pp 195–221

Kieser A (2004) The Americanization of academic management education in Germany. J Manage Inq 13(2):90–97. doi:10.1177/1056492604265301

Klerman DM (2002) Statistical and economic approaches to legal history. Univ Illinois Law Rev 2002(4):1167–1176

Klerman DM, Mahoney PG (2007) Legal origin? J Comp Econ 35:278–293

Krugman P (2009) How did economists get it so wrong? New York Times, September 2, 2009

Kuhn TS (1970) The structure of scientific revolutions, 2nd edn. University of Chicago Press, Chicago

La Porta R, Lopez-de-Silanes F, Shleifer A, Vishny RW (1998) Law and finance. J Polit Econ 106 (6):1113–1155

Lamprecht K (1896) Alte und neue Richtungen in der Geschichtewissenschaft (1896). R. Gartners Verlagsbuchhandlung, Berlin

Langdell CC (1871) A selection of cases on the law of contracts. Little, Brown and Co., Boston

Larenz K (1966) Über die Unentbehrlichkeit der Jurisprudenz als Wissenschaft. Berlin

Leiter B (2001a) Legal realism and legal positivism reconsidered. Ethics 111(2):278–301

Leiter B (2007) Naturalizing jurisprudence: essays on American legal realism and naturalism in legal philosophy. Oxford University Press, Oxford

Leiter B (2009) Naturalizing jurisprudence: three approaches. In: Shook J, Kurtz P (eds) The future of naturalism. Prometheus Books, Amherst, pp 197–207

Lieder J (2010) Legal Origins und empirische Rechtsvergleichung. Zur Bedeutung des Rechts für die Entwicklung von Kapitalmärkten und Corporate-Governance-Strukturen. Zeitschrift für Vergleichende Rechtswissenschaft 109:216–264

Likhovski A (2003) Czernowitz, Lincoln, Jerusalem, and the comparative history of American jurisprudence. Theor Inq Law 4:621–657

Llewellyn KN (1930) The bramble bush: some lectures on law and its study. Columbia University School of Law, New York

Llewellyn KN (1935) On what is wrong with so-called legal education. Columbia Law Rev 35 (5):651–678

Lobban M (2012) The varieties of legal history. Clio@Thémis 5:1–29

LoPucki LM (2016) Dawn of the discipline-based law faculty. J Leg Educ 65:506–542

Mæhle SS (2015) Rettsvitenskapelig forskningsmetodikk – i lys av grunnleggende forskningsverdier. Tidsskrift for Rettsvitenskap 128(2):125–157

Maitland FW (1911) Why the history of English law is not written. In: Fisher HAL (ed) The collected papers of Frederick William Maitland, vol I. University Press, Cambridge, pp 480–497

Malloy RP (2004) Law in a market context: an introduction to market concepts in legal reasoning. Cambridge University Press, Cambridge

Mäntysaari P (2005) Comparative corporate governance: shareholders as a rule-maker. Springer, Berlin Heidelberg

Mäntysaari P (2010a) The law of corporate finance: general principles and EU law. Volume I: Cash flow, risk, agency, information. Springer, Berlin Heidelberg

Mäntysaari P (2010b) The law of corporate finance: general principles and EU law. Volume II: Contracts in general. Springer, Berlin/Heidelberg
Mäntysaari P (2012) Organising the firm: theories of commercial law, corporate governance and corporate law. Springer, Berlin Heidelberg
Mäntysaari P (2013) Was sollte man tun? Ein Plädoyer für anwenderfreundliche Rechtswissenschaft. Rechtstheorie 44(2):189–207. doi:10.3790/rth.44.2.189
Mäntysaari P (2016a) Auditorier och retorik. Tidsskrift for Rettsvitenskap 129(1):1–42. doi:10.18261/issn.1504–3096–2016-01-01
Maslow AH (1966) The psychology of science: a reconnaissance. Harper & Row, New York
Mathiesen T (1973) Inledning. In: Edling S, Elwin G (eds) Rättssociologi: om lag, konflikt och behov. Wahlström & Widstrand, Stockholm, pp 9–14
McCloskey DN (1988) The rhetoric of law and economics. Mich Law Rev 86(4):752–767. doi:10.2307/1289214
Mestmäcker EJ (2007) A legal theory without law: Posner v. Hayek on economic analysis of law. Walter Eucken Institut, Beiträge zur Ordnungstheorie und Ordnungspolitik 174. Mohr Siebeck, Tübingen
Michaels R (2008) The functional method of comparative law. In: Reimann M, Zimmermann R (eds) The Oxford handbook of comparative law. Oxford handbooks in law. Oxford University Press, Oxford, Chapter 10, pp 339–382
Michaels R (2009) Comparative law by numbers? Legal origins thesis, doing business reports, and the silence of traditional comparative law. Am J Comp Law 57:765–795
Miles TJ, Sunstein CR (2008) The new legal realism. Univ Chicago Law Rev 75:831–851
Mosler H (1995) General principles of law. In: Bernhardt R (ed) Encyclopedia of public international law, vol II. North-Holland, Amsterdam, pp 511–527
Murray MD (2012) The Great Recession and the rhetorical canons of law and economics. Valparaiso University, Law Faculty Publications, Paper 40
Nobleman E (1961) Review of Roscoe Pound, Treatise on jurisprudence. Am Univ Law Rev 10:179–199
Olsen L (2004) Rättsvetenskapliga perspektiv. Svensk Juristtidning 89(2):105–145
Perelman C, Olbrechts-Tyteca L (1971) The new rhetoric: a treatise on argumentation. University of Notre Dame Press, Notre Dame
Petersen J (2014) Max Webers Rechtssoziologie und die juristische Methodenlehre, 2. Auflage. Mohr Siebeck, Tübingen
Posner RA (1975) The economic approach to law. Texas Law Rev 53:757–782
Posner RA (1995) Overcoming law. Harvard University Press, Cambridge
Posner EA (2002a) Book Review: Kraus, Jody S., and Walt, Steven D., eds., The jurisprudential foundations of corporate and commercial law. Ethics 112:626–628
Posner RA (2002b) Legal scholarship today. Harv Law Rev 115(5):1314–1326
Posner RA (2010) How judges think. Harvard University Press, Cambridge
Pound R (1910) Law in books and law in action. Am Law Rev 44:12–36
Pound R (1959) Jurisprudence, vol 1. West Publishing Co., St. Paul, Minn
Rabel E (1924) Aufgabe und Notwendigkeit der Rechtsvergleichung. In: Leser HG (ed) (1967) Ernst Rabel: Gesammelte Aufsätze, vol III. Mohr Siebeck, Tübingen, pp 1–21
Rabel E (1927) Rechtsvergleichung und internationale Rechtsprechung. Rabels Zeitschrift für ausländisches und internationales Privatrecht 1:5–47
Ragin CC (1987) The comparative method: moving beyond qualitative and quantitative strategies. University of California Press, Berkeley, Los Angeles, London
Rakoff TD (2002) Introduction to symposium: law, knowledge, and the academy. Harv Law Rev 115:1278–1287
Rhode DL (2002) Legal scholarship. Harv Law Rev 115(5):1327–1361. doi:10.2307/1342548
Ross A (1953) Om ret og retfærdighed. Nyt Nordisk Forlag Arnold Busck, Copenhagen
Ross A (1958) On law and justice. Stevens & Sons Limited, London

Ryan B, Scapens RW, Theobald M (1992) Research method and methodology in finance and accounting. Academic Press, London
Sandgren C (2005) Om teoribildning och rättsvetenskap. Juridisk Tidskrift 16(2):297–333
Sarat A, Anderson M, Frank CO (2010) Introduction: on the origins and prospects of the humanistic study of law. In: Sarat A, Anderson M, Frank CO (eds) Law and the humanities: an introduction. Cambridge University Press, Cambridge, pp 1–46
Schiff D (1981) N.S. Timasheff's sociology of law. Mod Law Rev 44(4):400–421. doi:10.1111/j.1468-2230.1981.tb02751.x
Schoonhoven CB (1981) Problems with contingency theory: testing assumptions hidden within the language of contingency "theory". Adm Sci Q 26(3):349–377
Schopenhauer A (1830) Eristische Dialektik: Die Kunst, Recht zu Behalten
Shapiro SJ (2006) What is the internal point of view? Fordham Law Rev 75:1157–1170
Sieber U (2010) Rechtliche Ordnung in einer globalen Welt. Die Entwicklung zu einem fragmentierten System von nationalen, internationalen und privaten Normen. Rechtstheorie 41(2):151–198. doi:10.3790/rth.41.2.151
Simon HA (1991) Organizations and markets. J Econ Perspect 5(2):25–44
Spencer N (2016) The evolution of the West: how Christianity has shaped our values. SPCK, London
Stigler GJ (1971) The theory of economic regulation. Bell J Econ Manage Sci 2(1):3–21
Stolleis M (2008) Rechtsgeschichte schreiben. Rekonstruktion, Erzählung, Fiktion? Jacob Burckhardt-Gespräche auf Castelen 21. Schwabe, Basel
Svensson M (2008) Sociala normer och regelefterlevnad: Trafiksäkerhetsfrågor ur ett rättssociologiskt perspektiv. Lund Studies in Sociology of Law 28, Lund
Teubner G (1998) Legal irritants: good faith in British law or how unifying law ends up in new divergences. Mod Law Rev 61(1):11–32. doi:10.1111/1468-2230.00125
Thüsing G (2015) Mit Arbeit spielt man nicht! Plädoyer für eine gerechte Ordnung des Arbeitsmarkts. C.H.Beck, München
Timasheff NS (1937) What is "sociology of law"? Am J Sociol 43(2):225–235
Tomlins C, Comaroff J (2011) "Law As...": theory and practice in legal history. Irvine Law Rev 1 (3):1039–1079
Ulen TS (2002) A Nobel prize in legal science: theory, empirical work, and the scientific method in the study of law. Univ Illinois Law Rev 4:875–920
Van de Mieroop M (2005) The invention of interest. Sumerian loans. In: Goetzmann WN, Rouwenhorst KG (eds) The origins of value. Oxford University Press, Oxford, pp 17–30
van Gestel R, Micklitz HW (2014) Why methods matter in European legal scholarship. Eur Law J 20:292–316. doi:10.1111/eulj.12049
van Gestel R, Micklitz HW, Maduro MP (2012) Methodology in the new legal world. European University Institute Working Papers LAW 2012/13
van Gestel R, Micklitz HW, Rubin EL (eds) (2016) Rethinking legal scholarship: a transatlantic dialogue. Cambridge University Press, Cambridge
Vaquero AN (2013) Five models of legal science. Revus 19:53–81. doi:10.4000/revus.2449
Vec M (2001) Chronik. Mit den Augen des Rechtshistorikers – Ein Symposion zur Methode der Rechtsgeschichte. Zeitschrift der Savigny-Stiftung für Rechtsgeschichte. Germanistische Abteilung 118(1):907–911. doi:10.7767/zrgga.2001.118.1.907
von Holderstein Holtermann J, Christensen MJ, Madsen MR (2013) Kan retsvidenskaben være empirisk? Om aktualiteten af Alf Ross' empiriske vending i retsfilosofien. Retfærd 36/141 (2):3–22
von Jhering R (1868) Ist die Jurisprudenz eine Wissenschaft? Jherings Wiener Antrittsvorlesung vom 16. Oktober 1868
von Kirchmann J (1848) Die Werthlosigkeit der Jurisprudenz als Wissenschaft. Verlage von Julius Springer, Berlin
von Ranke L (1885) Sämtliche Werke. Bd. 33/34. Duncker & Humblot, Leipzig

von Savigny FC (1814) Vom Beruf unsrer Zeit für Gesetzgebung und Rechtswissenschaft. Mohr und Zimmer, Heidelberg
von Savigny FC (1831) Of the vocation of our age for legislation and jurisprudence. Translated by Abraham Hayward. Littlewood & Co., London
von Savigny FC (1840) System des heutigen Römischen Rechts, Erster Band. Veit und Comp, Berlin
von Wright GH (1963) Norm and action: a logical enquiry. Routledge & Kegan Paul, London
Walker A (2014) Bramble bush revisited: Llewellyn, the Great Depression, and the first law school crisis, 1929–1939. J Leg Educ 64(2):145–180
Watson A (1974) Legal transplants: an approach to comparative law. Scottish Academic Press, Edinburgh
Weber M (1904–1905) Die protestantische Ethik und der Geist des Kapitalismus. Archiv für Sozialwissenschaft und Sozialpolitik 20(1):1–54, 21(1):1–110
Weber M (1922) Wirtschaft und Gesellschaft – Grundriß der verstehenden Soziologie. J.C.B Mohr (Paul Siebeck), Tübingen
Weber M (1949) The methodology of the social sciences. The Free Press, Glencoe
Wendell Holmes O (1897) The path of the law. Harv Law Rev 10:457–478
Wesel U (1974) Zur Methode der Rechtsgeschichte. Kritische Justiz 7(4):337–368
Whaples R, Morris AP, Moorhouse JC (1998) What should lawyers know about economics? J Leg Educ 48:120–124
Williamson OE (1985) The economic institutions of capitalism. The Free Press, New York
Woodward J (1958) Management and technology. Her Majesty's Stationary Office, London
Zahle H (2003) Legal doctrine between empirical and rhetorical truth. A critical analysis of Alf Ross' conception of legal doctrine. Eur J Int Law 14(4):801–815. doi:10.1093/ejil/14.4.801
Zimmerman JL (2001) Conjectures regarding empirical managerial accounting research. J Account Econ 32:411–427
Zweigert K, Kötz H (1996) Einführung in die Rechtsvergleichung auf dem Gebiete des Privatrechts, 3., neubearbeitete Auflage. Mohr Siebeck, Tübingen

Chapter 7
Anomalies of Normal Legal Science, Applications of User-Friendly Legal Science

7.1 General Remarks

The purpose of this chapter is to show that normal legal science already knows several examples of the user perspective and that many existing doctrinal disciplines could be upgraded into scientific disciplines within User-Friendly Legal Science. While Chap. 6 told you what User-Friendly Legal Science is not, this chapter will tell you what it might become.

We will have a brief look at four discursive formations as prototypes of what we here call the user-friendly research approach. Such examples are useful for the purposes of this book because each scientific discipline has its own story. Even a new scientific discipline has a history.[1] The new discipline of User-Friendly Legal Science will hopefully look more legitimate if it can be shown to reflect existing silent or tacit knowledge in legal scholarship and practice.[2]

These four examples show different approaches relating to the user. In these examples, the user can be anyone, the state, the firm or clear in other ways.

Moreover, one of the examples consists of a group of established legal disciplines that seem to exhibit at least some of the characteristics of User-Friendly Legal Science.

The three other examples are discursive formations that can be regarded as anomalies of legal science. They can be regarded as anomalies because they either do not fit within the definition of legal science or legal dogmatics or cannot be defined as an area of law in any meaningful sense.[3] These three discursive formations include legal rhetoric that does not fit within the definition of legal science, international law that has raised the question whether it really is 'law' and commercial law that either exists or does not exist as an area of law depending on the

[1]Kuhn TS (1970).

[2]Polanyi M (1967).

[3]For a very narrow view on legal science and legal discourse, see, for example, Tuori K (2006).

P. Mäntysaari, *User-friendly Legal Science*, DOI 10.1007/978-3-319-53492-3_7

jurisdiction. These discursive formations might nevertheless be upgraded into scientific disciplines within User-Friendly Legal Science.

Clear User, Legal Norms as Tools. The first example in this chapter consists of a group of established legal disciplines. It is characteristic of these disciplines that they have identified a clear user and a clear context and that the user's characteristic legal tools consist of legal norms (Sect. 7.2). It would be relatively easy to upgrade these disciplines into scientific disciplines within User-Friendly Legal Science.

Legal Rhetoric, Anyone as User. Legal rhetoric (Sect. 7.3) provides a different kind of example. Anyone can and does use rhetoric. Rhetoric is the oldest example of an independent area of scholarship that is based on the user perspective. In the legal field, one of the questions that it answers is how a person should argue in order to win an argument in a dispute about the interpretation of legal norms. Although it is a fundamental ingredient of legal dogmatics and there is no legal dogmatics without legal rhetoric, it is not recognised as a legal discipline in normal legal science. This is because the practices of legal rhetoric are not legal norms. One can say that legal rhetoric is an anomaly of legal science.[4] In User-Friendly Legal Science, however, it is possible to build a theory of legal argumentation from a user perspective and redefine legal rhetoric as a scientific discipline.[5]

International Law, the State as User. International law (Sect. 7.4) is a further anomaly of legal science. It is obviously closely connected to the interests of states. The development of international law shows how states have resorted to legal practices and legal thinking to protect their interests in relation to other states. Due to the sovereignty of states, and in the absence of an efficient enforcement mechanism, international law is largely used as a framework for legal rhetoric. The narrow point of view of doctrinal research does not reflect the reality of international politics and international law. User-Friendly Legal Science might therefore provide an alternative framework for international law.

Commercial Law, the Firm as User. Commercial law (Sect. 7.5) is again a bit different from the previous examples. From its beginnings in medieval Italy, it has been closely connected to the interests of traders and firms.[6] The codification of commercial law and the increasing regulation of business have raised the question of the interests and objectives served by commercial law. Interdisciplinary research (Sects. 6.2.3 and 6.3.4) and new regulation do not necessarily share the interests fostered by traditional commercial law. They can serve other purposes. User-

[4]For anomalies, see Kuhn TS (1970), Chapter 6.

[5]Mäntysaari P (2016a).

[6]See Ehrlich E (1913), pp. 398–399 on the connection of commercial law and living law: "Das einzige Rechtsgebiet, dessen Wissenschaft nicht bloß gelegentlich, sondern durchweg von dem tatsächlich Geübten ausgeht, ist das Handelsrecht . . . Das ist also das lebende Recht im Gegensatze zu dem bloß vor Gericht und den Behörden geltenden."

Friendly Legal Science could help to reconnect commercial law with its roots and redefine commercial law as a legal and scientific discipline.

7.2 Clear User and Legal Norms as Tools

One can distinguish between areas of law (collections of legal norms) and legal disciplines (the study of legal norms or other legal things). Since areas of law belong to legal dogmatics that is not at the core of this book, we will focus on legal disciplines only.

Main Points. It may be possible to upgrade various established legal disciplines into scientific disciplines within User-Friendly Legal Science. To do this, you would first need three fundamental things:

- the acceptance of the theory of User-Friendly Legal Science as the framework theory;
- the acceptance of its point of view (the hypothesis that users can use legal tools and practices in order to reach their objectives in different contexts); and
- the choice of a method that reflects the new point of view rather than the point of view of doctrinal research.

Some established legal disciplines are relatively easy to upgrade into these kinds of scientific disciplines. The task is easier where (a) the context and the user are relatively clear and well defined, (b) the user has relatively well-defined societal objectives in the chosen context and (c) the most important legal tools in the chosen context consist of laws and regulatory practices.

Clear User. On one hand, that user is often the state. The state has objectives in various contexts, and the state's most important legal tools often consist of legislation.

For example, the state must organise public administration. It may be possible to define the state's general objectives in this broad context. The state must also finance its activities. It uses taxation for this purpose. One may again be able to define the state's characteristic objectives. Criminal law provides a further example. The state uses criminal law for a purpose, and criminal law has well-known objectives.

On the other hand, the user of legislation and regulation is not always the state.[7] Non-state users may use legislation as a tool to attain their own objectives.[8] This explains, for example, why there is plenty of demand for professional lobbying services.

---

[7]Bourdieu P (1987), p. 839: "The law is the quintessential form of 'active' discourse, able by its own operation to produce its effects. It would not be excessive to say that it creates the social world, but only if we remember that it is this world which first creates the law."

[8]See, for example, Stigler GJ (1971); Vauchez A (2012); von Holderstein Holtermann J, Madsen MR (2015).

Such a non-state user can also be a non-human actor of the actor-network theory (ANT).[9] For example, one probably could define the objectives of 'gender equality' in a particular context such as employment. One might also be able to define the legal tools and practices that one tends to use in order to reach such objectives in that particular context. Moreover, one might be able to define the objectives of 'indigenous people' in the context of culture or land use and the characteristic legal tools and practices that help to reach such objectives. In both cases, the most important legal tools consist of mandatory laws.

Method Theories. In order to obtain better information about the user's societal objectives and the effect of the employment of the various legal tools and practices, these disciplines may have sought a closer connection to one or more non-legal scientific disciplines. For example, tax law may benefit from economics and criminal law from sociology.

It can be difficult to explain the role of such non-legal disciplines in doctrinal research. Interdisciplinary research does not cure the fundamental problems of doctrinal research (Sect. 6.2.3). In User-Friendly Legal Science, however, the role of such non-legal scientific disciplines can be to provide method theories that complement the main theories (Sect. 3.3).

Non-human Actors. There is plenty of room for new legal disciplines in User-Friendly Legal Science. For example, one can build a theory round a particular non-human actor of the ANT that to a large extent needs legislation or regulation for its protection.

The non-human actor should nevertheless be sufficiently easy to define. For example, 'ecology' certainly needs law for its protection,[10] but the notion of 'ecology' is rather vague.[11] Economic 'efficiency' provides a further example of a notion that is too vague to be used as a societal outcome worthy of protection (Sect. 6.3.4).

7.3 Legal Rhetoric

7.3.1 General Remarks

Legal rhetoric[12] should belong to your core competences if your profession is law.[13] James Boyd White put it this way: 'Legal knowledge is an activity of mind, a way

[9]In addition to Bruno Latour, the most well-known representatives of the actor-network theory include Michel Callon and John Law. See Latour B (2005). For the use of ANT in management accounting research, see Ahrens T, Chapman CS (2007).

[10]Capra F, Mattei U (2015), p. 14.

[11]See *ibid*, pp. 160–161.

[12]See, for example, Perelman C, Olbrechts-Tyteca L (1971); Perelman C (1977); Alexy R (2012); Gast W (2015); Graver HP (2011); Persson M (2007).

[13]von Jhering R (1858), Zweiter Theil, Zweite Abteilung, p. 322: "Der Zunft, an dem jeder Laie sich seines Laienthums bewußt werden muß, ... ist die juristische Methode. Dem Juristen sollte billigerweise nichts bekannter sein als sie, denn gerade sie ist es, die ihn zum Juristen macht. Und

of doing something with the rules and cases and other materials of law, an activity that is itself not reducible to a set of directions or any fixed description. It is a species of cultural competence, like learning a language; this may in fact be the closest analogy we have, for what a lawyer knows at the center is how to speak and write the language of the law, in actual situations in the world – how to use legal language to create legal meaning. Legal knowledge is in the end not factual but rhetorical and imaginative.'[14]

Legal rhetoric is at the core of doctrinal research. First, the point of view of doctrinal research is the interpretation and systematisation of legal norms. Second, its method consists of two elements: a theory of legal sources and legal rhetoric that seeks to justify the choice of arguments. This explains why deductive and inductive methods make little sense in legal dogmatics.[15]

The choice and relevant weight of legal arguments is, to a very large extent, not determined by legal norms. These choices depend, again to a very large extent, on subjective value preferences, the intended outcome and the perceived effect of the arguments.[16] A person arguing in the context of the interpretation of legal norms starts by choosing the premisses and applies useful arguments that are aligned with premisses.[17]

Legal rhetoric is thus a necessary ingredient of rational argumentation in the context of the interpretation of legal norms. Since rhetoric is not a scientific method, legal dogmatics is not a science. The originators of legal hermeneutics regarded legal dogmatics as an 'art'.[18]

Anomaly. Legal rhetoric is an anomaly of legal science[19]: it does not fit in the positivist understanding of legal argumentation, its existence means that there is no such thing as an 'internal point of view', it is not fully explained by the rational argumentation theory developed by the critics of legal positivism and you need legal rhetoric regardless of whether you apply the legal model, the attitudinal model or any other model for the court's legal decision-making.[20] We can have a brief look at these issues.

doch ist es nicht zu viel behauptet, daß ein eigentliches Bewußtsein über sie den meisten Juristen völlig fehlt, und daß unsere Wissenschaft alle anderen Gesetze besser kennt als die Gesetze ihrer selbst."

[14]White JB (2002), p. 1399.

[15]Hellner J (2001), pp. 69 and 71.

[16]Eckhoff T (1993).

[17]See already Augustine of Hippo, De doctrina christiana, Second Book, XXXIV and XXXVI.

[18]Kant I (1790), §§ 41 and 45; von Savigny FC (1840), § 32, p. 211. See also Samuelsson J (2013), p. 377.

[19]For anomalies, see Kuhn TS (1970), Chapter 6.

[20]Segal J, Spaeth H (2002), pp. 86–89.

Legal positivism was based on the idea that legal decisions could be logically derived from authoritative texts.[21] Kelsen's idea of 'pure law'[22] does not describe the use of legal rhetoric. Moreover, the view that there is only one correct decision for every case in law[23] does not explain the existence of different views about the interpretation of legal norms.

It is customary to distinguish between the law's internal and external points of view.[24] However, you could say that there is no such thing as the 'internal point of view' because the real people who decide on the law's 'internal point of view' exist outside the legal system. The choice of arguments and conclusions for the supposedly internal point of view can thus depend on private or political objectives outside the legal system. What remains is therefore an external point of view (that should be complemented by the point of view of User-Friendly Legal Science according to this book).

The 'internal point of view' can nevertheless be useful for various practical reasons. This is regardless of the fact that the 'internal point of view' is neither 'internal' nor a 'point of view'. The question of its functions is basically a question of the method supporting the point of view of legal dogmatics (that is, the interpretation and systematisation of legal norms):

- First, the method of the interpretation of legal norms is designed to give an element of predictability by limiting the primary sources and the legitimacy of arguments. Such limits and restraints are necessary to facilitate the rule of law. A 'virtuous circle' can follow.[25] Generally, there will be more social activity if risks and transaction costs are reduced. The interpretation of useful legal norms is no exception. The internal point of view can help to reduce perceived risk. It can increase public trust in the legal system by maintaining 'the autonomy of the legal field and its discipline-effect'[26] and by supporting 'the legitimacy of the office of the judge as quite other than that of a political or administrative decision-maker'.[27]
- Second, the method facilitates 'discursive closure'.[28] It provides a common language, that is, a set of rhetorical tools and practices. This can facilitate peaceful and rational argumentation between the parties. The method does not

[21]See Paso M (2014), p. 237.

[22]Kelsen H (1934).

[23]According to Dworkin, a proposition of law may be asserted as true if it is more consistent with the legal theory that justifies its prior application than is its contrary. Dworkin R (1977), pp. 339–340; Bowie NE (1977), p. 915.

[24]Hart HLA (1961/ 2012), p. 89. Max Weber distinguished between the intra juristic and the extra juristic perspective on legal matters in Weber M (1922), Second Part, Chapter VII, § 6, p. 492. For internal and external justification, see Paso M (2014), pp. 238–239.

[25]Acemoglu D, Robinson JA (2012), p. 307.

[26]Cotterrell R (1995), p. 53.

[27]*Ibid*, p. 92.

[28]See *ibid*, p. 100.

change the fact the interpretation of legal norms is a political or subjective activity.

- Third, the existence of a special method makes it possible to earn a living as a legal specialist or the law's gatekeeper.[29]

We can move on to the rational argumentation theory. The essence of the rational argumentation theory is rational justification: you need to convince others and be convinced in a way that is perceived as rational.[30] Since the rational argumentation theory is embedded in legal dogmatics, it must address the question of whether arguments are good or bad[31] and the acceptability of arguments for the purposes of legal dogmatics.[32] However, the rational argumentation theory does not describe how legal argumentation works in real life. First, while the rational argumentation theory focuses on what the decision-making of a fictive judge should be, it does not describe what it is. Second, the actual use of legal rhetoric in the everyday interpretation of legal norms by real people is not limited to court proceedings.[33] Third, everyday legal rhetoric is constrained by the likely effect of the arguments rather than their abstract legitimacy. Moreover, while justification can be internal or external, external justification plays a big role in legal practice.[34]

The use of legal rhetoric is not limited to court proceedings. It is of course applied in court proceedings as well. It is used regardless of how you describe the court's legal decision-making and regardless of whether you choose the legal model, the attitudinal model or any other model for the court's legal decision-making.[35] Under the legal model, the outcome of the interpretation of norms is determined by valid sources of law and valid interpretive methods applied to those sources. In this case, legal rhetoric is used to justify the intended outcome, the method, the choice of sources and the relevant weight of the sources. Under the attitudinal

---

[29]See *ibid*, pp. 92–93.

[30]Paso M (2014), p. 238.

[31]See, for example, McCloskey DN (1988), p. 757: "Take down a modern elementary textbook on logic ... and slowly read the section on 'fallacies.' Try to ignore the authoritarian and dismissive rhetoric with which the philosophers treat the 'fallacies,' and ask yourself – Are these not in fact the usual forms of legal reasoning? Are they really all wrong, to be discarded in serious conversation? Or should we rather make distinctions between good analogies and bad, good arguments from authority and bad, good rhetoric and bad?"

[32]See Paso M (2014), p. 237.

[33]Mäntysaari P (2016a).

[34]See Paso M (2014), p. 248; Mäntysaari P (2016a). The core of the decision is internal justification. However, there is a problem. Paso M (2014), p. 239: "[I]nternal justification does not answer the question of why a certain norm was chosen. The same applies to facts: Internal justification does not answer the question of why a certain fact was considered relevant while another was ignored." External justification is needed if the premisses cannot be derived from the law.

[35]Segal J, Spaeth H (2002), pp. 86–89.

model, the outcome is determined by the facts of the case and the ideological attitudes and values of the judges.[36]

User-Friendly Legal Science. It is possible to redefine legal rhetoric as an area of User-Friendly Legal Science[37] and as a scientific discipline. Its field consists of the legal system and society. Its context is the interpretation of legal norms. The user can be anyone using legal argumentation to prevail in the context of the interpretation of legal norms. The point of view of legal rhetoric is how the user can choose, use and combine arguments for the purpose of prevailing in the context of the interpretation of legal norms.

In the following, we can have a brief look at the history of legal rhetoric (Sect. 7.3.2) and legal rhetoric as a new discipline of User-Friendly Legal Science (Sects. 7.3.3 and 7.3.4).

7.3.2 Sophists, Rhetors and Law Teachers

It is not necessary to discuss the long history of rhetoric and legal rhetoric in great detail in this book.[38] A new discipline should nevertheless have roots. For this purpose, it suffices to highlight the close connection between rhetoric, advocacy and legal education in ancient Greece and Rome. To sum up, legal rhetoric preceded professional legal practice and legal education.

In ancient Greece, rhetoric was an informed way to convince other people. Sophists, Plato and Aristotle left their marks in its development. (a) Sophists turned rhetoric into a professional activity. They charged money for educating young noblemen.[39] Rhetoric played an important part in education, and an education in rhetoric was regarded as useful for people participating in legal proceedings.[40] (b) Since rhetoric was an informed way to convince other people and not a question of what was right or wrong, the activities of sophists were condemned by Plato in Gorgias[41] and Sophist.[42] In Phaedrus, however, he later found a connection between rhetoric and dialectic. According to Plato, both rhetoric and dialectic consist of processes that work as aids to speech and thought.[43] He made rhetoric the object of systematisation and theory building. (c) A follower of Socrates and

---

[36]*Ibid*, pp. 86–89.

[37]Mäntysaari P (2016a).

[38]See, for example, Cicero, De Oratore; Augustine of Hippo, De doctrina christiana; Schopenhauer A (1830); Perelman C, Olbrechts-Tyteca L (1971); Perelman C (1977); Gast W (2015).

[39]Plato, Sophist, 226a, Stranger: "Yes, and the sophist is nothing else, apparently, than the money-making class of the disputatious, argumentative, controversial, pugnacious, combative, acquisitive art, as our argument has now again stated."

[40]Plato, Sophist, 232d.

[41]Plato, Gorgias, 454e and 455a.

[42]Plato, Sophist, 233a and 233b.

[43]Plato, Phaedrus, 266b.

Plato, Aristotle studied rhetoric systematically in his book Rhetoric. Aristotle identified judicial (forensic) rhetoric as one of the three types of civic rhetoric.[44]

The business of rhetoric grew in size. It became a specialist activity in ancient Greece. For example, Demosthenes made a living as a logographer writing speeches for use in private legal suits.[45] Teachers of rhetoric (rhetors) were found in all Greek cities, educating young noblemen for a career in politics or law. The practice of employing Greek teachers was taken over by Roman patricians after the expansion of Rome in the Mediterranean area. It was customary for young noblemen to be sent to a grammaticus for early education and a rhetor for higher education.

There was at first no clear distinction between an education in rhetoric and legal education. In the kingdom era of Rome, both law and religion were the domain of the clergy. There was, however, a gradual movement towards greater specialisation, and one started to make a clearer distinction between religion and secular law. The study of law became distinct from religion and oratory.[46]

It became possible to study law. Tiberius Coruncanius is regarded as the first Roman to teach law in public (about the year 254 or 253 BC).[47] Servius Sulpicius Rufus, a contemporary of Cicero, is regarded as the founder of the systematic treatment of law. Cicero wrote that Rufus was the first lawyer of his time and alone understood it as science.[48]

Moreover, it became possible to practice law as a profession. There was a profession of legal advisors already before Cicero's time.[49]

In the time of Diocletian, state recognition seems to have been extended to the law schools of Rome and Berytus (modern Beirut) and later to the law schools of Constantinople, Alexandria and Cæsarea.[50] In 425 AD, two law professors each were made obligatory for the universities of Constantinople and Rome, the other professors teaching Latin language and literature, Greek language and literature, and philosophy.[51] Much later, the history of modern legal science begins with the teaching of Roman law at Bologna.[52]

---

[44]Aristotle, Rhetoric, First Book, Chapter 3, 1358b.

[45]For Greek law, see Szramkiewicz R, Descamps O (2013), Chapter I, § 3 B.

[46]See, for example, Cicero, De Oratore, First Book, sections 48, 159, 236; Pound R (1959), Chapter 2, § 2, p. 30.

[47]Sherman CP (1908), p. 500; Pound R (1959), Chapter 2, § 2, p. 30.

[48]Cicero, Brutus, section 152: "... postremo habere regulam, qua vera et falsa iudicarentur ..."

[49]See, for example, Cicero, De Oratore, First Book, sections 199–202.

[50]Sherman CP (1908), p. 503.

[51]See *ibid*, pp. 503–504.

[52]Pound R (1959), Chapter 2, § 6, p. 43.

7.3.3 User-Friendly Legal Rhetoric

Legal rhetoric is at the core of legal argumentation even in modern times.[53] There is plenty of literature.[54] User-Friendly Legal Science can nevertheless help to redefine it as a scientific discipline. We can try to define it in this and the following sections to show that it can be done.

The starting point is that virtually everybody uses legal tools and practices in daily life, at least in developed countries. Legal tools and practices are facilitated and influenced by laws, and even laws can be used as legal tools. You cannot take into account or apply laws without interpreting legal norms one way or another. Whether people reach their objectives depends on the interpretation of legal norms. For this to happen in a particular situation, a person needs to prevail when there are competing propositions.

Legal norms are therefore interpreted in various kinds of situations. They are mostly interpreted outside the court.[55] They can be interpreted by all kinds of people and not just by judges or lawyers.[56] Modern society is facilitated by a legal infrastructure and would not work if people had to turn to a lawyer or a judge every time they need to use legal norms: they use legal norms when crossing the street.

It is possible to build a theory that describes how people can use rhetoric to prevail in the context of the interpretation of legal norms.[57] By definition, such a theory is not normative. It cannot be assumed that people want to interpret legal norms in any particular way other than what serves their own purposes. If the theory were normative, it would lack scientificity.[58]

Discretion. Basically, people are free to use any arguments and techniques they like, but some arguments and techniques might be more likely to lead to the desired outcome than other practices. Argumentation in the context of the interpretation of legal norms is a special form of practical argumentation.[59]

---

[53]See, for example, Aune JA (1996); Latour B (2013), p. 366: "Cicero could take his place in the French Council of State or in the Luxembourg Tribunal without having to do anything except learn French!"

[54]See, for example, Perelman C, Olbrechts-Tyteca L (1971); Perelman C (1977); Gast W (2006); Gast W (2015); Alexy R (2012).

[55]See, for example, Alexy R (2012), C.I.1., p. 261.

[56]The traditional view is limited to disputes in the court. See, for example, Llewellyn K (1930), p. 3: "What these officials do about disputes is, to my mind, the law itself." Capra F, Mattei U (2015), p. 126: "According to a more realist legal vision, the last word in the law does not belong to the legal professionals at the top of the pyramid, such as a supreme court. Rather, it belongs to those at the bottom, because the usual decision maker is the one closest to the actual conflict, the interpreter who actually captures (or makes) the law in action in most cases."

[57]Mäntysaari P (2016a).

[58]Weber M (1904), Chapter I: "[D]enn wir sind der Meinung, daß es niemals Aufgabe einer Erfahrungswissenschaft sein kann, bindende Normen und Ideale zu ermitteln, um daraus für die Praxis Rezepte ableiten zu können."

[59]Alexy R (2012), Einleitung 2, p. 33 and C.III.1., p. 349.

There is no fundamental difference between legal argumentation in the context of the interpretation of laws and in the context of the interpretation of contracts. However, each of these two cases of legal argumentation has its own particular characteristics because of differences in the legal framework of interpretation in each case.

There is no fundamental difference between the argumentation of parties and the argumentation of judges. The same general theory can describe legal rhetoric in both cases. However, the argumentation of judges is a special case because of the regulation of their activities. Their argumentation is constrained by their legal duties[60] and particular legal rules regulating the legal decision-making process. For example, in legal dogmatics, one can distinguish between formal and substantive theories about reaching decisions.[61] While formal theories focus on the method, substantive theories focus on the substance of the decision. Formal theories thus identify the kinds of considerations that judges ought to weigh, but substantive theories specify the substantive criteria for decisions. Generally, a high level of legal pluralism is likely to increase the discretion of the judge and the opportunities to use legal rhetoric in creative ways. To what extent it is likely to undermine the rule of law can depend on the contents and efficiency of social norms.[62]

Core Concepts. We can define the core concepts of legal rhetoric as a discipline of User-Friendly Legal Science as follows:

- The field of legal rhetoric consists of the legal system and society. It is not limited to the legal system because the subjective preferences and interests that influence the use of arguments exist outside the legal system. The participants in this very broad field range from the common man and firms to lawyers, judges and states.
- The context can be defined as the interpretation of legal norms.
- The user can be defined as anyone using legal argumentation to prevail in this context.
- One can also define more specific contexts with more specific users such as legal argumentation in the context of the interpretation of contracts or legal argumentation by judges.
- The point of view of legal rhetoric is how the user can choose, combine and use arguments for the purpose of prevailing in the context of the interpretation of legal norms.

Theory Building. One can build a theory to describe the legal rhetoric that you can use for the purpose of prevailing in the context of the interpretation of norms. It can be regarded as the basic form of legal argumentation.

Language. Legal rhetoric has its own language due to its long historical roots and body of literature. For the sake of clarity and to connect with prior discourse,

---

[60]Mäntysaari P (2016a).

[61]Fallon RH Jr. (1999), pp. 562–563.

[62]For source pluralism in Nazi Germany and the German Democratic Republic, see Schröder J (2016).

we call the user here the speaker, the other party the opponent and the target group to whom the arguments are addressed the auditorium (or audience).

Outcome. The speaker chooses the intended outcome and the useful methods to produce it. While some people are constrained by their legal duties, most people are basically free to choose the intended outcome according to their subjective preferences but subject to social norms.

Auditorium. Both the speaker and the opponent choose their respective auditoriums.[63] Members of the auditoriums do the same. There can be different subjectively chosen auditoriums in the same context, for which reason participants may direct their respective messages to different audiences.[64]

The speaker chooses the auditorium according to what the speaker perceives as useful. The speaker is not prevented from choosing a fictive auditorium, such as a universal auditorium,[65] but the speaker's arguments are more likely to prevail where the chosen auditorium consists of real people who matter in the context.[66] In legal proceedings, for example, it may be useful to adapt the argumentation to the style and value preferences of the court[67] and less useful to choose an auditorium that consists of imagined wise and virtuous guardians[68] of justice who do not exist in the real world.

The choice of the auditorium thus depends on the interests of the speaker and the speaker's strategy.[69] For example, in the struggle for authority in legal science, it might be futile for a researcher-speaker to talk to direct competitors that have invested plenty of human capital in their own competing propositions and are market leaders in the scientific marketplace; the researcher might instead turn to the consumers of new propositions or choose a new scientific marketplace such as an international auditorium or a niche market.[70]

Types of Arguments. The weight of arguments depends on subjective preferences.[71] Since there can be different subjectively chosen auditoriums in the context, the arguments that prevail depend on subjective preferences, the allocation of power in the context and social norms. In other words, somebody will prevail regardless of who is 'right'.[72]

---

[63]Perelman C, Olbrechts-Tyteca L (1971), § 4; Alexy R (2012), A.IV.2, pp. 199–200 and A.IV.4, pp. 203–205.

[64]For example, while a terrorist on trial might direct his message to fellow extremists and sympathisers, the judge might direct her message to her own peers and the general public. One can also say that they act "strategically". Alexy R (2012), C.I.2, p. 270.

[65]Perelman C, Olbrechts-Tyteca L (1971), § 7; Alexy R (2012), IV.4, p. 203.

[66]See, for example, Llewellyn K (1930), p. 3.

[67]The leading predictive-explanatory theory of judicial decisions in political science is the "attitudinal model". See Segal J, Spaeth H (2002), pp. 86–89.

[68]Plato, Republic, 2.

[69]Bourdieu P (1975), p. 30.

[70]Compare Bourdieu P (1975), p. 23: "The struggle for scientific authority . . . owes its specificity to the fact that the producers tend to have no possible clients other than their competitors . . ."

[71]Alexy R (2012), C.II, p. 273.

[72]Schopenhauer A (1830).

The speaker can improve the chances of success by using legal rhetoric.[73] One can distinguish between several types of arguments and rhetorical techniques in the context of the interpretation of legal norms. The speaker uses (a) general research-related arguments and dogmatic arguments, (b) general rhetorical techniques and context-specific rhetorical techniques (Sect. 7.3.4), as well as (c) open arguments and hidden arguments.

Open Arguments and Hidden Arguments. Some arguments can be open in the sense that their apparent textual content is the same as their intended meaning. In order to achieve outcome 1, the speaker says A; on its face, A means X, and X is what the speaker intended to communicate. The use of open arguments tends to be limited to what is socially acceptable. For example, the speaker may refer to the clear wording of a statute when it is generally accepted that statutes should primarily be interpreted according to their clear wording. The speaker is less likely to use open arguments that are not socially acceptable because it is less likely that they will lead to the intended outcome.

Arguments can also be hidden in the sense that their apparent textual content is not the same as their intended meaning. In order to achieve outcome 2, the speaker says B; on its face, B means Y, but between the lines, B means Z, and Z is what the speaker intended to communicate. The use of hidden arguments is customary where it would not be socially acceptable to use them openly. The increased polarisation of society probably leads to increased use of open arguments as social constraints evaporate.

7.3.4 Arguments and Techniques

The speaker needs different kinds of arguments. Moreover, the speaker needs techniques to choose between potential arguments and to combine the various arguments. The techniques can belong to different fields such as the fields of rhetoric, scientific research or legal dogmatics. One can distinguish between general and context-specific techniques. General rhetorical techniques can be used in most contexts and are not context specific. Context-specific arguments and techniques are used in the particular context of the interpretation of legal norms.[74]

Compliance with General Research-Related Requirements. When the context is research related, legal argumentation should comply with general research-related requirements. They relate to research design and research ethics (Chap. 3).

---

[73]See, for example, Augustine of Hippo, De doctrina christiana, Fourth Book, II; Capra F, Mattei U (2015), p. 126: "Thus, the outcome of a legal conflict is not predictable with certainty (as the mechanistic vision claims) but is only probable, since we are not able to master all the factors that determine the prejudices of the interpreter."

[74]Mäntysaari P (2016a).

Doctrinal Arguments. The speaker needs a legal façade for the argumentation.[75] The legal façade consists of three kinds of arguments: rules on legal sources and the chosen legal norms, normative standards of interpretation and the general principles of the legal system.[76]

General Rhetorical Techniques. The speaker uses general rhetorical techniques when choosing and applying the doctrinal or research-related arguments. These techniques have probably been common knowledge since the antiquity.

General rhetorical techniques can help to convince the audience. For example, Aristotle distinguished between different ways to persuade the audience (ethos, pathos, logos), Cicero distinguished between different components of a speech, and the style of the speech plays an important role according to Augustine.[77]

You need rhetorical techniques even in research. Research design depends on the subjective preferences of the researcher (Sect. 3.1). General rhetorical techniques can help to increase the acceptance of the speaker's choices. For example, the acceptance of the research question can be increased by arguments that increase perceived ethos and logos. In doctrinal research, the acceptance of findings is particularly dependent on perceived ethos and logos because legal sources can be chosen, combined and interpreted in various ways.[78]

General rhetorical techniques can also provide counterarguments. Counterarguments such as argumentum ad hominem, argumentum ad rem and argumentum ad auditores help to reduce the perceived ethos and logos of the opponent.[79]

Context-Specific Rhetorical Techniques. The speaker uses particular context-specific rhetorical techniques in the context of the interpretation of legal norms.

The most important techniques relate to authority, proximity to the norm's undisputed area of application, similarity, internal logic and teleology. While many of the rhetorical techniques are perceived as legitimate ways of argumentation and called interpretation standards, some are customarily used in the context of the interpretation of legal norms for their usefulness despite the fact that they, according to the social norm, perhaps should not be used.

---

[75] See Ross A (1966), § 30, p. 179; Alexy R (2012), Einleitung 2, p. 38; Graver HP (2000), p. 457. See even Bourdieu P (1987), p. 818: "Furthermore, competition between interpreters is limited by the fact that judicial decisions can be distinguished from naked exercises of power only to the extent that they can be presented as the necessary result of a principled interpretation of unanimously accepted texts."

[76] See already von Savigny FC (1840), Chapter 4, § 33. See also Alexy R (2012), Einleitung 1, p. 21; Graver HP (2008), pp. 82–83 and 115; Peczenik A (2005), p. 249.

[77] See, for example, Augustine of Hippo, De doctrina christiana, Fourth Book, X.

[78] Malloy RP (2004), p. 16 gives an example of ethos arguments. According to Malloy, there are "four general justifications that are typically offered as a basis for private property rights over valuable resources. These justifications can be identified as approaches based on natural rights, distributive justice, economics, and identity."

[79] Schopenhauer A (1830).

Authority. Authority plays a big role in legal rhetoric.[80] There are various kinds of authority that the speaker can use in the context of the interpretation of legal norms. The speaker can use a factual position of power: at the end of the day, somebody will decide how legal norms are interpreted in the particular case, and in some cases it can be the speaker. The speaker can also refer to the authority of a single legal source (such as the wording of a statute or a particular judgment), the authority of the auditorium (such as the previous opinions of the audience), the majority view (contributing to herd behaviour in law),[81] legal science (which provides alternative arguments and alternative views), a single person (contributing to the Matthew effect in science),[82] the speaker's own authority ('trust me, I'm a lawyer', 'the nature of things'[83]) or science (see, for example, Sect. 6.3.4).[84]

Proximity to the Norm's Undisputed Area of Application. It is customary to interpret a legal norm on the basis of how closely the facts are connected to the norm's undisputed area of application.[85] Inside the norm's undisputed area of application, the speaker can choose between the application of the norm or teleological reduction (contra legem). In the border area, the speaker can choose a broad or narrow interpretation of the norm. Outside the core area of application, the speaker can decide to apply the norm analogically (ex analogia) or choose not to apply it (argumentum e contrario). These rhetorical techniques can be useful in the absence of clear rules on when to choose one alternative rather than the other.[86]

Similarity. Proximity to the norm's undisputed area of application is an application of a more general technique of similarity.[87] The speaker can seek to justify a certain interpretation of a legal norm by arguing that A is the same thing as B in relation to the undisputed cases that the norm is intended for or that A is not the same thing as B in relation to such typical cases. The question of similarity or differences plays a major role in the interpretation of legal norms because legal norms contain vague concepts.[88]

Internal Logic. Techniques that are based on internal logic refer, in particular, to (a) coherence,[89] (b) the internal systematisation of the law, (c) classification,

---

[80]Mäntysaari P (2016a), section 6.2.

[81]Sunstein CR (2001); Cheffins BR (2004).

[82]Merton RK (1973).

[83]See Larenz K (1969), pp. 388–394; Strömholm S (1975).

[84]For the use of economics, see Malloy RP (2004).

[85]Heck P (1914), p. 173 ("Begriffskern", "Begriffshof").

[86]See Ross A (1966), § 30, p. 180; Eckhoff T (1993), Chapter 5, II, p. 100: "Om begrunnelsene for å tolke en lov innskrenkende kan det ikke sies stort mer enn det som er sagt om lovtolkning i sin allminnelighet. Alle slags tolkningargumenter kan tenkes påberobt til støtte for innskrenkende tolkning."

[87]Mäntysaari P (2016a), section 6.4.

[88]See, for example, Eckhoff T (1993), Chapter 2, VI, p. 48 and Chapter 2, VIII, p. 54.

[89]See, for example, BVerfGE 19, 206, 219 on the separation of church and state under the German constitution. The outcome was motivated by the combined effect of many provisions: "Das Grundgesetz legt durch Art. 4 Abs. 1, Art. 3 Abs. 3, Art. 33 Abs. 3 GG sowie durch Art. 136 Abs.

(d) continuity in time, (e) proximity to the norm's undisputed area of application (such as argumentum a fortiori that consists of argumentum a maiori ad minus and argumentum a minori ad maius, analogy or teleological reduction), (f) the general principles that legal norms shall be aligned with and (g) indirect evidence (such as argumentum ad absurdum).[90]

Teleology. Teleological arguments focus on the effect of the proposed interpretation of the norm. The speaker can refer to (a) the actual or hypothetic effect, (b) societal effect or effect in the legal system and (c) effect in the particular case or as a general rule. There is a connection between teleological arguments and the norm's 'purpose'.[91]

Effect on Doctrinal Research. Defining legal rhetoric as a scientific discipline does not mean the end of doctrinal research. You obviously need useful information about what legal norms the court would be likely to apply and how the court would be likely to interpret them.[92]

However, you should distinguish between legal dogmatics and legal rhetoric. While legal dogmatics is designed to identify legal norms and define their normative content, legal rhetoric provides a toolbox of practices that you can use to increase the acceptance of the intended outcome. In other words, legal dogmatics focuses on the normative content and legal rhetoric on ways to justify any content.

Legal dogmatics can be improved by better knowledge of legal rhetoric in three main ways. It can increase the transparency of arguments (which can be open or hidden), provide a theoretical framework for the analysis of arguments and facilitate a more critical approach to the interpretation of legal norms.

At the same time, increased focus on legal rhetoric can mean more than just increased awareness of language and a belated 'linguistic turn' in legal dogmatics.[93] The use of legal arguments is rational only when it is aligned with the actual objectives of the 'speaker': the use of words reflects society.[94] Legal rhetoric could become the discipline that provides the theoretical framework to describe this behaviour.[95] It is already common knowledge that legal texts can be interpreted

1 und 4 und Art. 137 Abs. 1 WRV in Verbindung mit Art. 140 GG dem Staat als Heimstatt aller Staatsbürger ohne Ansehen der Person weltanschaulich-religiöse Neutralität auf. Es verwehrt die Einführung staatskirchlicher Rechtsformen und untersagt auch die Privilegierung bestimmter Bekenntnisse." You can find a further example in Leiter B (2001): "We prefer simpler explanations to more complex ones ... We prefer more comprehensive explanations ... We prefer explanations that leave more of our other well-confirmed beliefs and theories intact to those that don't ..."

[90]Mäntysaari P (2016a), section 6.5.

[91]*Ibid*, section 6.6.

[92]See, for example, Ross A (1958), p. 29 on the prognosis theory.

[93]The main principles of a linguistic analysis were set out in Wittgenstein L (1922). The phrase "the linguistic turn" was coined by Gustav Bergmann. Bergmann G (1964), p. 177. It was made popular in 1967 by Richard Rorty. Rorty R (1967), p. 3. For recent discourse in legal science and Koskenniemi, see Dellavalle S (2016).

[94]Wittgenstein L (1953), § 1 and § 43.

[95]See, for example, Paso M (2014); Paso M (2009).

'using methods significantly different from those which are traditionally adopted by legal scholars'.[96]

7.4 Development of International Law

7.4.1 General Remarks

International law used to be an anomaly of legal science. Due to its peculiar characteristics, it used to raise questions about whether it could be regarded as 'law'.

There were doubts because the benchmark was municipal law. International law obviously is not the same thing.[97] Unlike municipal law, international law is very closely connected to the actual practices of sovereign states.[98] Many of its rules might be regarded as moral rules in the absence of enforcement powers.[99] Moreover, international law cannot have a 'basic norm' (Grundnorm).[100]

It has nevertheless been accepted that not only municipal law but even international law can be regarded as 'law'. Different kinds of arguments have been used in favour of this conclusion.

There have been attempts to find a basic norm. Moreover, one has looked for de facto sanctions for the breach of international law. Hans Kelsen drew the conclusion that international law is of the same kind as municipal law, the difference being that international law is a 'primitive legal system'.[101]

H.L.A. Hart did not regard the search for a basic norm as very relevant: 'There is indeed something comic in the efforts made to fashion a basic rule for the most simple forms of social structure which exist without one.'[102] Hart described international law as a 'simple form of social structure' rather than a 'developed legal system'.[103]

---

[96]Banakar R, Travers M (2005), p. 137.

[97]Hart HLA (1961/ 2012), pp. 215–216.

[98]See, for example *ibid*, pp. 214, 220 and 224 on attempts "to reconcile the (absolute) sovereignty of states with the existence of binding rules of international law, by treating all international obligations as self-imposed like the obligation which arises from a promise".

[99]Ross A (1958), § 12; Hart HLA (1961/ 2012), pp. 225–227.

[100]Hart HLA (1961/ 2012), p. 233.

[101]Kelsen H (1934), pp. 131–132: "Das Völkerrecht weist den nämlichen Charakter auf wie das einzelstaatliche Recht. Es ist wie dieses eine Zwangsordnung . . . Die spezifischen Unrechtsfolgen des Völkerrechts sind: Repressalie und Krieg. Aber das Völkerrecht ist noch eine primitive Rechtsordnung . . . Es ist die Technik der Selbsthilfe, von der auch die Entwicklung der einzelstaatlichen Rechtsordnung ausgegangen ist."

[102]Hart HLA (1961/ 2012), p. 236.

[103]*Ibid*, p. 214: ". . . the rules for states resemble that simple form of social structure, consisting only of primary rules of obligation, which, when we find it among societies of individuals, we are accustomed to contrast with a developed legal system."

In any case, Jeremy Bentham pointed out already in the late eighteenth century that international law is sufficiently analogous to national (municipal) law to be intelligible to lawyers.[104] According to Hart, the analogy is 'one of content not of form' and that 'in this analogy of content, no other social rules are so close to municipal law as those of international law'.[105]

International law looks like an example of a traditional area of law that you could redefine and describe as an area of User-Friendly Legal Science. We can therefore have a brief look at its development (Sect. 7.4.2) and character as a potential scientific discipline (Sect. 7.4.3).

7.4.2 *Brief History of International Law*

International law has meant different things during the course of its development. It is characteristic of international law that it is 'law' between states and that the most important objectives are state objectives.[106] However, international law addresses phenomena that are older than states. These phenomena have changed over the course of time reflecting the development of contacts between societies. Moreover, the development of international law over time has followed the development of Western political organisation.

Depending on the era, one could say that international law relates to 'the ensemble of methods or devices which give an element of predictability to international relations', 'a more or less comprehensive substantive code of conduct applying to nations', 'a set of substantive principles applying uniquely to States as such' or 'the integration of the world at large into something like a single community under a rule of law'.[107]

States have used such legal tools for a long time. In ancient Greece, the interaction of the many small states was facilitated by an inter-state culture and particular rules of behaviour. In the Roman Empire, there were rules for interactions between Roman citizens and foreigners (jus gentium) but no rules for dealings with territories outside the Roman Empire. After the fall of the Roman Empire, the many entities of Europe found inspiration in Corpus Iuris Civilis and canon law—the most advanced sources of law of the time—when dealing with questions of interaction with other entities. The emergence of international trade made it necessary to protect the commercial interests of merchants and states by common rules.

Modern international law is connected to the emergence of nation states and the notion of sovereignty. According to its founding myth, international law began with

[104]Bentham J (1789), Chapter XVII, number XXV, note.

[105]Hart HLA (1961/ 2012), pp. 236–237.

[106]See, for example, Neff SC (2003), p. 42 and Kelsen H (1934), p. 132: "Das Völkerrecht verplichtet und berechtigt die Staaten."

[107]Neff SC (2003), p. 32.

the Peace of Westphalia in 1648. The Peace of Westphalia was followed by the growth of entities that were regarded as sovereign nation states, each with its own centralised system of government. The term international law was coined by Bentham.[108]

Modern international law is regarded as an instrument to reach political objectives, that is, 'the objectives of particular actors involved in hegemonic pursuits'.[109] International law is applied in the context of the international relations of states. In other words, 'international law exists to advance the repertory of substantive values, preferences, and practices that those in dominant positions seek to realize in the world'.[110]

7.4.3 International Law through the Lens of User-Friendly Legal Science

The step from the traditional to the user-friendly research approach would be small in international law. There is a clear user that has identifiable interests in the customary contexts of international law. The present primary sources of international law can say something about user objectives in the various contexts and about the legal tools and practices that the user can employ to reach its objectives.

The Users of International Law. Traditional international law is law between states. The state is a territorial unit that claims sovereignty, that is, unlimited power to regulate its internal and external affairs. An entity is a sovereign state where it has been recognised as one.

According to the positivist approach, the independent nation state was the 'fundamental unit' of international law, each state with its own distinctive set of national interests.[111] States act the way they see fit. This led to the instrumentalist approach. International law was regarded as 'a tool for the attainment of goals decided on by political processes'.[112]

However, the users of international law are not limited to states. They range from international organisations to other political operators and groups claiming

[108]Bentham J (1789), Chapter XVII, number XXV, note: "The word *international,* it must be acknowledged, is a new one; though, it is hoped, sufficiently analogous and intelligible. It is calculated to express, in a more significant way, the branch of law which goes commonly under the name of the *law of nations:* an appellation so uncharacteristic, that, were it not for the force of custom, it would seem rather to refer to internal jurisprudence. The chancellor D'Aguesseau has already made, I find, a similar remark: he says that what is commonly called *droit* des *gens,* ought rather to be termed *droit* entre *les gens.*"

[109]Koskenniemi M (2003), pp. 110–111.

[110]*Ibid*, pp. 110–111.

[111]Neff SC (2003), p. 42.

[112]*Ibid*, p. 42.

protection.[113] There can even be non-human users of international law under the actor-network theory (Sect. 7.2).

While states use the tools and practices of international law directly, non-state actors benefit from their use indirectly. Non-state actors may encourage states to pursue their ambitions on the platform of international law rather than unilaterally or through violence. A nicer world is obviously in the interests of most non-state actors.

Non-state actors can use the tools and practices of international law even directly depending on the context. First, international law can provide a platform on which claims can be made against states or the powerful. The tools and practices of international law can exist as 'a promise of justice' for the weak.[114] Second, non-state users can have specific interests that they pursue by means of these tools and practices (see below).

One may ask whether the users of international law could include the 'international community' for the purposes of User-Friendly Legal Science. While the 'international community' can sound appealing and might be used for rhetorical purposes, it is too vague as a user category.[115] Neither the objectives nor the legal means to reach them can be described in reliable ways unless the user category is defined narrowly as an ideal type and consists of users with homogeneous interests.

Contexts. Users have interests in the context of international relations between states or the accountability of states. It is possible to define even more specific contexts depending on the user. The existence of different kinds of users increases the number of the particular contexts in which the tools and practices of international law can be employed. Moreover, it increases the range of user objectives that are both user specific and context specific. We can have a brief look at the characteristic user objectives.

State Objectives. Obviously, the 'objectives of international law' depend on the perspective. In User-Friendly Legal Science, the core objectives are user objectives, and the 'objectives of international law' as such belong to the rhetoric that different kinds of actors use for the purpose of reaching their own objectives (Sect. 7.3.4). This seems to reflect how the 'objectives of international law' are understood in the field.[116] Different users can have different political preferences and different

[113]See, for example, Vauchez A (2012); von Holderstein Holtermann J, Madsen MR (2015).

[114]Koskenniemi M (2003), pp. 110–111.

[115]*Ibid*, p. 90: "If there is an 'international community', it is not a teleological but a practical association, a system not designed to realize ultimate ends but to co-ordinate practical action to further the objectives of existing communities."

[116]*Ibid*, p. 89: "International law certainly seeks to realize the political values, interests, and preferences of various international actors. But it also appears as a standard of criticism and means of controlling those in powerful positions."

objectives.[117] The rhetorical use of the 'objectives of international law' can play an important role in the context of the interpretation of international legal norms.[118]

International law mainly reflects state objectives. According to the traditional view, only state objectives count.[119] A brief analysis of the discourse can thus help to identify the objectives of states in this context.[120]

One can distinguish between fundamental objectives and complementary objectives. If it is accepted that the state can have objectives, the fundamental objective of the state must be its own existence. In traditional international law, the highest objective of the system of international law is indeed the existence and survival of states.[121] International law discourse indicates what things are regarded as essential for the existence and survival of states in their relation to other states.

There are even complementary objectives. Mere existence and survival is not enough to satisfy the state's interests. Relations between states have become more complex. The state has objectives in a variety of new contexts due to the emergence of new technologies, economic and political integration, new ideas about justice and fairness and other things. Consequently, the national interest is served in new ways by means of the tools and practices of international law.

Wolfgang Friedmann distinguished between 'international law of coexistence' and 'international law of cooperation'. The scope of 'international law of cooperation' has increased as cooperation has become the best way to serve the national interest.[122]

The customary topics that could be said to belong to 'international law of coexistence' in international law textbooks[123] include, for example, (a) the existence of a state, the territory of a state, the principle of sovereignty and the modalities relating to the existence of sovereign states (such as recognition, limitations of sovereignty, responsibility and representation); (b) war or peace (conduct, neutrality, demilitarisation); (c) issues relating to treaties; and (d) conflict resolution, as well as legal argumentation. These topics seem to reflect the fundamental objectives of states in this very broad context.

---

[117] *Ibid*, p. 90.

[118] *Ibid*, p. 89: "Instrumentalism and formalism connote two opposite sensibilities of what it means to be an international lawyer, and two cultures of professional practice, the stereotypes of 'the advisor' to a powerful actor with many policy-alternatives and 'the judge' scrutinizing the legality of a particular international behaviour."

[119] Kelsen H (1934), p. 132: "Das Völkerrecht verplichtet und berechtigt die Staaten." Koskenniemi M (2003), p. 94: "But the Westphalian myth leaves also unexplained why only State objectives count."

[120] Koskenniemi M (2003), p. 90: "To enquire about the objectives of international law is to study the political preferences of international actors – what it is that *they* wish to attain by international law."

[121] *Ibid*, p. 95: "State objectives and State survival remain the highest objectives of the System."

[122] Friedmann W (1964).

[123] For example, Brownlie I (1990); Evans MD (2003); Hakapää K (2010).

The customary topics that could belong to 'international law of cooperation' relate to trade and finance, communications, technical and scientific standardisation and the quality of life. While some of these topics reflect fundamental objectives and things that are 'essential to the survival of States',[124] others could be regarded as complementary objectives. For example, facilitating trade belongs to the fundamental objectives of the state. Trade has played a major role in international law. Modern international law has fostered 'global freedom of economic intercourse on a liberal capitalist basis'.[125]

Non-state Objectives. Non-state objectives have played a growing role in traditional international law, and there are non-state actors that use international law.

Some of the non-state actors are international organisations that exercise international public authority. Such organisations must address all the issues that must be addressed by self-contained entities generally.[126] Moreover, such organisations need legitimacy (member state consent to the institution's foundational act, legitimacy beyond such member state consent) and a way to facilitate effective regulation.[127]

There are even other kinds of non-state actors. The fact that they can have objectives in this context can be illustrated with the UN regulatory framework. The UN Charter addresses several objectives of human beings and peoples: (a) The purposes of the United Nations include several issues relating to the quality of life. Any individual in the Western world, the values of which the UN Charter originally reflects, is expected to prefer 'respect for human rights and fundamental freedoms' and freedom from discrimination on the basis of 'race, sex, language, or religion'.[128] According to Western values, the same principles should be extended to other people as well.[129] (b) Peoples are expected to want 'equal rights and self-determination'.[130] The UN Declaration on the Rights of Indigenous Peoples is evidence of the particular objectives of indigenous peoples.

The environment could be regarded as a user under the actor-network theory. The United Nations Environment Programme (UNEP) can be seen as a primary source that provides evidence of this non-human actor's objectives.

[124]Koskenniemi M (2003), p. 92; Watts A (2001), p. 7: "International trade and commerce, international finance, international communication – all are essential to the survival of States, and all require an international legal system to provide a stable framework within which they may function."

[125]Neff SC (2003), p. 45.

[126]You can find an example in Mäntysaari P (2005), section 2.3 and Mäntysaari P (2010a), section 8.2.

[127]See von Bogdandy A, Goldmann M, Venzke I (2016), Part I on "the regulatory requests surrounding international institutions".

[128]Article 1(3) of the UN Charter.

[129]Matthew 7:12; Luke 6:31.

[130]Article 55(1) of the UN Charter.

Legal Tools and Practices. States and non-state users of international law can use both international law as such and particular international law tools and practices. In other words, 'international law operates . . . as a relatively autonomous formal technique as well as an instrument for advancing particular claims and agendas in the context of political struggle'.[131]

International Law as Such. States benefit from international law as such in four main ways. They relate to culture, behaviour, argumentation and governance.

International law is 'a more or less comprehensive substantive code of conduct'[132] that applies to states. It can be used to define or delimit the respective spheres within which each state is entitled to exercise its authority.[133] It can help to create a culture of civilised and ethical behaviour between states.[134]

International law can thus be used as a framework that acts as a constraint on the behaviour of other states. It can influence the behaviour of states even though its sanctions are often limited to public disapproval.[135] A state may prefer to interpret international law in ways that restrict the behaviour of other states but protect its own sovereignty and discretion.

International law can provide arguments that a state uses in the national interest to make its own actions look more legitimate and reasonable or to show other states' actions in a bad light. International law thus provides a framework for legal argumentation and rhetoric.[136] For example, in most cases practitioners choose the 'routine application of standard solutions', but they 'often allow the reason for the rule to override the rule' as they 'believe the rule itself has no intrinsic worth'.[137] They seek 'something practical'.[138] International law is seen instrumentally, and its formality does not seem to bear any particular merit.[139] The sources of international law—and the 'rules of recognition' that used to be lacking[140]—are now set out in Article 38 of the Statute of the International Court of Justice.[141]

---

[131] Koskenniemi M (2003), p. 96.

[132] Neff SC (2003), p. 32.

[133] Koskenniemi M (2003), p. 95, citing Brierly JL (1944), p. 3.

[134] Koskenniemi M (2003), p. 93.

[135] Ross A (1958), § 12.

[136] Koskenniemi M (2003), p. 96: "I will argue that international law operates – and should operate – as a relatively autonomous formal technique *as well as* an instrument for advancing particular claims and agendas in the context of political struggle." See also Marxsen C (2016).

[137] Koskenniemi M (2003), pp. 98–99.

[138] *Ibid*, p. 100.

[139] *Ibid*, p. 101 on interdisciplinary studies in the 1990s.

[140] Hart HLA (1961/ 2012), p. 214: "It is indeed arguable . . . that international law not only lacks the secondary rules of change and adjudication which provide for legislature and courts, but also a unifying rule of recognition specifying 'sources' of law and providing general criteria for the identification of its rules."

[141] Article 38(1) of the Statute of the International Court of Justice; Scobbie I (2003), p. 62.

A state can benefit from international law even internally. International law can act as a constraint on the state's actions internally and facilitate better governance.

Particular Tools and Practices. International law provides various kinds of tools and practices. International law discourse provides information about them.

As regards international law of coexistence, the customary tools obviously include diplomatic relations, treaties, dispute resolution systems and international organisations. The early standard practices that helped to increase predictability in interstate relations related especially to diplomatic relations, treaty making and the conduct of war.[142]

Arthur Nussbaum gives early examples of treaties: an agreement between the rulers of the city-states of Lagash and Umma in Mesopotamia setting a proscribed boundary between their two states and an agreement between Ramses II of Egypt and the king of the Hittites establishing 'eternal peace and brotherhood' between their two nations.[143] The practice of the arbitration of disputes was developed in the Greek city-states.[144] The UN is an example of international organisations. Its purposes include maintaining international peace and security and strengthening universal peace.[145]

As regards international law of cooperation, one of its most important contexts is trade. Treaties are important in this context as well. You need treaties to ensure fair treatment and to facilitate maritime trading.[146] There are several examples: International trade in Northern Europe was regulated by the legal framework of the Hanseatic League for hundreds of years. In the seventeenth century, European states built up a network of bilateral treaties of friendship, commerce and navigation with a high degree of standardisation.[147] By the beginning of the twentieth century, a deeper level of economic integration through international treaties had already 'helped to provide the necessary legal infrastructure for improvements in international communication and transportation'.[148]

Method. Traditional international law has its own methods. They seem to be influenced by three things. First, legal rhetoric plays an important role for practitioners because international law is regarded as an instrument to reach political objectives.[149] Second, it is customary for researchers to choose the doctrinal

---

[142]Neff SC (2003), p. 33: "... a number of fairly standard practices emerged, which helped to place inter-State relations on at least a somewhat stable and predictable footing. This was true in three areas especially: diplomatic relations, treaty-making, and the conduct of war. A major additional contribution of the Greek city-States was the practice of arbitration of disputes ..."

[143]Nussbaum A (1954), pp. 1–2.

[144]Neff SC (2003), p. 33.

[145]Article 1 of the UN Charter.

[146]Neff SC (2003), p. 36.

[147]*Ibid*, p. 40.

[148]*Ibid*, p. 45.

[149]See Dellavalle S (2016): "The practical consequence that Koskenniemi draws from his legal theory is that precisely because the legal language has no truth content in itself, it is up to the legal professional to give a sense to the law according to his/her priorities. In other words, exactly the

approach and use its methods. Third, the interdisciplinary approach is a way to increase the scientificity of research. Researchers search for scientificity in the theories and methods of sociology or history.

There is awareness of the nature of the primary sources of international law. It is partly based on international treaties.[150]

Like in all doctrinal research, the coherence of legal propositions plays an important role. Obviously, there would be no system building without coherence over time (continuity)[151] and inside the system.[152] In order to interpret and understand their source materials, researchers take into account the context and the intentions of the originator.[153]

Where researchers look for scientificity in the theories and methods of sociology or history, one may ask how to draw a line between international law research on one hand and sociology or history on the other.[154]

The choice of the user-friendly-legal-research approach could bring several benefits. It could provide a clearer point of view, a better distinction between the domain theories of international law and its method theories, a better distinction between the discipline-specific primary sources and other sources and a better understanding of how the scientific methods of social sciences can be applied in international law research. Moreover, the findings of the user-friendly research approach could be used even in doctrinal research in which teleological arguments play a prominent role.

---

lack of a truth content in the legal language enables the legal professional to use the law as an instrument at the service of his/her – lastly not rationally justifiable – preferences."

[150]See, for example, Articles 31–32 of the 1969 Vienna Convention on the law of treaties.

[151]Orford A (2013), p. 176: "If we want to understand the work that a particular legal argument is doing, we have to grasp both aspects of law's operation—the way it relates to a particular, identifiable social context, and the way in which it gestures beyond that context to a conversation that may persist—sometimes in a neat linear progression, sometimes in wild leaps and bounds—across centuries."

[152]Dellavalle S (2016), Chapter II: "Koskenniemi's epistemology is, at first, a legal epistemology, addressing mainly the question whether legal propositions contain a provable and coherent reference to phenomena, facts or actions, and thus to a 'true' knowledge of the world." Chapter IV: "[T]he legal system described by legal positivists and system theorists is assumed to be internally coherent insofar as it is regarded as rooted in a consistent idea of rationality. On the contrary, one of the most essential tenets of Koskenniemi's epistemology consists precisely in the assertion that the linguistic analysis of the legal discourse demonstrates its lack of internal consistency."

[153]Orford A (2013), p. 170.

[154]*Ibid*, pp. 170 and 177; von Holderstein Holtermann J, Madsen MR (2015).

7.5 Development of Commercial Law

7.5.1 *General Remarks*

Commercial law (le droit commercial, Handelsrecht)—also known as corporate and commercial law (Handels- und Gesellschaftsrecht)—is without doubt a very important area of law. Modern society relies on commercial enterprises and commercial exchanges. This makes commercial law a major source of income for legal practitioners. It tends to provide the largest share of revenue for leading global law firms. And since clients pay so much for legal advice in corporate and commercial matters, it must be important for clients as well.

However, commercial law is an anomaly. It is anomaly because it has been difficult to define it in a meaningful way in normal legal science.

In this section, we will try to define commercial law as a scientific discipline. We will start with a brief history of commercial law (Sect. 7.5.2). The key point is that the interests of firms played a major role in the development of early commercial law. The interests of commercial enterprises influenced the great codifications of commercial law in France and Germany as well. We will therefore have a look at the firm as the default user in French and German commercial laws (Sect. 7.5.3) before identifying the main approaches that scholars have used when defining commercial law as an area of law (Sect. 7.5.4). Finally, we will define commercial law as a scientific discipline in User-Friendly Legal Science (Sect. 7.5.5).

7.5.2 *Brief History of Commercial Law*

The history of commercial law shows that traders and firms have played an important role in the development of commercial law and in commercial law discourse.

Time before Commercial Law. The roots of commercial law can be traced back to the roots of civilisation itself. National and international trade flourished in Egypt already in the pre-dynastic period.[155] Specialisation and the loss of self-sufficiency meant that people needed to exchange goods and services. In Mesopotamia, this led to the invention of writing, credit and interest.[156]

Research in the history of commercial law customarily starts with classical Roman law and Justinian's Corpus Iuris Civilis that was a codification of classical Roman law. However, while the law of obligations had already reached an advanced level, the Roman and Byzantine economies were agrarian, and Roman law was not designed for commercial practice. Most of commercial law was developed much later.

---

[155] Szramkiewicz R, Descamps O (2013), Chapter I, § 2 A.

[156] *Ibid*, Chapter 1, § 2 B; Van de Mieroop M (2005), pp. 17–18.

Lex Mercatoria. Commercial law started to develop independently of Roman law as lex mercatoria in the Middle Ages.[157]

Chronologically, lex mercatoria is divided into three stages,[158] although the stages may be a matter of taste.[159] The first was the period of *customary* commercial law from the twelfth to the fifteenth centuries. The driving force was the Italian mercantile community.[160] The second was the period of *codification* (incorporation) of lex mercatoria into the various municipal or state systems of law. Lex mercatoria was, to a large extent, replaced by national commercial codes and state regulation of commercial exchanges.[161] The third stage was the *modern* lex mercatoria characterised by the existence of large multinational firms, international rule-making organisations and other global players. We can have a closer look at the second stage that seems to be the most relevant for the purpose of defining commercial law as an area of law.

Codification. From the sixteenth century, there were attempts to systematise the body of first-stage rules according to jurisprudential criteria. The first national commercial code was the French Ordonnance sur le Commerce (1673). It was complemented by Ordonnance sur la Marine (1681). In these ways, the customs and usages of merchants were embodied in French law.[162] In addition to French law, Dutch commercial laws and practices played an important role in continental Europe.

Continental European countries can thank France for laying the foundations for much of the legislation and doctrinal research in the area of commercial law. After the French revolution, five legal codes ('les cinq codes') were adopted under Napoléon I between 1804 and 1810. Code civil, the 1803 civil code, was complemented by Code de commerce, the 1807 commercial code. Code civil and Code de commerce shaped commercial law in continental Europe. French law was used as a model even in the great German codifications (Bürgerliches Gesetzbuch 1896 and Handelsgesetzbuch 1897).[163]

---

[157] See, for example, Van Caenegem RC, Johnston DEL (1992), pp. 83–85.

[158] Schmitthoff CM (1961).

[159] See, for example, Michaels R (2007), p. 448.

[160] See also Neff SC (2003), p. 36.

[161] See Szramkiewicz R, Descamps O (2013) on French law; Schmoeckel M, Maetschke M (2016) on German law; Trakman LE (1983). See also Scott HS (1978), p. 738: "In any case, statutory rules are principally designed to alter rather than to 'codify' the existing legal regime. They reflect concern with the ability of various transactors, whether merchants or consumers, to protect themselves in the marketplace, and they are ultimately distributional in character. Since they are designed to alter the existing order or to remedy market failure or inefficiency, statutory commercial rules are unlikely to be optional – mere backstops for existing merchant practices."

[162] Trakman LE (1983), p. 25; Szramkiewicz R, Descamps O (2013), Chapter III.

[163] This can be contrasted with the earlier 1861 Allgemeines Deutsches Handelsgesetzbuch (ADHGB) of the German Federation. As the ADHGB was not complemented by a general private law code, it regulated many questions belonging to general private law.

The legal developments in France and Germany are representative of what happened in continental Europe.[164] Commercial law is influenced by either French or German commercial law in many continental European and other countries.

In continental Europe, traditional commercial law is a normative area of law. To a large extent, the respective scopes and contents of the French and German codes reflect the interests of the main users of commercial law, that is, commercial enterprises (firms). This is hardly surprising. The prosperity of nations depends on production and commerce, and it is in the self-interest of nations to facilitate commercial transactions and the growth of commercial enterprises.[165] It has also been in the self-interest of people who want to amass fortunes.[166]

In both France and Germany, one can distinguish between commercial law in the narrow sense (questions regulated in the commercial code) and in the broad sense (commercial questions regulated outside the commercial code).

In French law, a distinction is made between commercial law (le droit commercial) and business law (le droit des affaires). While commercial law is based on Code de commerce, business law has a broader scope.[167] These areas share their general characteristics to a very large extent.[168] French commercial law regulates three issues: commercial acts (les operations commerciales, 'actes de commerce'), traders (les commerçants) and businesses (le fonds de commerce).

German commercial law is originally based on the Handelsgesetzbuch (HGB). On one hand, HGB is part of German private or civil law. On the other, German commercial law also belongs to a broader area called business law (Wirtschaftsrecht).[169] One can distinguish between private business law (Wirtschaftsprivatrecht) and public business law (Wirtschaftsverwaltungsrecht).

The development of commercial law followed a different path in England. The use of medieval lex mercatoria was restricted in various ways. Commercial practices had to be aligned with the rules of positive law.[170] Lord Mansfield is regarded as the founder of English commercial law.[171] He pioneered the reception into

---

[164]Trakman LE (1983), p. 25.

[165]Boisguilbert P (1695); Chydenius A (1765); Turgot ARJ (1776); Smith A (1776).

[166]Stigler GJ (1971); Fisk C, Gordon RW (2011), p. 539: "Of course, one of the core insights of legal history since Hurst and Horwitz has been that legal regimes facilitate particular economic arrangements and distributions of wealth and that people who are motivated largely by the desire to amass fortunes have been influential creators of the tapestry of law for centuries."

[167]Guével D (2012), p. 23, Introduction, no 21: "On peut donc postuler que le droit des affaires est. compose du droit de commercial ainsi que d'un ensemble de règles (empruntées à d'autres matières) pouvant intéresser l'enterprise privée, le professional et/ou les activités économiques ou professionelles)".

[168]*Ibid*, pp. 23–26, Introduction, nos 23–33.

[169]See, for example, Roth GH (1994), § 1.3.a.

[170]Trakman LE (1983), p. 27.

[171]Especially for his work in cases such as: Pillans & Rose v Van Mierop & Hopkins [1765] 3 Burr 1663; and Carter v Boehm [1766] 3 Burr 1905. Lord Mansfield was born William Murray in Scotland in 1705.

English law of the practices of continental and British merchants (international lex mercatoria). However, there is no commercial code in England. The notion of commercial law can therefore be used in an open and flexible way in English law.[172]

Characteristics. The history of commercial law and business practices form the traditional basis of modern commercial law discourse. Commercial law builds on the practices of firms in commercial transactions.

Commercial law facilitates and fosters commercial exchanges. For example, commercial contracts are necessary in all transactions between firms, and firms need to use one or more business entities in all commercial transactions. Therefore, both commercial contract law and company law fall within the scope of commercial law in continental Europe.[173]

The deep characteristics of commercial law are said to include its long historical roots, its close connection to actual market practices and expected market behaviour, its international nature and its dynamic nature.[174] Commercial law therefore respects party autonomy and favours clear rules.[175] These characteristics are reflected in the scope and provisions of commercial law in various ways.[176]

Modern commercial law discourse is not fully aligned with such characteristics. Commercial law discourse tends to focus on legal norms rather than practices and expectations. However, commercial law discourse can say something useful about the user. We will study the user in the following section (7.5.3).

7.5.3 The User Perspective in French and German Commercial Laws

The issues of commercial law discourse reflect the interests that discourse participants prefer to further. Since these interests can be identified, one can even identify the default or characteristic user of commercial law. In French and German commercial laws, the characteristic user seems to be the firm. One can therefore say that Code de commerce and the Handelsgesetzbuch are prototypes of legislation that reflects the user perspective. Focusing on the interests of the firm does not seem

---

172 See Goode RM (1998), p. 8.

173 Goode takes a more limited view in common law countries. Goode RM (1988), p. 141; Goode RM (1998), p. 3.

174 Roth GH (1994), § 1.2.b. Compare Goode RM (1988), p. 141.

175 Roth GH (1994), § 1.2.b: "Auf eine kurze Formel gebracht: Das Handelsrecht ist charakterisiert durch eine tendenziell stärkere Betonung des Verkehrsinteresses gegenüber dem Bestandsinteresse, der Privatautonomie und Selbsverantwortlichkeit gegenüber dem sozialen Rechtsschutz und der Rechtssicherheit und Rechtsklarheit gegenüber der Einzelfallgerechtigkeit." Szramkiewicz R, Descamps O (2013), Chapter I, § 1(6): "Il est: international, individualiste, laic, conventionnel, restitutif et non répressif, non formaliste." See also Goode RM (1988), p. 148.

176 See, for example, Guével D (2012), pp. 23–26, Introduction, II, nos 23–32.

obvious in the light of modern international discourse.[177] This makes it worthwhile to have a closer look at the user in traditional French and German commercial laws.

Issues of Commercial Law. The issues of commercial codes have largely been dictated by the needs of commerce.[178]

In France and Germany, the choice of the issues addressed by the commercial codes is meaningful in the light of the chosen default user of the codified rules. The HGB regulates business forms, financial information (bookkeeping, accounting, auditing) and commercial contracts. The scope of Code de commerce is slightly broader. For example, Code de commerce protects freedom of competition and facilitates the rescue of enterprises. Both codes seem to focus on the fundamental needs of the firm (see Sect. 7.5.5).

This can be contrasted with the Uniform Commercial Code (UCC) (see Table 7.1). Unlike Code de commerce and the HGB, the UCC does not reflect an ambition to create a system of commercial law based on the interests of the firm.[179]

French and German commercial laws define the default user of commercial law. The core concepts in this respect are the business, the firm and traders.

The User in French Law. French commercial law regulates three issues: commercial acts (les operations commerciales, 'actes de commerce'), traders (les commerçants) and businesses (le fonds de commerce). In addition, the core notions of French business law include the enterprise (l'enterprise). The business, the trader and the enterprise mean different things.

The business (le fonds de commerce) is a legal notion that originates in French law. It is regarded as one of the objects of regulation. Title IV of Code de commerce regulates various transactions whose object is a business.

The business consists of various elements. Many of these elements have been mentioned expressly in the Code.[180] First, there is no business without commercial *customers*. The customer base is thus an indispensable element of the business.[181] Second, the existence of a customer base is supported by *intangible* elements such

[177]The firm is not to be confused with a network of contracts or a legal entity. For the opposite view, see Jensen MC, Meckling WH (1976), p. 311; Orts EW (2015), pp. 28 and 53.

[178]Roth GH (1994), § 1.2.b: "Inhaltlich lassen sich die besonderen Charakteristika des Handelsrechts unschwer von den aus dem genannten wirtschaftlichen Zusammenhang erwachsenden Bedürfnissen her erklären." Guével D (2012), p. 23, Introduction, no 21: "On peut donc postuler que le droit des affaires est. compose du droit de commercial ainsi que d'un ensemble de règles (empruntées à d'autres matières) pouvant intéresser l'enterprise privée, le professional et/ou les activités économiques ou professionelles)."

[179]See also Goode RM (1988), p. 141: "[Commercial law] possesses four characteristics. It is based on transactions, not on institutions; it is concerned primarily with dealings between merchants . . .; it is centred on contract and on the usages of the market; and it is concerned with a large mass of transactions . . ."

[180]Article L. 142–2 of the Code de commerce.

[181]Guével D (2012), p. 75, Chapter 1, Section 3, B, no 130: "La clientele est un élément du fonds de commerce . . . Mais c'est son élément essentiel, un élément indispensable, puisque, comme on l'a vu, de fonds doit être exploité pour exister . . .".

Table 7.1 Code de commerce, HGB and the UCC

Code de commerce	HGB
First Book. Commerce in general (including the definition of commercial acts, traders, and businesses). Second Book. Commercial companies. Third Book. Certain forms of sales and exclusivity clauses. Fourth Book. Freedom of pricing and competition. Fifth Book. Payment instruments and guarantees. Sixth Book. Rescue of enterprises in economic difficulties. Seventh Book. Jurisdiction in commercial matters. Eighth Book. Regulated professions. Ninth Book. Overseas matters.	First Book. Merchants. Second Book. Business Entities and the Silent Company. Third Book. Accounts. Fourth Book. Commercial Contracts. Fifth Book. Sea Trade.

UCC
Article 1. General Provisions. Article 2. Sales. Article 2A. Leases. Article 3. Negotiable Instruments. Article 4. Bank Deposit. Article 4A. Funds Transfers. Article 5. Letters of Credit. Article 6. Bulk Transfers and Bulk Sales. Article 7. Warehouse Receipts, Bills of Lading and Other Documents of Title. Article 8. Investment Securities. Article 9. Secured Transactions.

as the business name (le nom commercial), the visual identity (l'enseigne), intellectual property rights (la propriété intellectuelle), licences and authorisations, and rights to premises (les droits conférant la jouissance de locaux). Third, the customer base is supported by *tangible* elements such as stock of finished products or parts (le stock) and raw materials (le materiel et l'outillage).

However, the business is more than its elements. The business is deemed to possess certain general characteristics. According to case law, it is a particular kind of *whole* (universalité). It must be something that is *exploited*. If it is not exploited, it is not a business. Each business has its *unique* characteristics. Businesses are thus not the same. A business is regarded as a *movable* (un bien mobiliar) and *intangible* asset (un bien incorporeal). Its nature must be *commercial* (un bien de nature commerciale), and it must have *customers*.[182]

One can distinguish between the business (in French commercial law) and the enterprise (in French business law). Unlike the business (le fonds de commerce), there is no general legal definition of the enterprise in French law.

In the sociological sense, enterprises—firms—are regarded as the most important participants in market economy.[183] An enterprise consists of capitalistic ele-

[182]*Ibid*, pp. 72–74, Chapter 1, Section 3, A, nos 125–127.

[183]*Ibid*, p. 85, Chapter 2, Section 1, § 1, no 146: "L'enterprise devrait être au cœur de droit des affaires. On considère souvent que l'enterprise constitue l'élément micro-économique fundamental en économie libérale." See already Weber M (1922).

ments and human elements under one direction. The different elements are combined, first, by various kinds of contracts and, second, by common interests.[184]

Since the enterprise exists as a general notion in sociology rather than in law, the enterprise is not a legal person.[185] On the other hand, the enterprise can be the object of legal regulation[186] and is the object of quite extensive legal regulation in market economy. In the legal sense, the meaning of this notion depends on the context.[187]

While the enterprise is not a legal person, a trader can be. There is a simple definition of traders in Code de commerce: traders carry out commercial acts as part of their usual profession.[188] Traders include companies that are regarded as traders due to their business form (par la forme),[189] certain groups of traders (les associés commerçants) and, according to a presumption, certain entities subject to registration obligations (les commerçants par la publicité légale).[190]

There is thus a system consisting of an enterprise, a business and a trader. An enterprise consists of a business and a management. The management does not seem to be an integral part of a business. An enterprise belongs to a trader. A trader can be a legal entity. A legal entity—a trader—can also be part of an enterprise that belongs to another trader higher up in the chain. For example, a large group of companies can be regarded as an enterprise that belongs to the parent company.[191]

The User in German Law. German commercial law has traditionally been defined as the special private law of the trader ('Sonderprivatrecht des Kaufmanns'). However, the notion of the trader (der Kaufmann) reflects the state of commerce before the age of capitalism and industrialisation. Modern German commercial law therefore distinguishes between the trader (der Kaufmann), commercial business (Handelsgewerbe), the firm (das Unternehmen) and the carrier of the firm (der Unternehmensträger).

A trader is a person that carries out commercial business (Handelsgewerbe).[192] There are various kinds of traders. For example, some traders are traders due to their business form (Formkaufmann). Therefore, commercial companies (Handelsgesellschaften) are traders.[193]

[184]Guével D (2012), p. 88, Chapter 2, Section 1, no 155: "[L]'enterprise devrait être une entité autonome, à la fois sujet et objet de droit, comprenant un élément capitalistique, un élément humain et une direction indépendante, agrégés par des contrats et regroupés autour d'un intérêt commun spécifique, non nécessairement lucratif."

[185]*Ibid*, p. 86, Chapter 2, Section 1, § 1, no 149: "L'enterprise n'a pas la personnalité morale en France."

[186]*Ibid*, p. 87, Chapter 2, Section 1, § 1, no 149.

[187]*Ibid*, p. 86, Chapter 2, Section 1, no 149: "La définition juridique de l'enterprise n'est que purement doctrinale et peut donc varier d'uin auteur á l'autre."

[188]Article L. 121–1 of Code de commerce.

[189]Article L. 210–1 of Code de commerce.

[190]Article L. 123–7 of Code de commerce.

[191]Guével D (2012), pp. 88–89, Chapter 2, Section 1, § 1, no 156.

[192]§ 1(1) HGB.

[193]§ 6(1) HGB.

By definition, a commercial business (Handelsgewerbe) is a business that is carried out by a trader.[194] Not expressly defined in the HGB, such a business means an activity (other than a professional activity) that is recognisable, independent, planned and carried out for a certain period of time for the purpose of making a profit.[195]

The firm (das Unternehmen) has not expressly been defined in the HGB. On one hand, it could mean business operations (Gewerbebetrieb),[196] the legal entity to which the business operations belong[197] or both the legal entity and its business operations[198] according to the wording of the HGB. On the other, one could also say that the firm relates to the organisation, assets and operation of the entity. The firm benefits from a business form that provides legal personality and asset partitioning.[199]

German legal science distinguishes between the firm and the legal entity. The firm (das Unternehmen) belongs at law to a legal entity that acts as the 'carrier of the firm' (Unternehmensträger).[200] However, the firm (das Unternehmen) has its own interests (Unternehmensinteresse).

The Firm. Both French and German commercial laws have thus developed new concepts such as the enterprise or the firm to describe market participants. Old concepts such as traders and legal entities are not sufficient to align commercial law with actual market behaviour. The interests of the enterprise/the firm have become more important in commercial law for obvious reasons. Firms organised in various ways are the most important participants in market economy. They produce most goods, and most people earn their living as their employees or contractors.

The enterprise/the firm is not the same thing as the legal entity. For example, the recognition of the interests of the enterprise or the firm has made it easier to recognise that the business of modern firms is not limited to the confines of one legal entity. In German law, the regulation of company groups (Konzernrecht) and the duties of good faith ('Treu und Glauben', § 242 BGB) between group members make it easier to manage a firm that uses a fleet of legal entities.[201] In French law, the 'Rozenblum' doctrine, which is based on the case law of Cour de cassation,[202] serves the same purpose but is more limited.[203] According to the Rozenblum

---

[194]§ 1(2) HGB.

[195]Führlich ER (2006), § 3.I.1: "Unter einem Gewerbe ist jede * äußerlich erkennbare, * selbständige, * planmäßig, auf gewisse Dauer, * mit Gewinnerzielungsabsicht ausgeübte Tätigkeit, * die nicht ‚freier Beruf' ist, zu verstehen."

[196]§ 1(2) HGB and § 6(2) HGB.

[197]§ 2 HGB.

[198]§ 15(4) HGB.

[199]See, for example, § 33(2) HGB, § 105(2) HGB and § 264b HGB.

[200]One can see evidence of this also in § 3(1)(2) GmbHG and § 23(2)(2) AktG. See, for example, Priester HJ (2004), p. 252.

[201]Mäntysaari P (2005), p. 363.

[202]La Chambre Criminelle de la Cour de cassation, 4 February 1985.

[203]See Hofstetter K (1990).

judgment, financial transfers (financial assistance) may take place between legal entities that belong to the same group provided that certain conditions are met.[204]

The distinction between the enterprise/the firm and its legal entities is well known even in other areas of law such as EU competition law.[205]

The Interests to Be Served by Commercial Law. French and German commercial laws show that it is legitimate to choose the firm as the user of legal tools and practices in commercial law discourse. The commercial codes of these two countries seem to be focused on the interests of firms. Rather than treat firms as a black box, French and German commercial laws try to define the firm's elements. The guiding light is not abstract 'efficiency'.[206]

7.5.4 Earlier Approaches

There are many ways to define commercial law as an area of law. One can distinguish between five main approaches.

The first, as we have seen, is codification specific. Commercial law is regarded as an area of law at least in countries that have adopted a commercial code. It is indeed more difficult to define this area of law in a meaningful way in the absence of a code.[207] However, even where there is a general commercial code, it can be difficult to explain why certain areas of law belong or do not belong to commercial law.[208] Commercial codes do not address the same issues worldwide.[209] Moreover,

---

[204]In particular, it must be compatible with group policy, there must be some return for the company providing the assistance and no disruption of the balance of mutual obligations, and the financial assistance should not exceed the capacity of the company. See also Commission Staff Working Document, An EU Framework for Cross-border Crisis Management in the Banking Sector, SEC(2009) 1407, paragraph 60.

[205]Articles 101, 102 and 107 of the TFEU. For example, the European Commission (SA.38373) took the view that the way to establish the taxable profits for two Irish incorporated companies of the Apple group did not correspond to economic reality. The European Commission decided that the practices of Ireland amounted to prohibited state aid to Apple.

[206]For the very different US view, see Kraus JS, Walt SD (2000), p. 1: "Efficiency is the dominant paradigm in contemporary corporate and commercial law scholarship. The jurisprudential foundations of corporate and commercial law, then are the foundations of efficiency analysis." For a critique, see Posner EA (2002); Eidenmüller H (2005), pp. 169–170, 487 and 490; Mestmäcker EJ (2007), p. 13; Mäntysaari P (2012), section 3.6.

[207]See Goode RM (1998), p. 8. For example, there is no such code in the Nordic countries and most common law jurisdictions.

[208]For example, it is assumed that company law is at the core of German commercial law, but much of German company law is regulated outside the German commercial law code (HGB). Goode argues that company law does not belong to a commercial law code. Goode RM (1988), p. 141.

[209]Compare the Code de commerce (France) and the Uniform Commercial Code (USA).

commercial law cannot be limited in any meaningful way to what was regarded as important for firms a long time ago in a different kind of society.

The second approach is to define commercial law as the regulation of commerce or as legal norms that are important for business. Such a broad approach can also be coupled with the use of a broad notion such as 'business law', 'le droit des affaires' or 'Wirtschaftsrecht' to describe the area of law. However, this approach is rather arbitrary and futile because virtually any legal norm can be relevant for at least some firms in a market economy,[210] and there should be a clearer distinction between commercial law and the rest of the legal system.[211] It is difficult to define commercial law if your starting point is legal norms.

The third approach is subjective. Subjective preferences, political preferences or the private interests of legal scholars who want to gain access to funding and/or academic positions allocated to 'commercial law research' can play a role in the choice of issues claimed to belong to commercial law.[212]

The fourth approach builds on past discourse. While the history of commercial law discourse could be helpful, it is not sufficient when defining modern commercial law. Past notions of commercial law can be products of the time and based on subjective preferences.[213]

Finally, one can choose to study legal tools and practices through the lens of the firm.[214]

The problems that you face when trying to define commercial law as an area of law are linked to the absence of theory.[215] There cannot be a norm-based universal theory of commercial law because there are too many legal norms that are relevant for firms, the norms are too heterogenic and the norms do not share the same public policy objectives. For the same reasons, it is hardly possible to build a norm-based theory of business law, le droit des affaires or Wirtschaftsrecht.

This brings us back to User-Friendly Legal Science. It is easier to build a theory of commercial law if you study the legal field through the lens of the firm and redefine commercial law as a user-friendly scientific discipline (Sect. 7.5.5).

---

[210]For legal history, see Schmoeckel M, Maetschke M (2016), pp. 3–4, number 5.

[211]Kant I (1783), § 1.

[212]For example, Finnish commercial law used to consist of the same issues as German commercial law for the most part of the twentieth century. What was perceived as commercial law in Finland changed in the 1980s due to the political preferences of a generation of legal scholars. While the starting point of German commercial law was and still is the perspective of the trader or the firm, the increasingly leftish Finnish commercial law scholars were more interested in how business could be regulated. See Mäntysaari P (2011); Mäntysaari P (2014).

[213]For example, Goode argues that company law does not belong to a commercial law code. Goode RM (1988), p. 141. Companies have nevertheless been regulated in the French and German codes.

[214]See, for example, Ehrlich E (1913), pp. 398–399; Goode RM (1988), p. 141.

[215]Druey JN (2009); Fleischer H (2007); Mäntysaari P (2012), section 3.1.

7.5.5 User-Friendly Commercial Law

One can build theories to describe how firms use legal tools and practices to reach their objectives in different contexts. Since each firm has a management that uses legal tools and practices on the firm's behalf in order to reach its objectives, we can call this form of commercial law Management-Based Commercial Law (MBCL).[216]

General MBCL. One can distinguish between general MBCL as a broad scientific discipline and the branches of MBCL. We can first have a look at general MBCL.

The Firm as the User. The starting point is that there are firms. For the purposes of MBCL, the firm is defined as an organisational construction. Firms consist of people working as organised teams. The firm can thus be regarded as a particular kind of organisational construction competing against other firms in the market.

The firm is an ideal type. There is wide range of firms in real life. However, they are similar to some extent. The behaviour of firms can be understood better by focusing on typical behaviour (Sect. 2.2).

The firm is not a normative concept for the purposes of MBCL. For example, it is not the same thing as the trader (commerçant, Kaufmann) in commercial law, and it does mean the business form of the organisation (the company, the legal entity).

The distinction between the firm (or the enterprise) and its business form (the legal entity) is of fundamental importance here. In practice, one could of course say that it is the legal entity that does various kinds of things. For example, various acts must be attributable to a legal entity and various assets must be allocated to it.[217] However, the entity is just a legal tool. The choice of the 'perspective' of a mere technical tool does not help to explain its existential questions such as why the tool was chosen and used in the first place. In order to describe rational behaviour at theory level, it is better to say that the firm does the doing and the legal entity is a way to keep score.[218]

The Field and the Context. The field of MBCL consists of two overlapping fields or coupled systems, that is, market economy and the legal system. The firm acts in many different contexts in this broad field. The most general context in this field consists of transactions in the broad sense. For general MBCL, we can thus define the context as transactions in general.[219]

The Ultimate Goal of the Firm. It is assumed that the firm has interests. If one assumes that the firm has its own interests, the ultimate goal of the firm must be its

---

[216] Mäntysaari P (2010a); Mäntysaari P (2011); Mäntysaari P (2012); Mäntysaari P (2014).

[217] See, for example, Mäntysaari P (2002) on the Finnish corporation as an actor; Orts EW (2015) on the firm as a business person.

[218] Mäntysaari P (2010), p. 172.

[219] For differences between MBCL and transaction cost economics, see Mäntysaari P (2012), section 4.9.

own long-term survival in a competitive environment.[220] This goal facilitates the rational decision-making of the firm.

The Objectives of the Firm. There is a connection between the ultimate goal of the firm and its more specific objectives.

Rational firms do useful things to survive. The choice of useful ways to ensure the long-term survival of the firm is likely to increase the firm's long-term survival chances. Choices that do not serve this purpose are likely to reduce the firm's long-term survival chances.[221]

Depending on the circumstances, different things may help the firm to survive (contingency theory).[222] It is nevertheless clear that most firms must make a profit and create value over a long period of time in order to survive in the long term.[223]

Generally, each firm tends to manage four things in all transactions[224]: (1) cash flow and the exchange of goods and services, (2) risk, (3) principal–agency relationships and (4) information. Each firm does this because firms tend to act in rational ways. In the financial sense, rational decision-making is based on expected return (number 1 on the list) and perceived risk (2). There is also a social dimension. The firm cannot survive unless many internal and external parties contribute to its survival by acting according to its interests. There is a large number of relationships with the firm as the principal and many other parties as the firm's agents (3).[225] Moreover, rational decision-making is always based on information (4).[226]

Levels of Decision-Making. The firm manages these four things at the strategic level, the operational level and the transaction level.[227]

The Legal Tools and Practices of the Firm. The firm tends to use five types of generic legal tools and practices in all transactions.[228] They include (a) a business form, (b) contracts,[229] (c) regulatory compliance and organisation of the firm's internal activities, (d) generic ways to manage principal–agency relationships and (e) generic ways to manage information. The French and German codes contain examples of many of these tools.

---

[220] Alchian AA (1950).

[221] *Ibid.* See also Freeman RE (1984).

[222] Woodward J (1958); Schoonhoven CB (1981).

[223] Alchian AA (1950); Friedman M (1970).

[224] Mäntysaari P (2010a); Mäntysaari P (2012), section 4.5.

[225] For the traditional use of principal-agent relationships in economics, see Jensen MC, Meckling WH (1976); Alchian AA, Demsetz H (1972); Fama EF, Jensen MC (1983a); Fama EF, Jensen MC (1983b). For the development of agency theory, see Eisenhardt KM (1989).

[226] For a historical survey, see Stiglitz JE (2002).

[227] Mäntysaari P (2010a), section 4.3, section 7.2, section 7.3; Mäntysaari (2012), section 4.7.

[228] Mäntysaari P (2010a), section 1.1; Mäntysaari P (2012), section 4.6.

[229] Transaction cost economics explains market mechanisms with the notion of contracts. Williamson OE (1998); Williamson OE (2005). However, these contracts are fictive rather than legal contracts. Moreover, contracts are not the only legal tool used in transactions according to MBCL.

Branches of MBCL. We have discussed general MBCL. When the context is defined as transactions in general, firms share their general objectives and use the same types of legal tools and practices. In particular contexts, the firm has even particular objectives and uses particular legal tools and practices. General MBCL is thus complemented by the branches of MBCL. The branches of MBCL are 'functional'.[230] Unlike the traditional dogmatic areas of law, they can be regarded as scientific disciplines.

One can design such new scientific disciplines by taking the following steps. One should identify a particular commercial context, the particular aspects of the objectives of firms in the context, the particular manner of reaching them with general legal tools and practices, and the particular legal tools and practices used by firms in that context.[231]

Method Theories. The main theories—the theory of User-Friendly Legal Science and the theory of MBCL—and the context-specific theories can be complemented by method theories depending on the research project. For example, institutional economics (transaction cost economics) can provide many useful method theories.[232] Economic theories can thus be used as method theories in commercial law scholarship without the researcher having to adopt the point of view of economics as such. Depending on the study, the researcher may find useful method theories even in business economics.

References

Acemoglu D, Robinson JA (2012) Why nations fail: the origins of power, prosperity, and poverty. Crown Business, New York

Ahrens T, Chapman CS (2007) Management accounting as practice. Accounting Organ Soc 32 (1/2):1–27

Alchian AA (1950) Uncertainty, evolution, and economic theory. J Polit Econ 58(3):211–221

Alchian AA, Demsetz H (1972) Production, information costs, and economic organization. Am Econ Rev 62(5):777–795

Alexy R (2012) Theorie der juristischen Argumentation. Die theorie des rationalen Diskurses als Theorie der juristischen Begründung. 7. Auflage. Suhrkamp, Frankfurt am Main

Aristotle, Rhetoric

Augustine of Hippo (426–427) De doctrina christiana

Aune JA (1996) On the rhetorical criticism of judge Posner. Hastings Constitutional Law Q 23 (3):658–669

Banakar R, Travers M (2005) Studying legal texts. In: Banakar R, Travers M (eds) Theory and method in socio-legal research. Hart Publishing, Oxford and Portland Oregon, pp 133–137

---

[230] For functional branches of commercial law, see, for example, Eidenmüller H (2007), p. 486; Fleischer H (2007), p. 50.

[231] See Mäntysaari P (2010a), section 1.1 (law of corporate finance) and section 8.2 (law of corporate governance); Mäntysaari P (2012) (law of corporate governance, company law); Mäntysaari P (2015), section 2.5 (electricity supply); Mäntysaari (2016c) (company law).

[232] See, for example, Grundmann S (2015); Engelbrekt AB (2013).

Bentham J (1789) An introduction to the principles of morals and legislation. Clarendon Press, Oxford (1907 reprint of 1823 edition)
Bergmann G (1964) Logic and reality. University of Wisconsin Press, Madison
Boisguilbert P (1695) Le Détail de la France, la cause de la diminution de ses biens et la facilité du remède en fournissant en un mois tout l'argent dont le Roi a besoin et enrichissant tout le monde
Bourdieu P (1975) The specificity of the scientific field and the social conditions of the progress of reason. Soc Sci Inf 14(6):19–47. doi:10.1177/053901847501400602
Bourdieu P (1987) The force of law: toward a sociology of the juridical field. Hastings Law J 38:814–853
Bowie NE (1977) Taking rights seriously. By Ronald Dworkin. Massachusetts: Harvard University press. 1977. Pp. 563. Catholic Univ Law Rev 26(4):908–923
Brierly JL (1944) The outlook for international law. The Clarendon Press, Oxford
Brownlie I (1990) Principles of public international law, Fourth edn. Clarendon Press, Oxford
Capra F, Mattei U (2015) The ecology of law: toward a legal system in tune with nature and community. Berrett-Koehler Publishers, Inc., Oakland
Cheffins BR (2004) The trajectory of (corporate law) scholarship. Cambridge Law J 63 (2):456–506. doi:http://dx.doi.org/10.1017/S0008197304006658
Chydenius A (1765) Den Nationnale Winsten. Lars Salvius, Stockholm
Cicero, Brutus
Cicero, De Oratore
Cotterrell R (1995) Law's community: legal theory in sociological perspective. Clarendon Press, Oxford
Dellavalle S (2016) Law as a linguistic instrument without truth content? On the epistemology of Koskenniemi's understanding of law. Max Planck Institute for Comparative Public Law & International Law (MPIL) Research Paper No. 2016–08
Druey JN (2009) The practitioner and the professor – is there a theory of commercial law? In: Tison M, De Wulf H, Van Der Elst C, Steennot R (eds) Perspectives in company law and financial regulation: essays in honour of Eddy Wymeersch. Cambridge University Press, Cambridge, pp 607–616
Dworkin R (1977) Taking rights seriously. Duckworth, London
Eckhoff T (1993) Rettskildelære. 3. utgave. Tano, Oslo
Ehrlich E (1913) Grundlegung der Soziologie des Rechts. Duncker & Humblot, München and Leipzig. English edition: Ehrlich E (1936) Fundamental principles of the sociology of law. Harvard University Press, Cambridge
Eidenmüller H (2005) Effizienz als Rechtsprinzip. Die Einheit der Gesellschaftswissenschaften 90. Mohr Siebeck, Tübingen
Eidenmüller H (2007) Forschungsperspektiven im Unternehmensrecht. Zeitschrift für Unternehmens- und Gesellschaftsrecht 36(4):484–499
Eisenhardt KM (1989) Agency theory: an assessment and review. Acad Manag Rev 14(1):57–74
Engelbrekt AB (2013) Institutionell teori och metod. In: Korling F, Zamboni M (eds) Juridisk metodlära. Studentlitteratur, Lund, pp 239–272
Evans MD (2003) International law, First edn. Oxford University Press, Oxford
Fallon RH Jr (1999) How to choose a constitutional theory. Calif Law Rev 87(3):535–579
Fama EF, Jensen MC (1983a) Separation of ownership and control. J Law Econ 14(2):301–325
Fama EF, Jensen MC (1983b) Agency problems and residual claims. J Law Econ 14(2):327–349
Fisk C, Gordon RW (2011) Foreword: "law as . . .": theory and method in legal history. UC Irvine Law Rev 1(3):519–541
Fleischer H (2007) Gesellschafts- und Kapitalmarktrecht als wissenschaftliche Disziplin – Das Proprium der Rechtswissenschaft. In: Engel C, Schön W (eds) Das Proprium der Rechtswissenschaft, Recht-Wissenschaft-Theorie, vol 1. Mohr Siebeck, Tübingen, pp 50–76
Freeman RE (1984) Strategic management. A stakeholder approach. Cambridge University Press, Cambridge (originally published in 1984)

Friedman M (1970) The social responsibility of business is to increase its profits. The New York Times Magazine, September 13, 1970
Friedmann W (1964) The changing structure of international law. Columbia University Press, New York
Führlich ER (2006) Wirtschaftsprivatrecht. Basiswissen des Bürgerlichen Rechts und des Handels- und Gesellschaftsrechts für Wirtschaftswissenschaftler und Unternehmenspraxis. 8., aktualisierte und überarbeitete Auflage. Verlag Franz Wahlen, München
Gast W (2006) Juristische Rhetorik. 4., neu bearbeitete Auflage. C.F. Müller Verlag, Heidelberg
Gast W (2015) Juristische Rhetorik. 5., überarbeitete und erweiterte Auflage. C.F. Müller Verlag, Heidelberg
Goode RM (1988) The Wilfred Fullagar memorial lecture: the codification of commercial law. Monash Univ Law Rev 14(3):135–157
Goode RM (1998) Commercial law in the next millenium. The Hamlyn lectures. Forty-ninth series. Sweet & Maxwell, London
Graver HP (2000) Keiserens garderobe: Eckhoffs rettskildelære og utfordringer fremover. Tidsskrift for Rettsvitenskap 113(4):429–476
Graver HP (2008) Vanlig juridisk metode? Om rettsdogmatikken som juridisk sjanger. Tidsskrift for Rettsvitenskap 121(2):149–178
Graver HP (2011) Rettsretorik. En metodlære. Fagbokforlaget, Bergen
Grundmann S (2015) Kapitel 3. Privatrecht und (Institutionen-)Ökonomik. A. Thema, Theorien und Kontext, Diskussion. In: Grundmann S, Micklitz HW, Renner M (eds) Privatrechtstheorie. Mohr Siebeck, Tübingen, pp 167–195
Guével D (2012) Droit de commerce et des affaires, 4e edn. LGDJ, Paris
Hakapää K (2010) Uusi kansainvälinen oikeus. Helsinki, Talentum
Hart HLA (2012) The concept of law, 3rd ed. With an introduction by Leslie Green. Oxford University Press, Oxford
Heck P (1914) Gesetzesauslegung und Interessenjurisprudenz. Archiv für die civilistische Praxis 112:1–318
Hellner J (2001) Metodproblem i rättsvetenskapen. Studier i förmögenhetsrätt, Jure, Stockholm
Hofstetter K (1990) Parent responsibility for subsidiary corporations: evaluating European trends. Int Comp Law Q 39(3):576–598. doi:https://doi.org/10.1093/iclqaj/39.3.576
Jensen MC, Meckling WH (1976) Theory of the firm: managerial behavior, agency costs and ownership structure. J Financ Econ 3(4):305–360
Kant I (1783) Prolegomena zu einer jeden künftigen Metaphysik die als Wissenschaft wird auftreten können. Johann Friedrich Hartknoch, Riga
Kant I (1790) Kritik der Urteilskraft. Lagarde and Friedrich, Berlin and Libau
Kelsen H (1934) Reine Rechtslehre: Einleitung in die rechtswissenschaftliche Problematik, 1. Aufl. Deuticke, Leipzig Wien. / Jestaedt M (ed) (2008) Studienausgabe. Mohr Siebeck, Tübingen
Koskenniemi M (2003) What is international law for? In: Evans MD (ed) International law. Oxford University Press, Oxford, pp 89–114
Kraus JS, Walt SD (2000) Introduction. In: Kraus JS, Walt SD (eds) The jurisprudential foundations of corporate and commercial law. Cambridge studies in philosophy and law. Cambridge University Press, Cambridge, pp 1–11
Kuhn TS (1970) The structure of scientific revolutions, Second edn. University of Chicago Press, Chicago
Larenz K (1969) Methodenlehre der Rechtswissenschaft, 2. Aufl. Springer, Heidelberg
Latour B (2005) Reassembling the social: an introduction to actor-network theory. Oxford University Press, Oxford
Leiter B (2001) Explaining theoretical disagreements. Univ Toronto Law J 51(4):367–398
Llewellyn KN (1930) The bramble bush: some lectures on law and its study. Columbia University School of Law, New York

Malloy RP (2004) Law in a market context: an introduction to market concepts in legal reasoning. Cambridge University Press, Cambridge
Mäntysaari P (2002) Osakeyhtiö toimijana. Helsinki, WSOY
Mäntysaari P (2005) Comparative corporate governance: shareholders as a rule-maker. Springer, Berlin Heidelberg
Mäntysaari P (2010a) The law of corporate finance: general principles and EU law. Volume I: Cash flow, risk, agency, information. Springer, Berlin Heidelberg
Mäntysaari P (2011) Handelsrättens teori: en teoretisk referensram för handelsrättslig forskning. Tidsskrift for Rettsvitenskap 124(2):197–226
Mäntysaari P (2012) Organising the firm: theories of commercial law, corporate governance and corporate law. Springer, Berlin Heidelberg
Mäntysaari P (2014) Kauppaoikeuden teoriasta. Lakimies 112(3):347–367
Mäntysaari P (2015) Användarperspektivet i rättsvetenskap: Bättre juridik med en vetenskaplig metod. In: Korhonen P, Saranpää T (eds) Isännän ääni: Juhlakirja Erkki Kustaa Rintala 1935–31/5–2015. Helsinki, Talentum, pp 489–505
Mäntysaari P (2016a) Auditorier och retorik. Tidsskrift for Rettsvitenskap 129(1):1–42. doi:10.18261/issn.1504-3096-2016-01-01
Mäntysaari P (2016c) Osakeyhtiöoikeuden teoriasta. In: Myllly UM, Nyström P, Viinikka T, Oikeuden ja talouden rajapinnassa: Juhlakirja Matti J. Sillanpää 60 vuotta. Edita, Helsinki, pp 159–180
Marxsen C (2016) International law in crisis: Russia's struggle for recognition. Max Planck Institute for Comparative Public Law and International Law, MPIL Research Paper No. 2016–05
McCloskey DN (1988) The rhetoric of law and economics. Mich Law Rev 86(4):752–767. doi:10.2307/1289214
Merton RK (1973) The Matthew effect in science. In: Merton RK (ed) The sociology of science. Theoretical and empirical investigations. University of Chicago Press, Chicago, pp 439–459
Mestmäcker EJ (2007) A legal theory without law: Posner v. Hayek on economic analysis of law. Walter Eucken Institut, Beiträge zur Ordnungstheorie und Ordnungspolitik 174. Mohr Siebeck, Tübingen
Michaels R (2007) The true lex mercatoria: law beyond the state. Indiana J Global Legal Stud 14 (2):447–468
Neff SC (2003) A short history of international law. In: Evans MD (ed) International law. Oxford University Press, Oxford, pp 31–58
Nussbaum A (1954) A concise history of the law of nations. Macmillan, New York
Orford A (2013) On international legal method. London Rev Int Law 1(1):166–197. doi:10.1093/lril/lrt005
Orts EW (2015) Business persons: a legal theory of the firm. Oxford University Press, Oxford
Paso M (2009) Viimeisellä tuomiolla – Suomen korkeimman oikeuden ja Euroopan yhteisöjen tuomioistuimen ennakkopäätösten retoriikka. Helsinki, Lakimiesliiton kustannus
Paso M (2014) Rhetoric meets rational argumentation theory. Ratio Juris 27(2):236–251
Peczenik A (2005) Juridikens allmänna läror. Svensk Juristtidning 90:249–272
Perelman C (1977) L'empire rhétorique. Rhétorique et argumentation. J. Vrin, Paris
Perelman C, Olbrechts-Tyteca L (1971) The new rhetoric: a treatise on argumentation. University of Notre Dame Press, Notre Dame
Persson M (2007) Retorik och juridik: Teori och metod. Demosthenes, Uppsala
Plato, Gorgias
Plato, Phaedrus
Plato, Republic
Plato, Sophist
Polanyi M (1967) The tacit dimension. Routledge & Kegan Paul, London
Posner EA (2002) Book Review: Kraus, Jody S., and Walt, Steven D., eds., The Jurisprudential Foundations of Corporate and Commercial Law. Ethics 112:626–628

Pound R (1959) Jurisprudence, vol 1. West Publishing Co., St. Paul
Priester HJ (2004) Beginn der Rechtsperson – Vorräte und Mäntel. Zeitschrift für das gesamte Handels- und Wirtschaftsrecht 168(3):248–264
Rorty R (1967) Metaphilosophical difficulties of linguistic philosophy. In: Rorty R (ed) The linguistic turn. Recent essays in philosophical method. University of Chicago Press, Chicago, pp 1–41
Ross A (1958) On law and justice. Stevens & Sons Limited, London
Ross A (1966) Om ret og refærdighet: en indførelse i den analytiske retsfilosofi. 2. opl. Nyt Nordisk Forlag, Copenhagen
Roth GH (1994) Handels- und Gesellschaftsrecht. Das Recht des kaufmännischen Unternehmens, 4. Aufl. Verlag Franz Wahlen, München
Samuelsson J (2013) Hermeneutik. In: Korling F, Zamboni M (eds) Juridisk metodlära. Studentlitteratur, Lund, pp 371–393
Schmitthoff CM (1961) International business law: a new law merchant. In: St J MacDonald R (ed), 2 Current law and socieal problems. University of Toronto Press, Toronto, pp 129–153
Schmoeckel M, Maetschke M (2016) Rechtsgeschichte der Wirtschaft: Seit dem 19. Jahrhundert. 2., überarbeitete und ergänzte Auflage. Mohr Siebeck, Tübingen
Schoonhoven CB (1981) Problems with contingency theory: testing assumptions hidden within the language of contingency "theory". Administrative Sci Q 26(3):349–377
Schopenhauer A (1830) Eristische Dialektik: Die Kunst, Recht zu Behalten
Schröder J (2016) Rechtswissenschaft in Diktaturen: Die juristische Methodenlehre im NS-Staat und in der DDR. Verlag C.H. Beck, München
Scobbie I (2003) Some common heresies about international law: sundry theoretical perspectives. In: Evans MD (ed) International law, First edn. Oxford University Press, Oxford, pp 59–87
Scott HS (1978) The risk fixers. Harv Law Rev 91(4):737–792
Segal J, Spaeth H (2002) The Supreme Court and the attitudinal model revisited. Cambridge University Press, Cambridge
Sherman CP (1908) Study of law in Roman law schools. Yale Law J 17(7):499–512. Faculty Scholarship Series. Paper 4434
Smith A (1776) The wealth of nations
Stigler GJ (1971) The theory of economic regulation. Bell J Econ Manag Sci 2(1):3–21
Stiglitz JE (2002) Information and the change in the paradigm in economics. Am Econ Rev 92 (3):460–501. doi:10.1257/00028280260136363
Strömholm S (1975) Zum Begriff der "Natur der Sache": Gedanken eines skandinavischen Juristen. Rabels Zeitschrift für ausländisches und internationales Privatrecht 39(4):702–714
Sunstein CR (2001) Foreword: on academic fads and fashions. Mich Law Rev 99:1251–1264
Szramkiewicz R, Descamps O (2013) Histoire du droit des affaires. 2e édition. LGDJ, Paris
Trakman LE (1983) The law merchant: the evolution of commercial law. Fred B. Rothman & Co., Littleton, Colorado
Tuori K (2006) Self-description and external description of the law. NoFo 2:27–43
Turgot ARJ (1776) Réflexions sur la formation et la distribution des richesses
Van Caenegem RC, Johnston DEL (1992) An historical introduction to private law. Cambridge University Press, Cambridge
Van de Mieroop M (2005) The invention of interest. Sumerian loans. In: Goetzmann WN, Rouwenhorst KG (eds) The origins of value. Oxford University Press, Oxford, pp 17–30
Vauchez A (2012) Keeping the dream alive: the European Court of Justice and the transnational fabric of integrationist jurisprudence. Eur Polit Sci Rev 4(81):51–71. doi:10.1017/S1755773911000105
von Bogdandy A, Goldmann M, Venzke I (2016) From public international to international public law: Translating world public opinion into international public authority. Max Planck Institute for Comparative Public Law and International Law, MPIL Research Paper Series No. 2016–02
von Holderstein Holtermann J, Madsen MR (2015) European new legal realism and international law: how to make international law intelligible. Leiden J Int Law 28(2):211–230

von Jhering R (1858) Geist des römischen Rechts auf den verschiedenen Stufen seiner Entwicklung. Druck und Verlag von Breitkopf und Härtel, Leipzig

von Savigny FC (1840) System des heutigen Römischen Rechts, Erster Band. Veit und Comp, Berlin

Watts A (2001) The importance of international law. In: Bryers M (ed) The role of law in international politics: essays in international relations and international law. Oxford University Press, Oxford, pp 5–16

Weber M (1904) Die "Objektivität" sozialwissenschaftlicher und sozialpolitischer Erkenntnis. Archiv für Sozialwissenschaft und Sozialpolitik 19(1):22–87

Weber M (1922) Wirtschaft und Gesellschaft - Grundriß der verstehenden Soziologie. J.C.B Mohr (Paul Siebeck), Tübingen

White JB (2002) Legal knowledge. Harv Law Rev 115(5):1396–1431

Williamson OE (1998) Transaction cost economics: how it works; where it is headed. De Economist 146:23–58

Williamson OE (2005) Transaction cost economics. In: Menard C, Shirley MM (eds) Handbook of new institutional economics. Springer, Dordrecht, pp 51–65

Wittgenstein L (1922) Tractatus Logico-Philosophicus: Logisch-philosophische Abhandlung. Kegan Paul, London

Wittgenstein L (1953) Philosophische Untersuchungen. In: Anscombe GEM, von Wright GH, Rhees R (eds) Werkausgabe, Band 1. Suhrkamp, Frankfurt (1984), pp 224–485

Woodward J (1958) Management and technology. Her Majesty's Stationary Office, London

Chapter 8
Conclusions

Legal science should comply with the customary requirements as to scientificity. The narrow focus of doctrinal research causes problems that are not limited to the lack of scientificity. The problems include, for example, the fact that legal science is less relevant than it could be and its short shelf life.

Replacing doctrinal research with the multidisciplinary approach or law-and-something disciplines is not the best answer for four main reasons. First, law-and-something disciplines do not treat legal science as an independent scientific discipline. Second, while legal science should reflect the complex nature of society and law by choosing a holistic perspective, other social sciences are free to choose other approaches. Non-normative social sciences do not need to reflect real-life complexity as closely as law does. Third, the values that the theories of other social sciences are based on do not necessarily reflect the complexity of the legal system and the value basis of the legal system. Fourth, theories originating in other social sciences can and have become irritants in legal science and the legal system.

User-Friendly Legal Science provides an alternative. It has its own point of view, theories and methods. It can be seen as a design science that delivers constructions. In this sense, law is indeed one of the professions.

User-Friendly Legal Science chooses neither 'the internal point of view' nor 'the external point of view'. Its point of view is how users can use legal tools and practices to reach their objectives in different contexts. This research approach is designed to focus on the game that the users of legal tools and practices really play. It would not reflect societal reality to reduce the players of this game to mere spectators of other games such as legal dogmatics.

User-Friendly Legal Science can bring many benefits. First, it can facilitate scientific theory building and the use of scientific methods in legal science. You can describe societal reality through the lens of the use of legal tools and practices in the language of legal science. Second, it can strengthen legal science in the competition for hegemony against established scientific disciplines. It takes a theory to beat a theory. This new discipline can produce the theories that legal science needs in order to prevail in the competition for hegemony. Third, User-

P. Mäntysaari, *User-friendly Legal Science*, DOI 10.1007/978-3-319-53492-3_8

Friendly Legal Science provides a way to unify legal research over national boundaries and to cope with the problems of legal pluralism and the arbitrariness of politics. Fourth, it can produce knowledge that is relevant for most people. Most people use legal tools and practices for the purpose of reaching their objectives in various kinds of contexts.

User-Friendly Legal Science can vastly increase the scope of legal science and make it more useful. We can conclude with words ascribed to Sir Isaac Newton: ‘I seem to have been only like a boy playing on the seashore, and diverting myself in now and then finding a smoother pebble or a prettier shell than ordinary, whilst the great ocean of truth lay all undiscovered before me.’

MIX
Papier aus verantwortungsvollen Quellen
Paper from responsible sources
FSC® C105338

If you have any concerns about our products,
you can contact us on
ProductSafety@springernature.com

In case Publisher is established outside the EU,
the EU authorized representative is:
Springer Nature Customer Service Center GmbH
Europaplatz 3, 69115 Heidelberg, Germany

Printed by Libri Plureos GmbH
in Hamburg, Germany